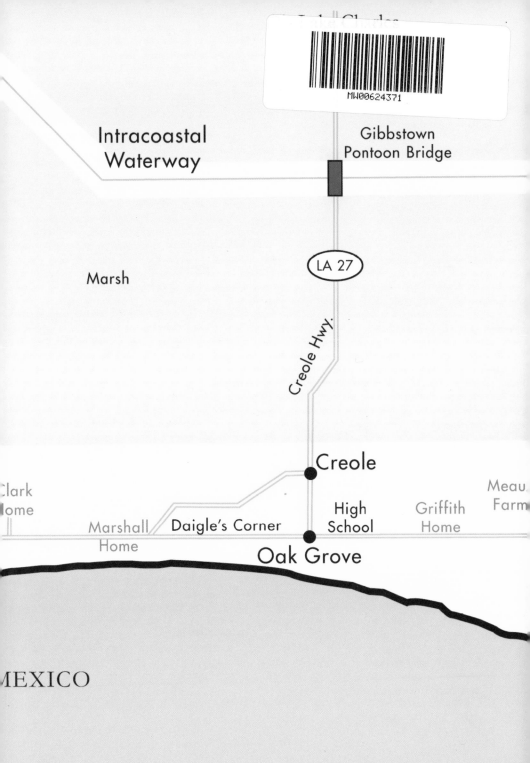

Intracoastal
Waterway

Gibbstown
Pontoon Bridge

LA 27

Marsh

Creole Hwy.

Creole

Clark
ome

Meau
Farm

Marshall
Home

Daigle's Corner

High
School

Griffith
Home

Oak Grove

MEXICO

RON PARISH, LOUISIANA

HURRICANE
AUDREY

To Cathy Mac —
— a survivor of
Audrey

Cathy Cagle Post
June 27, 2007
50th Anniversary
of Audrey

HURRICANE AUDREY

THE DEADLY STORM OF 1957

CATHY C. POST

PELICAN PUBLISHING COMPANY
GRETNA 2007

The word "Pelican" and the depiction of a pelican are trademarks
of Pelican Publishing Company, Inc., and are registered in the
U.S. Patent and Trademark Office.

Library of Congress Cataloging-in-Publication Data

Post, Cathy C.
  Hurricane Audrey : the deadly storm of 1957 / by Cathy C. Post.
    p. cm.
  Includes bibliographical references and index.
  ISBN 978-1-58980-458-6 (hardcover : alk. paper)
  1. Hurricane Audrey, 1957. 2. Cameron Parish (La.)—History—20th
century. 3. Disaster victims—Louisiana—Cameron Parish—Biography. 4.
Cameron Parish (La.)—Biography. 5. Cameron Parish (La.)—Social condi-
tions. I. Title.
  F377.C25P67 2007
  551.55'209763520904—dc22

                                              2006103402

Maps by Cathy C. Post

*The excerpt from Geneva Griffith's "Lagniappe Two" column appeared in the October
13, 2005, issue of the* Cameron Parish Pilot *and is reprinted here with permission.*

Printed in the United States of America
Published by Pelican Publishing Company, Inc.
1000 Burmaster Street, Gretna, Louisiana 70053

To Cameron Parish
and to my friends, Geneva Griffith, Leslie Griffith,
and "The Ladies of the Storm"

Contents

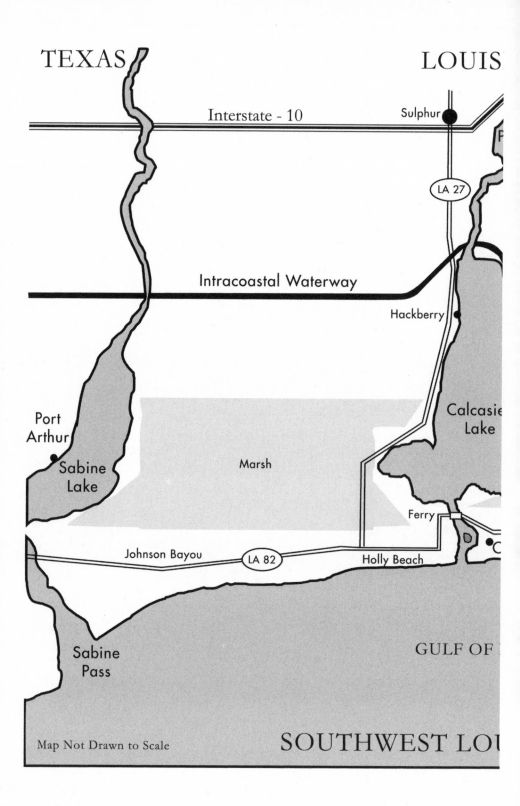

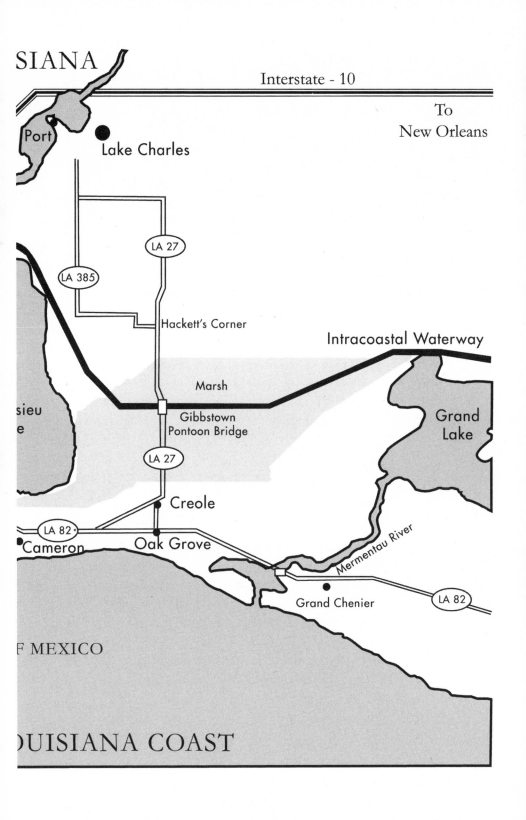

Index of Families
Discussed in This Book

Bartie:
  Raymond Bartie, Sr.
  Maybell Bartie
    Eugene Bartie, age 14
    Leda Mae Bartie, 13
    Rose Lee Bartie, 11
    Robert Lee Bartie, 10
    Raymond Bartie, Jr., 8
    Walter Bartie, 2
	For many years, the Bartie family lived and worked on the Johnny Meaux farm in Oak Grove. The farm was about a mile away from the Griffith residence.

Broussard:
  Whitney J. Broussard, Sr.
  Clara Ellender Broussard
    Whitney Broussard, Jr., 18
    Mary Ann Broussard, 15
    Ethel Broussard, 13
    Elaine Broussard, 10
    David Broussard, 5
    Richard Broussard, 3
    Helen Broussard, 18 months
	The Broussard family lived in Cameron, where Whitney was the principal at Cameron Elementary School. Clara and Whitney were both teachers. The Broussard family also owned a motel near their home.
	
	Mr. Broussard's parents, Numa and Helen Conner Broussard, lived 15 miles to the east in Creole.

Cagle: Alice Cagle Marshall, 61 Brown ("Tootie") Marshall, 57—Alice's husband Regina Davis Phillips—Alice's daughter; married to Walter Phillips; the Phillipses lived in Lake Charles with their children Joseph Maxwell Cagle, 38—Alice's nephew; married to Mary Belle Cagle; the Cagles lived in Lake Charles with their eight children; Joe owned and operated Cagle Chevrolet Theda Cagle Heath—Alice's niece; married to Charles C. Heath; the Heaths lived in Lake Charles	Alice Cagle Jeffries, a widow and retired schoolteacher, married Brown Marshall, a cattleman from Cameron. They lived along the coast at Daigle's Corner, between Cameron and Creole. Alice remained close to her daughter, Regina, and numerous relatives in the large Cagle family, who lived 35 miles due north in Lake Charles.
Carter: O. B. Carter, 55—sheriff of Cameron Parish	A lifelong resident of Cameron Parish, Sheriff Carter and his wife had many relatives in the area. Those mentioned briefly in this book were two prominent physicians in Creole—retired physician Dr. S. O. Carter (the sheriff's father); and the doctor's grandson, Dr. Stephen Carter, and his wife, Ducie (Geneva Griffith's friend).

	The two Creole doctors were also friends with Dr. Cecil Clark and his wife, Sybil, in the nearby town of Cameron.
Clark: 　Dr. Cecil Clark, 32 　Sybil Baccigalopi Clark 　　John Clark, 8 　　Joe Clark, 7 　　Elizabeth Dianne Clark, 3 　　Celia Marie Clark, 18 months 　　Jack Benjamin Clark, 3 months 　Zulmae Dubois, 53—nanny to the Clarks' five children	Young Dr. Cecil Clark was the only physician in the town of Cameron. His wife, Sybil, a nurse, worked alongside him at their small medical center. There were two other physicians in nearby towns in the parish (Dr. Carter and Dr. Dix).
DeBarge: 　Tommy DeBarge, 84 　Sidney DeBarge, 85	Elderly brothers Tommy and Sidney DeBarge shared a home in Cameron. Tommy's preferred mode of transportation was his sturdy, dependable bicycle.
Griffith: 　D. W. Griffith, 36 　Geneva Ellerbee Griffith, 35 　　Leslie Griffith, 11 　　Cherie Griffith, 5	The Griffiths lived in Oak Grove, east of Cameron. Geneva worked in the Cameron Parish Courthouse. D.W. was a boat captain for Pure Oil Company, servicing the offshore oilrigs.

Papa and Nannie Griffith— D.W.'s parents; lived in Port Arthur, Texas	The Ellerbee family—Geneva's parents—like D.W.'s lived in Port Arthur, Texas.
Marshall (see also Cagle): Brown ("Tootie") Marshall, 57 Alice Cagle Marshall, 61 Regina Phillips—Alice's daughter; lived in Lake Charles Joseph M. Cagle—Alice's nephew; lived in Lake Charles	Brown Marshall, a longtime cattleman in Cameron Parish, also operated a meat-processing plant near their home at Daigle's Corner, between Cameron and Creole. Alice's large Cagle family of sisters, brothers, nieces, and nephews lived in Lake Charles.
Meaux: Johnny Meaux Esther Nunez Meaux	Johnny Meaux, politician and country farmer, was a relative of the Griffith and Welch families. A Louisiana state representative for almost 30 years, he always maintained his home and farm in Oak Grove (near Geneva and D. W. Griffith's home). For several decades, the large Bartie family lived and worked on the Meaux farm.

Welch: Wynona ("Nona") Welch	Miss Nona Welch, D. W. Griffith's aunt, was the registrar of voters in Cameron Parish. She and Geneva Griffith both worked at the courthouse. Miss Nona was also related to the Davis family (of the historic Austin Davis House).

Preface

In all of recorded United States history, only one hurricane has taken a direct path, an unwavering, head-on course, before it struck the coastline of the United States. In June of 1957 Hurricane Audrey formed deep in the Gulf of Mexico in the Bay of Campeche, along the twenty-first parallel, 460 miles south of Cameron, Louisiana. It took direct aim at the small towns along this coast and moved due north for four days.

The populace was poised to evacuate, but then something went horribly wrong for the people along the Louisiana coast, resulting in a massive death toll. Despite its unwavering course, Audrey left over five hundred dead in its wake—almost two hundred of them children—making it one of the worst natural disasters in Louisiana history.

Why did so many people die in that enlightened, modern age of weather forecasting? While the world did not have weather satellite technology in 1957 for photographs, Audrey was the first hurricane to be tracked by radar. The country also had maritime reporting from ships at sea, as well as precise aerial reconnaissance. These U.S. Navy airplanes, the Storm Trackers, flew into storm systems and gathered all the necessary data for the National Weather Bureau—the exact wind speed, the barometric pressure, the precise location, and also the forward movement of the hurricane.

In the aftermath of the huge storm, Cameron Parish Assistant District Attorney Jennings B. Jones filed a lawsuit in U.S. Federal Court on behalf of numerous families against the Weather Bureau—*Whitney*

Bartie v. United States of America. It was the first case of its kind.

This book is a historical account, a memoir of the Griffith, Clark, Bartie, Marshall, Cagle, and Broussard families, and a chronicle of their battle for survival during Hurricane Audrey as well as their struggle to rebuild their lives in the aftermath of the deadly storm.

This is their story.

CHAPTER 1

Monday, June 24, 1957— Birth of a Storm

Monday, June 24, 1957
The Cameron Parish Courthouse
Cameron, Louisiana

Summer in the Deep South will jolt a person's senses. It's the hot, humid stillness that becomes so oppressive. If a person is lucky enough to live along the coastal beaches, however, the gulf breeze will transform a sweltering day into a pleasurable experience. In Louisiana, a cool day is heavenly, but a cool breeze is absolutely divine.

Geneva Griffith tapped her fingers to the beat and hummed along with Frank Sinatra as he crooned a tune on the car radio. She reached across the dash to increase the volume, then rolled the window down a bit more. Her long, brown hair ruffled against the blue scarf tied about her neck. It wasn't quite nine o'clock, but the heat was barely tolerable during her fifteen-minute drive to work that morning along the Louisiana coast highway. Throughout Oak Grove, farmers were already busy in the fields with the first summer harvest of their crops. She passed South Cameron High School, then Daigle's Corner, and soon after approached the outskirts of Cameron.

Turning right onto Smith Circle, Geneva arrived at the courthouse and eventually found a parking spot close to the trunk of a shady oak. The tree-lined streets surrounding the courthouse were bustling with pedestrians and leisurely small-town traffic. A multi-aged group of children rode their bikes on the dusty gravel road alongside the building.

With towels over their shoulders, they pedaled off to the beach a few miles away.

With her sack lunch and straw purse in hand, Geneva waved in passing at Thomas DeBarge, Alvin Dyson, and Sheriff O. B. Carter, who stood chatting near the front steps of the building.

DeBarge sat poised on the seat of his black bicycle with one foot planted firmly on the sidewalk. At eighty-four years old, Tommy kept in shape by accident. When his last car broke down after two decades of service, he decided to purchase a less expensive mode of transportation, one that fit the size of his pension check. To his way of thinking, if he bought a new Chevy, the car would undoubtedly outlive him anyway. The choice was simple, so for several years now he had been riding around town on the sturdy black bike, running errands and visiting longtime friends. Within a few months his muscles toned and firmed. His old heart beat stronger beneath his deep summer tan. Tommy experienced stamina and strength that he never expected to have in his old age.

The man lived a simple life and had no need to travel far from Cameron, where he shared a home with his widowed brother, Sidney DeBarge. A year older than Tommy, Sidney moved slowly about the house and had little use for either a car or a bike. He preferred his comfortable rocker on the wide front porch of his home.

"Nonsense, Tommy. I don't need a bicycle," he often repeated with a dismissive wave of his weathered hand. "I get plenty of exercise from this hoe." Formerly an oil-refinery worker and sheriff's deputy, Sidney now wanted to do nothing more strenuous than tilling his highly productive garden. At eighty-five, he was entitled.

"Good morning, Geneva," hailed the sheriff as she approached the steps. "How's D.W? Will he be in town for the Fourth of July parade?"

"Yes, sir. He's due home in five days. We'll be here for the big barbeque that afternoon, too. His folks will be driving over for the day as well. See you there!" A low-flying Pan Am Clipper passed overhead as Geneva entered the building.

"Maybe John Paul could have several of his new marsh buggies in the parade, too? Most folks have never seen them, and the barbeque and the parade would be the perfect opportunity to showcase that new vehicle, don't you think?" suggested the sheriff to Dyson, the Louisiana state representative from Cameron Parish.

Mr. Dyson's nonstop schedule this Monday included a meeting at Geneva's office, the Department of Agriculture. With a nod and a wave goodbye, Dyson parted from the group and entered the courthouse, removing his straw hat. His forehead dripped with perspiration in the early-morning heat. Removing his handkerchief, he wiped his brow then followed Geneva into the Agriculture Department.

The Griffith family had roots in Cameron Parish for over 150 years. Geneva and her husband, D.W., lived on thirty acres of lush, scenic land filled with grassy fields, marshland, and huge oak trees overlooking the Gulf of Mexico. The young couple built their home in Oak Grove on a low-lying ridge facing the gulf, just two miles from the beach. It was an idyllic place to raise their two children, son Leslie, eleven, and daughter Cherie, five.

Louisiana Highway 82, the two-lane coastal road, stretched in front of their home, heading eastward to Grand Chenier and westward to Cameron, fifteen miles away. Between the highway and the sandy beaches of the gulf, sage-green patches of marsh grass swayed in the breeze. The centuries-old ecosystem of both the coastal and inland marshes of the Louisiana coast was a prime factor in preserving the natural abundance of wildlife in the area. These green and gold marsh grasses more recently served an aesthetic purpose by hiding the wooden boardwalk roads that led to the numerous oil wells in the coastal marsh. The short, stocky pumping mechanisms had long ago replaced the tall derricks. Now, the view from the front patio of the Griffith home was unencumbered, stretching over the rose garden, across the manicured lawn, down to the coastal highway, then out to the marsh and finally the sandy beach. On a clear day Geneva could catch a glimpse of the whitecaps crashing onto the beaches of Oak Grove. The low rhythmic sound of the waves was ever present, a soothing acoustic shadow.

Behind the Griffith home was a large green barn, with an adjoining cattle pen with nearly one hundred head of cattle. There were horses

This photograph was taken shortly after Geneva and D.W. Griffith married, while he was in the U.S. Coast Guard stationed at Port Aransas, Texas. The young couple lived in the lighthouse that year.

in the stalls and chickens in the coop. The farm-fresh eggs from their hens tasted better than any store-bought eggs from the grocer.

The *L*-shaped, three-bedroom home was built on low piers a foot and a half high. To take advantage of the gulf breeze, the front door opened onto a six-feet-wide concrete porch that ran the length of the house. From this cement patio, red brick trim rose two feet upward, gracing the front of the home. This inviting entrance was adorned by Geneva's lush rose garden. The deep floral scent of her pink floribunda and her long-stemmed red tea roses often carried on a gentle evening breeze through open windows into the living room. When Geneva played at her piano, their fragrance was especially enjoyable, almost inspiring.

D.W.'s aunt, Nona Welch, was the local registrar of voters, and she also worked in the courthouse near Geneva's office. The Welches, the McCalls, the Meauxs, and the Griffiths were family, and several of the relatives lived near Geneva and D.W.'s home in Oak Grove.

Cameron Parish embodied all that is good about small-town living, especially this rural closeness of friends and relatives. With fewer than four thousand residents in the entire parish, most people knew their neighbors well. Add to that setting the spicy Cajun culture, and you had a lively blend of hardworking people who went about their daily lives with a distinct *joie de vivre*—a joy of living.

The majority of people in Cameron Parish were Cajuns—a name derived from "Acadians"—those hardy descendants of the French-Canadian settlers who came south from Acadia, present-day Nova Scotia. Peasant families from the French provinces of Normandy and Brittany had sailed across the Atlantic to Canada, spurred by a promise of land ownership from the French government. With property deeds in hand, the French-speaking Roman Catholics forged towns, communities, and livelihoods out of the land of Acadia. These original European settlers prospered and multiplied over the next hundred years.

Between 1620 and 1713, the French settlement in the New World changed hands politically many times but always remained loyal to France. Finally, a 1713 treaty with the British changed their lives forever.

Refusing to swear allegiance to England, the Acadians faced harsh consequences. Families were persecuted, arrested, and finally deported from the prosperous colony they had established a century before. Herded like cattle onto waiting ships in the harbor, many families became lost from one another. The British troops separated these devout Catholic families in a historic period referred to as *Le Grand Dérangement*, scattering them across the Western Hemisphere in a political storm.

Over time, word spread among the exiles of a sympathetic Spanish-speaking Catholic settlement along the Louisiana coast, and the Acadians began a long journey to the Deep South. Decades after the deportations began in Nova Scotia, many of the French families were finally reunited in Louisiana. Arriving in 1763, the resilient Acadians—roughly three thousand of them—sought and found refuge in the coastal plains and along the bayous of the hot, humid wilderness. They spread out in search of land they could call their own.

In much the same manner as they had established their colonies in Nova Scotia, the Acadians worked hard to provide a good life in Louisiana. The French settlers trusted few people, keeping to themselves except for trading fur pelts with their Spanish neighbors. They also became successful farmers and fishermen once again. Most importantly, the Spanish governing officials respected the Acadians' fierce ethnic loyalty to their homeland. Over time, the area along the Louisiana coast came to be known affectionately as Acadiana.

The Cajuns continue to be a fiercely proud and independent people, a distinct culture within this large country. Their descendants thrive in the cities and bayous of Cajun country, where their seventeenth-century French dialect is still spoken today. In Cameron Parish their herds of cattle are a vital part of the economy. In spite of the early generations' hardships, the Cajun of the 1900s enjoyed an uncomplicated life, with simple pleasures.

As this particular summer began—in 1957—life was good in the Bayou State. Within a matter of days, however, the Cajuns and fellow citizens of Cameron Parish would be required to draw upon those same strong characteristics of the exiled Acadian ancestors—a love of their land, an unshakable faith, and a determined will to survive.

Monday, June 24, 1957
The Johnny Meaux farm
Oak Grove, Louisiana

"I'm sorry to interrupt your day, Raymond."

"No, ma'am, not at all. I appreciate the break. We've been at it for hours." The genial black man closed the trunk of the older lady's car. "Okay, ma'am, you're good to go." He doffed his frayed straw hat with a warm smile and headed back to the barn, where he had been unloading a flatbed truck full of peas.

"Thanks again, Esther!" Alice waved to her friend as she rolled down the window of the car. The morning was promising to turn into another blistering day, and Alice had a lot to do before leaving for Lake Charles tomorrow. The dust from the long driveway hung in the still air as she stopped, then shifted into first gear and pulled out onto the main road. Her home was only about five minutes away, and it felt good to start the day outdoors.

Alice delighted in getting some of the first yield from Johnny Meaux's crop of field peas. She drove away from the Meaux farm with four bushels of peas in her trunk. Alice and her friend Johnny Meaux had known each other for years through the Louisiana political scene, but she was even closer to Johnny's wife, Esther. Alice was twenty years older than Esther but neither of them noticed or cared. In a small rural community, age is less a factor in friendships.

Alice and her new husband, Brown Marshall, lived in a rambling, two-story home on the coast highway between Cameron and Creole. She was adjusting well to her new home and her new life. With a trunk full of farm-fresh vegetables, Alice passed the Welch home, then the Griffith home, where Johnny Meaux's nephew lived. She noted how the deeply forested cheniers blended the small villages into one larger close-knit community. For the hundredth time, she marveled at the peace and contentment she found in her husband's hometown.

Alice Cagle Jeffries, a former schoolteacher, had been a widow in her late fifties with no intention of remarrying until she met Brown Marshall from Cameron, Louisiana. Marshall, called "Tootie" by most who knew him, was also widowed. The tall cattleman commanded attention just by entering a room, and Alice thought he looked much like her movie hero, John Wayne. At five foot five, Alice barely reached his shoulder, but she had spunk, and that's what caught and held his interest. Her soft brown eyes sealed the deal. The two met four years ago, fell in love, and married in a simple civil ceremony.

"I used to be tall and thin, but somewhere along the way, I turned into a short, fat grandmother," Alice remarked to her reflection in the full-length mirror on her wedding day. Turning a bit left, then right, she smoothed the creamy beige silk fabric of her suit over her some- what plump midriff. A lamp softly lit her bedroom. Alice tilted the mahogany-framed mirror a fraction to get a better view of the skirt's hem, making sure it was just right. Her light brown hair was mostly gray now, and she kept it in a short, fashionable bob with soft loose curls. The long heavy drapes hanging at the two bedroom windows had been drawn against the summer heat that prevailed outside. The room was cool despite the flurry of activity as she prepared for the small wedding ceremony.

Alice had shopped at Muller's and finally chose the lovely suit for her wedding day. The well-tailored jacket hung gracefully over the straight skirt. The soft hue of the silk enhanced her pale-pink, porcelain com- plexion, and she fairly glowed with happiness. Alice's sister had been telling her since she was a teenager that her flawless skin was her best feature, and she openly wished she too had been blessed with it.

At nearly sixty, Alice Cagle was plump and precious—and still had great skin.

"Momma, hush! You look beautiful. You look *especially* beautiful today. Your hair looks great, too. Now turn around and let me pin the corsage to your jacket," her daughter said laughingly.

"Now, Regina, you know it's true. Had I been young and thin, Brown Marshall would have swept me off my feet," she continued as Regina pinned the lavender-colored orchid securely to the fabric. "But since I'm older and wiser, I'll just settle for being in love. Who would have thought?" The grandmother smiled. She reached up and placed her hand against Regina's cheek.

Alice Cagle Jeffries with daughter Regina Davis Phillips and granddaughter Kathleen Phillips, circa 1951.

"At least Brown's home is nearby. Cameron is so close we will still see each other often."

"That's true, Momma. Besides, the children are excited about you living near the beach, so we may become real pests by visiting too often!"

Above everything else in the world, Alice loved her daughter. At thirty-five, Regina Davis Phillips shared many of her mother's characteristics, including her inexhaustible energy. Those around Regina soon found out that they needed to keep up with her pace or they would quickly fall behind.

Alice was also one of the best cooks in the large Cagle family. Her love of cooking showed in the way she taught her daughter to actually enjoy being in the kitchen. It was one of the greatest gifts she could give to her child, because it was so personal—a lifelong gift, something that money couldn't buy. The fact that Alice was so good at it didn't hurt either. Her 1912 cookbook won first place in a state contest.

"What should I call him?" Regina had asked her mother after she first met Mr. Marshall. "Brown is a strange first name, definitely unusual. Is that why everyone calls him 'Tootie'? But wait—Tootie is even more unusual than Brown. Hmmm, actually, the name 'Brown' is intriguing. It's starting to grow on me. Yes, I definitely like it."

The wedding had been three years ago. Life in Cameron was simple and good for the newlyweds. Mr. Marshall enjoyed his work and had no plans to retire, even though he was nearing sixty. Hard work had kept him in fit physical condition. He boasted a thick head of smooth, brown hair graying slightly at the temples and a deep tan from a lifetime in the sun, and a broad cowboy smile surfaced often from beneath the brim of his beige Stetson hat.

Marshall's large cattle operations in Cameron Parish made up a vital part of the local economy. The business included a large herd of cattle and a livestock slaughterhouse that processed a great deal of the stock from the area farmers and ranchers.

The Marshall home was as close to the beach as you could get, separated from the sandy shores by the coast highway and a narrow coastal marsh. The large, two-story Victorian home was built during the Roaring Twenties and had withstood several hurricanes and tropical storms. In 1938, an unnamed hurricane hit the Louisiana coast just east of Cameron, but the home survived in spite of being flooded by a foot of water. Situated at Daigle's Corner on the front ridge of the oak forest, the Marshall home offered Alice a quiet, rural setting in which to spend her later years.

Alice spent the rest of Monday morning shelling field peas at her kitchen table. In the heat of the afternoon she turned on the small fan nearby. The nine-foot ceilings usually helped circulate the warmer air away from the floor, but today the heat was stifling. When the fan no longer made a difference, she moved her small operation outside onto the wide veranda. From there she could hear the sound of the breakers on the beach and could listen to the caw of the seagulls as they hovered and swayed on the warm air currents along the coast. Today a somewhat warmer breeze blew in from the beach and through the tall oak trees that bordered the road in front of her home. She could usually count on this steady gulf breeze that blew off the water, over the narrow strip of land that formed the coastal communities, and then continued blowing northward out across the marsh beyond the small town of Cameron. But lately the weather seemed unusually hot with no relief in sight.

Alice crossed her ankles and placed the wide bowl on her lap, relaxing on the long, metal porch glider as she continued to shell more peas. She glided back and forth effortlessly as she worked to separate each long purple hull from the row of peas hidden inside. The glider had just the right amount of soft, comforting squeak in its hinges—the perfect porch partner.

Two projects topped her list of chores this week—getting plenty of peas in the freezer and making fig preserves. She was just about ready to check this one off her list. When the shelled peas filled the large ceramic bowl, Alice took a break to stretch her legs. The figs on her fruit trees would soon be ready to pick. Once the figs reached the ripe stage, the birds would begin their own harvesting. Alice was concerned she would end up with little or no fig preserves to show for this year if she waited too long to pick the tender fruit. For perfect preserves, timing was essential.

The Cagle family would later note that the fig trees in Cameron Parish would play a strange, dramatic role in Hurricane Audrey.

Moving down the wide cement steps of the veranda, Alice walked to the backyard of the house to check on the two fig trees. The dense, freshly mowed lawn tickled her toes through her open-toed espadrilles. Grasshoppers hummed in the grass here and there, a summer symphony that halted abruptly as the bugs moved quickly to escape her steps. On the fig trees, the wide, flat, green leaves hid the fruit from marauding birds for the time being. All over the gulf coast, fig trees were heavy with their fruit. A close inspection and a bit of fig squeezing showed the need for just a few more days to ripen to the perfect stage.

In Lake Charles, Alice's daughter had several fig trees that were ready to pick, so tomorrow Alice planned to drive there for the annual culinary event. Mother and daughter enjoyed the joint effort and now included the granddaughters, Kathleen, Frances, and Elizabeth, in the fun. The ladies would spend a day picking and peeling the figs, visiting and chatting all the while. The next day they would cook batch after batch on the stove until the juices and sugar became a translucent, thick syrup with chunks of tender fruit, ready to be placed in sterilized jars. They would put up dozens of jars of sweet, dark-brown fig preserves for the family to enjoy throughout the next year.

An hour before dinnertime Alice's first chore was finished. She poured all of the peas into freezer containers lined up on her kitchen countertop. She then labeled two containers for Regina, which Alice would deliver tomorrow. Alice often made the drive back and forth to Lake Charles by herself.

"It's a short drive. It's only an hour, for heaven's sake. And besides, I'm old, but I'm not dead," she often told her husband, asserting her driving rights. She didn't want to end up like her sister-in-law, Ona Cagle.

Alice's brother Robert had always driven his wife, Ona, everywhere she needed to go, and Ona had only recently learned to drive after his death five years ago. Now in her early sixties, she had never quite gotten the knack of sharing the road. Cars routinely swerved along Prien Lake Road to avoid her approach from the opposite direction. Her son Joe had given her a shiny gray Chevrolet with an automatic shift, but it didn't improve her driving skills in the least.

Alice never wanted to lose her driving skills, skills she learned from her brothers decades ago. More importantly, she always wanted to be mobile, able to drive to Lake Charles at the drop of a hat. To this Southern lady, mobility was the key to seeing family and friends.

Alice's grandchildren had been down last week to swim at the beach, one of the kids' favorite outings. Alice, too, loved the beach, so long as she had her wide-brimmed straw hat. The bright sun off the sand always hurt her eyes, but sunglasses and her trusty hat made it enjoyable. She and Regina would hold the smaller children's hands and wade out into the waves, much to their delight, while the older ones dove beneath the waves and swam with ease in the undulating surf.

Above all, however, Alice's grandchildren enjoyed the car ride across the Calcasieu Ship Channel on the ferry at the western edge of town. Standing at the rail, the children watched the seagulls, as the gray and white birds dipped and swooped in the breeze like trapeze artists, all the while searching for food. Unlike a circus safety net, the deep green water allowed the gulls to dive beneath the waves to capture fish in their sharp beaks. If the birds flew too close to the rail with their loud caws, the children shrieked with laughter.

Despite its small size, the port of Cameron was once the busiest port in the nation, due to the fishing industry. The shipping pace had slowed somewhat in the past decade, but the area was still a hub of seagoing vessels, many traversing the waters north to the port of Lake Charles.

The ferry provided more than transportation across the busy ship channel. It was a lifeline that allowed Highway 82, which stretched along the gulf coast, to continue west to Port Arthur, Texas.

Powered by two GM 150-horsepower engines, the ferry carried fifteen or twenty cars on each crossing. It sported one large wooden lifeboat and a glass-enclosed wheelhouse atop the first floor's engine room. The skipper had a clear view of the wide ship channel at all times. As with the noise of the seagulls overhead, the children squealed and covered their ears when the skipper sounded the loud horn upon approaching the dock.

In less than fifty-two hours, however, the powerful ferry, along with its skipper and chief engineer, would be embroiled in a life-or-death struggle just to stay afloat.

Monday, June 24, 1957
Campeche Bay, off the coast of Mexico
400 miles due south of the Louisiana coastline

New Orleans Weather Bureau Bulletin, 10:30 P.M. CST, June 24, 1957:

A TROPICAL DEPRESSION WAS LOCATED IN THE

GULF OF MEXICO ABOUT 300 MILES SOUTHEAST OF BROWNSVILLE TEXAS AT 10:30 PM CST. HIGHEST WINDS ARE ESTIMATED ABOUT 35 TO 40 MPH. INDICATIONS ARE FOR NORTHWARD MOVEMENT OF THE DEPRESSION. SMALL CRAFT ALONG THE LOWER TEXAS COAST SHOULD NOT VENTURE INTO THE OPEN GULF. NEXT RELEASE WILL BE AT 4 AM CST UNLESS DEVELOPMENTS WARRANT AN EARLIER RELEASE.

CHAPTER 2

Tuesday—
Life Before Audrey

Tuesday, June 25, 1957
The Whitney Broussard home
Cameron, Louisiana

"Sorry, ma'am. It's just too heavy. We can't lift it. You will have to make other arrangements to haul it off to the dump."

That's what the garbage men had told Clara Broussard when she finally removed the brick mantel from the fireplace and set the heavy load on the curb for pick-up. It had taken some time to chip the bricks away from the wall one by one, but it was worth the effort. Clara had never wanted the fireplace in her home. She had grown up with fireplaces and considered them a mess, just one more thing to clean. Plus, a popping log often caused sparks to fly, and she was afraid the house would catch fire. It wasn't safe, and she had babies to protect. Clara didn't want the fireplace, and she wasn't going to have it. It was just that simple.

It had taken a while to convince her husband, Whitney, however. He enjoyed spending cold winter evenings in front of the fire. Winters in the Deep South were short lived, lasting only three or four months at best. The rustic scent of the burning oak logs, together with the warmth and crackle of the flickering orange flames, was something to savor. It was a lovely focal point of the living room, but it had become a bone of contention. Gentle persuasion prevailed, however. With a smile and shake of his head, Whitney relented to Clara's gentle pleadings, never suspecting how quickly the fireplace would disappear from their home.

Clara was on a mission. As soon as Whitney left for work the next morning, she began removing the bricks. She could repair the abrasions and board up the opening on the wall later. For now, Clara hammered and chipped away at the mortar between the bricks. Each time she had amassed a stack of bricks on the floor of the living room, the petite woman carried an armload out to the curb and dumped it unceremoniously in a large empty trashcan. Her dress took a beating, and her dark hair was flecked with ash and gray mortar, but she rarely looked more energized, more determined. Clara's slender arms could hold just so many bricks at a time, so the project required many trips to the trashcan.

When will I ever find time to take a load of bricks to the dump? thought Clara that day as the garbage truck pulled away. "Too heavy? Well, we'll see about that. This trashcan won't be too heavy for too long."

Over the course of a few weeks, Clara removed one armload of bricks from the trashcan and deposited it in another can, which soon became filled with the usual refuse. Each time the garbage truck made its rounds through the neighborhood, an armload of bricks was surreptitiously removed with the trash. The tiny, dark-haired beauty smiled knowingly from her kitchen window as the last of the fireplace was finally hauled away from the Broussard home.

Several years had passed since Clara effectively circumvented the system that day. Now at the age of forty, she continued to use a combination of gentle persuasion and firm resolve to accomplish her everyday tasks—a skill learned years ago when she first came to Cameron to teach school.

Clara's husband, Whitney Broussard, had been the principal at Cameron Elementary School for many years, and as a result, most of the children in town knew him by name. Amazingly, he somehow managed to know most of their names, too, and over time had developed a special rapport with the children of Cameron Parish. No matter where he was in town, it seemed there was always a child greeting him with a wave and a smile. Some people are beloved in their communities, and this man was one of those.

At six foot two, Whitney was easy to spot in a sea of little students. His own seven children thought their daddy had the longest legs in the world. Clara, too, had noticed how tall he was when they were first

SCHOOL DAYS 1956-'57
Cameron Elem.

Whitney Broussard, principal of Cameron Elementary School.

introduced a couple of decades ago. But at a petite five foot one, she noticed that most people were tall compared to her. What struck Clara in Whitney's case were his eyes, a deep hazel green. Clara could have sworn that those eyes actually sparkled when he looked at her that day back in 1936.

Clara Ellender had come to Cameron Parish from Bourg, Louisiana to teach school. She met the tall Cajun with the green eyes a few days after arriving in town. She and her roommate decided to rent a room at the Broussard home. The new boarders found the accommodations to be just as good as all the glowing referrals they had heard. After a four-month courtship, Clara and Whitney were married. After seven children, the sparkle was still there. Until the day he died, Whitney adored his precious, gentle Clara.

On any given day Whitney was a busy man. In addition to being the school principal, he also owned and operated the Broussard Motel, which was located across the street from the school, near the intersection of Louisiana Highway 82 and Dan Street. The Broussard family resided on Dan Street in a small, quiet, residential neighborhood. Their property was framed on all sides by a stand of tall, old pine trees. The pines often swayed in the gulf breeze and offered a welcome shade in the hot summer months. In the days to come, these pines with their deep taproots would help save the Broussard family home from total destruction.

But on this summer morning, Clara was going to drive into town for a few errands, including taking some of the children for check-ups and immunizations at Dr. Clark's clinic. Her day was shaping up to be a busy one and she wanted to get an early start.

Tuesday, June 25
Dr. Clark's clinic
Cameron, Louisiana

The plaques and certificates on the wall of the small hospital didn't tell the whole story, only the beginning. Dr. Cecil Clark was a tiger. More specifically, he was a Louisiana State University Bengal Tiger.

Clark graduated from LSU School of Medicine in Baton Rouge, after returning as a veteran from World War II. Clark spent his internship in New Orleans, where he met a young nurse, Sybil Baccigalopi, a red-haired, green-eyed beauty. As it turned out, Sybil was from Grand Chenier, Louisiana, only a few miles from his home in Cameron Parish.

Sybil had just received her "cap"—her degree in nursing. She often observed the intern with his patients, and she grew to respect his skill as a doctor. It seemed only natural that he became her mentor. Respect grew into love, and after a one-year courtship the two were married. The twenty-seven-year-old doctor began his medical practice in the gulf-side community of Cameron in 1952, where the doctor established the twelve-bed Cameron Medical Center. While functioning as superintendent of the new hospital, Sybil also served as her husband's anesthetist.

During those past five years, Dr. Clark had become a welcome addition to the small number of physicians practicing in Cameron Parish. There was Dr. George Dix, also an LSU graduate, who operated the Dix Clinic in nearby Creole. Then there were the two Dr. Carters—Dr. Stephen Carter, who lived in Creole as well, and the older Dr. S. O. Carter, his grandfather, now retired. Dr. Carter, Dr. Carter, and Dr. Clark—sometimes newcomers got the names mixed up, being that they were so similar, but the locals rarely did. The number of doctors was small, but what they lacked in numbers, they each made up in dedication.

There was something inherently good about this new doctor, too. Everyone who worked with Cecil Clark realized he was somewhat special, but they couldn't quite put their finger on what made him so. Yes, he was a good doctor, a dedicated physician. He was a loving husband to his wife, Sybil, and a devoted father to his five young children. And yes, there were several important diplomas and certificates on the walls of his office at the hospital, but his most hard-earned certificate was yet to be awarded. Dr. Cecil Clark's most important achievements would come in the days and weeks that lay ahead. This young man would become a great man.

Tuesday was a day much like any other at the hospital. Dr. Clark reached for the thick patient files located on the shelf near the next examining room. He read the names and smiled.

"And what's this . . . are these my beautiful Broussard babies?" he asked warmly, as he opened the door to find the Broussard family. "Hi, Mrs. Broussard. How are you? Is Whitney relaxing a bit during his summer break? Richard, you are growing so tall. You're not a baby anymore, are you? And David, you must be almost ready to start first grade now, huh. Did you know that your mother used to be my teacher?"

The conversation flowed easily between the doctor and these patients. They were longtime friends and it showed. Clara and Whitney Broussard were several years his senior but had so many things in common with the younger doctor and his wife. Besides, Mrs. Clark grew up in Cameron Parish, and she had known the Broussards all her life, long before she married the Tiger from LSU.

His nurse administered immunization shots to two of the children. They both received a small red sucker as a treat.

"And how is Richard this morning? I see you are not scheduled for a shot today."

Not one to miss out on a red sucker, the dark-haired three-year-old replied seriously, "Dr. Clark, I've had a headache all day. My brain hurts."

From her chair next to the examining table, Clara smiled and said she thought it might be just a little summer cold.

"Oh, I see. Well, let's take a look. Would a sucker make it feel any better?"

Richard nodded his head pitifully, then smiled as the nurse pulled out another sucker. The doctor placed his stethoscope against the small chest for a quick listen, then quickly looked down Richard's throat before the sucker commandeered the space. Happy to get out of the doctor's office without so much as a band-aid or a shot, Richard led the family down the hall and into the lobby, waving goodbye to Nurse Clark, the doctor's wife.

Noon, Tuesday, June 25
Office of Cagle Chevrolet
Lake Charles, Louisiana

"Tropical Storm Audrey is officially a hurricane," reported the newsman on the office radio.

"Hey, Bob. Could you turn that up?"

Joe Cagle walked out of his oak-paneled office to better listen to the bulletin from the Weather Bureau. Bob Self was the office manager at Cagle Chevrolet and had been for years. He was also one of Joe's best friends. The two men strained to hear as Bob leaned across his desk to turn up the volume.

"A navy reconnaissance plane flying above the tropical depression Tuesday morning reported that the storm had become a hurricane with a well-defined eye. Winds were recorded at 75 miles an hour. The

This photograph of Joe Cagle was taken in Baton Rouge while he attended Louisiana State University, circa 1942.

Weather Bureau named the hurricane Audrey, the first storm of the season. The storm center is located at latitude 22.5 and longitude 93.0 with little forward movement at this time. In its present location, Hurricane Audrey is 525 miles due south of Lake Charles. Paul Cook, chief meteorologist at the Lake Charles Weather Bureau, said the storm is still too far south to say exactly where it will hit. Stay tuned throughout the day for more updates on Hurricane Audrey as they become available."

With this noon broadcast, the official hurricane watch had begun along the entire gulf coast. From the Texas coastline all the way to the Florida Keys, national and local news carried reports of the hurricane's formation and location. Those communities along the coast realized that there was no way to predict at this early stage where it would make landfall, because hurricanes in the past moved toward the coastline at an angle, often veering and changing course several times.

But Hurricane Audrey was to break all the rules.

Tuesday, June 25
The Cameron Parish Courthouse
Cameron, Louisiana

Eating lunch at her desk that Tuesday, Geneva listened to the talk around the water cooler with interest. News of a hurricane in the gulf meant that crews on the oilrigs would begin evacuating to shore within hours. For Geneva, this development meant that her husband would be home soon, probably by early tomorrow, as soon as his boat could transport the last of the roustabout crews to safety.

One of Geneva's co-workers, a newcomer to the area, looked worried. He was getting teased because he was the only person on Geneva's floor who was overly concerned about the storm out in the gulf. The new Veteran's Affairs officer recently moved with his wife and children from north Louisiana to Cameron. The couple had never before experienced a hurricane but had heard about the danger posed by the powerful storms. Most of the folks working in the courthouse had weathered several hurricanes during their lifetimes in Cameron Parish. The storms were a fact of nature in coastal communities. Depending on the weather forecasts, the locals would either ride out the storms or evacuate to Lake Charles if the hurricane was a bad one.

One storm vet explained to the newcomer, "No need to panic, really. It's way too soon to evacuate. If it becomes a bad hurricane, and it heads our way, then we point our cars north and drive. Besides, it gets expensive staying in a hotel and eating in restaurants for days on end. Better to wait till the time is right. No need to panic. No need at all."

Geneva and D.W. had both lived all their lives along the gulf coast, growing up in Port Arthur, Texas, only a one-hour drive from their home in Oak Grove. Their parents still lived in Port Arthur and were often in touch with the young family. Storm preparations were nothing new to Geneva, and this particular Tuesday was no different. First things first—if a hurricane is brewing out in the gulf, and it could be heading your way, you go to the store. Late Tuesday afternoon, Geneva pulled in to the parking lot at Mr. Be's in Creole and stocked up on canned goods, batteries, kerosene, and the like.

"Hey there, Geneva!"

"Ducie! Hello. How's that new baby today?"

Geneva leaned over her friend's shopping cart to gently stroke the pale-brown fluff of new hair beginning to grow on the infant's tiny head. Ducie Carter lived in Creole, and she was a close friend. Ducie's husband, Stephen, was also their family doctor.

"Well, he's almost sleeping through the night now, so I'm actually beginning to catch up on my sleep. But you know, I'm so tired from chasing after the twins all day that a full eight hours of shut-eye wouldn't make any difference. I have resigned myself to being tired for a few years to come," Ducie said with a laugh as she reached down to caress the twins' shoulders as they held the hem of her skirt. "I guess that's why God gives us children when we are young, when we can handle anything, huh."

The two young mothers laughed and chatted as they chose their fresh produce. Ducie was fit and trim and had already lost her baby weight. She didn't need any makeup, nor did she have much time for it. Her cheeks glowed with good health and good humor.

"Geneva, did you hear about the storm out in the gulf? I understand it became a hurricane today, and they named it Audrey."

"Yeah, I heard it on the radio. I thought I'd stock up on a few canned goods just in case. D.W. will be coming home from offshore tomorrow, but I don't want to wait until the last minute to get everything ready."

"Same here. Stephen's schedule is nonstop, as you know, so I try to do all the household stuff myself. Besides, I think hurricane season is the only time I ever remember to pick up fresh batteries and freezer tape. Why is that?" The friends waved goodbye as Ducie headed to the checkout counter.

After the bag boy loaded the groceries and supplies in her trunk, Geneva pulled out of the parking lot and onto the Creole highway for the ten-minute drive home. The afternoon heat was stifling, and her dress felt damp against her skin. She would be home soon, and her workday would be winding down. The children's babysitter, Bernice, would be there, as usual, watching the kids till she returned. Thank goodness for Bernice. Leslie and Cherie enjoyed her company. They especially enjoyed playing Go Fish with Bernice.

At the stop sign, Geneva turned left onto the coast highway and passed the hand-painted yard sign *Crabs for Sale*. Blue crabs from the warm waters of the gulf were a Southern delicacy. Sometimes Geneva made crab stew, but today the sign made her think of a mess of boiled crabs simmering on the stove. When the crabs were dropped into boiling water, their brown shells streaked in blue would turn a bright red. Her family also relished the addition of corn on the cob and red potatoes dropped into the spicy, seasoned water. To really enjoy a crab boil, the family would often have dinner outside on a picnic table topped with newspaper to absorb the juices. *I'll have to stop and get a few dozen crabs while D.W. is home.*

Geneva couldn't help but look toward the gulf as she cruised down the highway, checking out the skies overhead. *Nothing amiss there.* A handful of fluffy cumulus clouds dotted the brilliant, pale-blue sky. Frank Sinatra crooned "Summer Winds" over KLOU on her car's radio, causing her thumbs to involuntarily tap to the beat on the steering wheel. *You gotta love Sinatra.* Geneva pressed lightly on her brake as she approached a slow-moving, older-model truck ahead of her sedan. It seemed that the only time this highway was the least bit busy was from five to six o'clock, when people headed home from work in Cameron. In the mornings, what few commuters there were all rushed down the road trying to get to work on time, so the pace was noticeably quicker. When the oncoming traffic allowed, Geneva passed the truck with ease and waved at the two gray-headed passengers, Numa and Helen Conner Broussard, inside.

She knew that these were Whitney Broussard's parents. Simply put, Geneva Griffith knew everybody. Since taking a job as a freelance reporter with the *Cameron Pilot* in 1956, Geneva often contributed human-interest stories and community-event articles for the small local newspaper, which was established that same year. Readership was picking up, and the steady increase in subscriptions foretold a healthy future for the new business. The owner-editor, Jerry Wise, had a small but dedicated staff. With her full-time job at the courthouse, Geneva took on reporting assignments as time allowed. She was quickly becoming well known by all the residents of Cameron Parish by covering the local fairs, festivals, and numerous other community gatherings.

Most people in Calcasieu and Cameron parishes subscribed to the long-established *Lake Charles American Press* for their daily information. The Sherman family owned a publishing empire that included many newspapers across the country. The thick, comprehensive newspaper was a highly respected source for local, area, and world news and offered both a morning and evening edition in peak times. For the people of Cameron, however, the *Pilot* filled a special niche.

Geneva did not have an assignment due to the editor for several days, so tonight could be spent relaxing with the children.

Tuesday afternoon, June 25
The Johnny Meaux farm
Oak Grove, Louisiana

After attending a police jury meeting that afternoon, Johnny

Meaux marveled at the growth and progress he'd witnessed in Cameron Parish over the past decade. Postwar America was thriving and the economy was good. Even in the small rural communities of the Deep South, business development was on the rise. It was the best of both worlds.

We even have our own newspaper now, he thought with pride as he flipped to the second page of the *Pilot*. "The parade next week will be a good gathering for the parish, don't you think, Esther?" he asked his wife.

The two escaped the sweltering heat that had plagued the area for the past week by enjoying a gentle breeze under the shade of the front porch that late afternoon. June bugs flew with abandon this time of year. The beetles' lazy buzz always heralded the hottest months of the year. One small specimen settled on Meaux's newspaper, and he leisurely brushed it away.

Near the barn, Raymond Bartie removed his straw hat and used the damp bandana around his neck to wipe his forehead. It had been a long day for the field hands on the Meaux farm, but this would be the last load of the afternoon. The men had just finished hauling a flatbed truckload of field peas to the large red barn, where they offloaded the harvest into the remaining empty storage bin. Several of the Bartie children were playing in the loft of the barn, but they came down the ladder when their father and older brother Eugene approached.

Work was hard on the Meaux farm, but the business was a success, due in large part to the dedication of the Bartie family. Raymond had lived and worked here for over ten years. He and his wife, Maybell, lived in a house across the field from the Meaux home. Several of their six children were born and reared on this land he had grown to love. Like most men who had a connection with the earth, Bartie dreamed of one day owning a piece of farmland, but in the 1950s, money was often scarce for a black family in the Deep South.

Scooting all the little ones out, Mr. Bartie closed the barn doors behind them, and the group began the walk across the field to the Bartie home. Following their energetic romp, Bartie noticed how much his children had grown lately. The well-worn path bore the foot-prints of his barefoot children, while fourteen-year-old Eugene's boot prints seemed as large as Raymond's own. The boy was almost a man, and Raymond looked at his son with pride, recalling the long hours they worked side by side in bringing in this crop.

As they approached the steps of the whitewashed wooden house, the youngest Bartie, two-year-old Walter, waited impatiently at the screen door to greet his father. The aroma of freshly baked cornbread hot from the oven emanated from Maybell's kitchen at the rear of the house. Raymond could swear he smelled okra and field peas simmering on the stove. This was his favorite part of the day—coming home to his family, and Maybell's cooking. Maybell Bartie had a talent for making simple things special, like the freshly cut bouquet of wild sunflowers on the table. The long stems were artfully arranged in a simple glass vase as if from a florist. Her home, like her kitchen, was warm and inviting, and filled with love.

"How's my little man?"

Bending low, Raymond lifted the toddler into the air amid squeals of delight.

Tuesday evening, June 25
Oilrig platform off the Louisiana coast

Capt. D.W. Griffith, Geneva's husband, removed his cap and wiped his brow with the back of his rolled-up shirtsleeve. Griffith found pleasure in his career as a boat captain for Pure Oil Company, and worked ten days on, five days off. Another shift had just ended on the oilrig, and dinner was being served to the tired, apprehensive crew. Before D.W. joined his friends in the cafeteria, he paused outside on the deck. The weather was tolerable for the moment, but clouds had moved in to form the beginnings of an overcast sky to the south of the oilrig. Boat captains were constantly attuned to weather conditions, and D.W. was no exception. He had also noticed something unusual— a slight change in the currents that day around the oilrigs. He had plied these waters for years and knew the currents well. As the afternoon progressed the currents went from somewhat odd to downright strange. Griffith attributed the strange movement to the advancing storm. He had never observed this change in ocean movements before and could think of no other reason except the hurricane.

At noon Tuesday, he and the other captains had been alerted by short-wave radio that the tropical storm had been upgraded to a hurricane. All the oilrig personnel on the Texas and Louisiana coasts were busy securing the massive rigs for the advancing storm. Evacuation of the roustabout crews had already begun by the service boats and helicopters belonging to the oil companies from Galveston, Texas to Grand Isle, Louisiana. Captain Griffith would have all his passengers back on land by Wednesday morning.

"Griffith, what the latest on the hurricane?" asked a stocky, deeply tanned man headed toward the cafeteria. Even the strongest roustabouts were cautious when it came to storms at sea. The two shook hands then faced south to watch the skies.

"She's clocked at 100 miles per hour now, up from 75 miles per hour at noon. The four o'clock report from the Weather Bureau said she had not changed course and was still headed due north, moving slowly toward the Louisiana-Texas border. If nothing changes, landfall is expected to be early Friday morning. But then, hurricanes often seem to veer off to the northeast once they get near land. If that happens Audrey might hit east of Cameron, and we will be just fine. But as you can imagine, that would be bad for Vermilion Parish. Either way, Mark, it's never a good thing when a big one hits the gulf coast."

"Do you think this will be a big one?"

"I don't know. Too soon to tell. All I do know is we're going to remove as much sensitive equipment from the rig as we can over the next couple of hours, load up the last of the guys, then we're out of here. The pogy boats have all headed to shore as of noon today."

"Well, don't take the cook just yet." The older man patted D.W. on the back and said his goodbyes. With one last glance backward, Mark looked at the darkening clouds in the far distance as he walked off the open deck into the mess hall.

Some oilrigs were much farther out in the gulf than the one on which D.W. stood this Tuesday afternoon. Oil companies built their massive rigs on the gulf's continental shelf, which is sort of a submerged extension of the coastline, not out in the deeper waters. The continental shelf off the Cameron coast extended 100 miles from shore. This was the widest shelf in the Gulf of Mexico, providing the longest span of relatively shallow water. Louisiana's geographic shelf contributed significantly to the ability of an oil company to access the oil deposits below.

Gov. Earl K. Long made certain that the tax revenues for Louisiana included taxes on oil pumped from its ground. In the week before Audrey, the state issued eighty-four drilling permits along the Louisiana coastline. The state coffers were full, and Governor Long was duly respected for taking care of the common man. Roads and schools were built in abundance. Long loved the people of Louisiana, and the voters loved him right back. In the weeks to come, Gov. Earl Long would fight one of his greatest battles to protect and defend the common man of Cameron Parish.

Tuesday evening, June 25
The Whitney Broussard home
Cameron, Louisiana

After visiting the doctor's office that morning, Clara Broussard and the children stopped at the market to get fresh gulf shrimp. Clara was a meticulous housekeeper, with an easy, gentle flow in her daily routine of cooking, cleaning, and minding the seven children all at the same time. On this Tuesday evening, she prepared gumbo for dinner, and the thick soup was simmering on the stove. Steam rose from the large metal pot, and the savory aroma of bay leaf and garlic filled the kitchen. Her husband would be coming home from his office at the motel within the hour.

Thirteen-year-old Ethel readied the seafood, peeling the shrimp with surprisingly deft fingers for a novice cook. Her mother had taught her early on how to cook gumbo, and Ethel knew just when to add the shrimp and crabmeat to the savory broth.

Barely eye level to the countertop, three-year-old Richard snuck a treat for himself from a platter of food, carefully positioning a pitted black olive on each of his tiny fingertips. Ethel and her little brother exchanged secretive glances, and the toddler got an approving, conspiratorial wink from his sister. Suppressing a smile, Ethel moved to place salad, garlic bread, and Tabasco sauce on the table.

In the dining room, Clara removed the delicate Noritake plates from the large china cabinet and set the stack at the end of the table. The softly intricate Seren Garden pattern was a nice complement to the cream-colored dining-room walls. Elaine, ten, helped set the table for the evening meal, and began her well-honed routine of placing one plate in front of each chair, returning several times to the stack of china plates to complete her mission. Soon the table was beautifully appointed with napkins and silverware as well.

It wasn't the china and crystal that were important to Mrs. Broussard. It was her family that was important. The Broussard children grew up knowing that laughter and giggles were perfectly welcome on top of a china place setting. Saying grace at the beginning of a family meal came as easily to the children as breathing in the aromas of a home-cooked meal. Good table manners were taught so gently and consistently to the little ones that they had no idea they were learning life lessons over a bowl of seafood gumbo.

After dinner that evening, the family gathered as they always did to say the rosary. Like the majority of families in Cameron Parish, Whitney and Clara were devout Catholics, and they had taught their young children to recite the rosary at an early age. With toddlers in the mix, this pious nightly gathering was sometimes a three-ring circus, but a holy one nonetheless.

Neither Whitney nor Clara caught the evening news and weather report that night about the hurricane that was churning out in the gulf. As their rosary was ending, the phone began to ring.

"Hello? Son! It's so good to hear your voice! How are your classes?"

Whitney Broussard, Jr., attended college "up north" in St. Louis and had extended his stay for the summer session. His life for the next few years was mapped out perfectly. He was realizing his dream, but it hurt

In the living room of the Broussard home in Cameron, 1956: David, age four; Elaine, age nine; and Richard Broussard, age two.

being so far from the family he loved. It would be Christmas before he was due home for a long holiday break, but Hurricane Audrey would soon change all those well-laid plans.

Tuesday evening, June 25
The Griffith home
Oak Grove, Louisiana

That evening after supper, Geneva restocked her cupboards with the new provisions. Tomorrow she would top off the lanterns with kerosene. For now that chore could wait. Tonight all she wanted to do was cuddle on the sofa with Leslie and Cherie to watch some television. At ten o'clock, she listened to the weather report on the short-wave radio before going to bed.

"This is Hurricane Advisory number three issued by the New Orleans Weather Bureau at 10:00 P.M. CST, today, June twenty-fifth. Continue hurricane watch along Louisiana and Texas coasts with the greatest threat to the Louisiana coast. Hurricane Audrey is increasing in size and at 10:00 P.M. was centered near latitude 23.7, longitude 93.4, or about 500 miles southwest of New Orleans. It is moving slowly northward. Highest winds are estimated 100 miles per hour near the center and gales extend out 125 miles from the center. Indications are for northward movement about 7 miles per hour for the next twelve hours with a slow turn toward the north-northeast Wednesday. Seas and tides will increase along the Louisiana and Texas coasts and small craft in this area should remain in port. The next advisory will be issued at 4:00 A.M. CST."

Geneva again thought of all the people on the rigs, who would soon be evacuated because of the storm. D.W. would indeed be home tomorrow after his scheduled ten-day stint out in the gulf was cut short.

But there was something important that few realized. Not only were the offshore workers going to have to go ashore quickly to be safe from this storm, they were going to have to go much farther inland than Cameron to avoid the deadly wrath of Hurricane Audrey.

Tuesday evening, June 25
Home of Regina and Walter Phillips
Lake Charles, Louisiana

At the end of her long day, Alice Marshall was glad to be off her feet. She and the girls had picked figs for several hours, and she was tired. It was eight o'clock and the sun was finally beginning to fade outside. She relaxed in an easy chair in front of the television, hoping to stay awake long enough to hear the ten o'clock news. Regina's husband, Walter, had come home that evening from his print shop on Common Street with news of a hurricane out in the gulf. He said the storm would likely hit Thursday night or Friday morning.

Regina took extra care with the girls' bath that evening, making sure the shampoo removed all the tree sap from her daughters' hair. All three were sticky from head to toe from crawling beneath the low-hanging branches of the fig trees then climbing the limbs to reach the fruit at the top.

After dinner, Alice read little Elizabeth several stories, while Kathleen and Frances lay on the carpet watching TV at their grandmother's feet. Now the day was winding down, and the grownups waited to hear the latest reports on Hurricane Audrey.

The evening edition of the *Lake Charles American Press* showed large two-inch-tall headlines reading, *HURRICANE FORMS IN GULF. A*

Alice Cagle Marshall (center) with her sister, Nan Cagle Cooley, and granddaughters, Elizabeth, Frances, and Kathleen Phillips, 1953.

map accompanied the article on the front page, showing Audrey out in the Gulf of Mexico with a huge arrow pointed directly at Lake Charles. Just as Alice finished reading the paper, her husband called from their home in Cameron, concerned about the news of the hurricane.

"I suppose it's too soon to predict where it will strike along the coast, but we should make some kind of plan for the next few days," Brown spoke into the phone. "Assuming Audrey stays on its current course toward the Texas-Louisiana border, it's supposed to arrive sometime Thursday or Friday. If so, we will stay Wednesday night in Lake Charles."

"Yes, of course. Better to be safe," Alice responded, nodding.

"I will have to work all day tomorrow," her husband continued, "to close up the business and secure the house against the hurricane winds. I have shutters and extra boards in the tool shed for the windows that I will nail up before I leave. And I will try to move some of your furniture up off the floor as well—just in case."

"Okay, honey, that sounds like a plan. But wouldn't you like some help? I can be there in the morning bright and early," Alice offered. "We could drive back up to Lake Charles together tomorrow evening."

"Actually, I'd rather have both vehicles in Lake Charles, just in case there is coastal flooding. So stay put. I'll be there tomorrow evening."

Close to the Marshall home, the waves lapped rhythmically onto the sandy beach, pushing white foam and bubbles as far up the gentle slope as possible before pausing, then retreating back to form another wave. A woman's soft laughter carried on the gulf breeze, over a haunting love song in the background. The two lovers strolled at the water's edge, enjoying the view of the beach stretching down the coast. An intensely beautiful sunset bathed the whitecaps, shimmering off the liquid surface of the waves, while overhead clouds reflected the deep, rich gold and pink colors of the setting sun. The few remaining people on the beach set ablaze a small bonfire of graying driftwood, which crackled and spit orange flames into the wind. The two young lovers began to dance slowly at the water's edge, and thought that a more romantic setting could not be found anywhere in the world. Across the sunset sky behind them, a flock of gray pelicans flew low over the waves.

CHAPTER 3

Wednesday—
The Best-Laid Plans

Wednesday, June 26, 1957
Home of Joe Rutherford
Oak Grove, Louisiana

It was time to brand the cattle, but the cattle disagreed. Roundup time was a great adventure for Dr. Cecil Clark's two sons, Joe and John. They wanted to learn how to "brand cows and be real cowboys." Dr. Clark's stepfather, Joe Rutherford, was just the person to teach them. He'd been branding his own cattle for almost fifty years right here in Oak Grove, about fifteen miles from Cameron. Rutherford's longtime friend and fellow cattleman, Conway LeBleu, would be joining the roundup, too.

John Clark, eight, was older than Joe, who had just finished the first grade. Both boys spent the night with their grandparents that Tuesday, so they could get up with the chickens, literally, and don their cowboy gear. Dr. Clark's mother, Bessie Rutherford, fixed them a huge breakfast to start the workday with her husband.

"After the roundup, we will spend the afternoon at the beach. I'll pack some Cokes in the ice chest, too. Would you like that?"

Eight-year-old John couldn't decide which adventure was going to be more fun. That morning he was indeed a real cowboy. That afternoon he was body surfing in the smaller waves at Rutherford Beach. The boys had heard the grownups talking about the storm out in the gulf. "A hurricane," they had said. Joe searched the skies above, but everything looked fine to the seven-year-old.

Playing at the water's edge, the Clark boys each built a sandcastle.

They were over a foot tall and had shells imbedded in the wide bases and sides. The boys were good at customizing their castles, too. They knew how to dribble just the right mixture of sand and water atop the castles to make weird, lumpy spires and shapes. Each boy claimed that his castle was the biggest and strongest and could withstand any hurricane. They finally came up with a suitable contest.

"Whoever's sandcastle outlasts the storm will win a nickel. Okay?" They shook hands on the bet and dashed off once again into the blue-green surf, laughing and hollering into the wind. Some of the brothers' best times were spent together on Rutherford Beach.

Neither castle would survive the storm. Neither would all of their family.

Dr. Cecil Clark took this snapshot of his family enjoying a day at the beach. This photograph was taken in June 1957, one week before Audrey. It was on a roll of film being processed at Mac's Camera Shop in Lake Charles when the storm hit. From left: John, age eight; Sybil, holding daughter Elizabeth, age three; and Joe, age seven.

Wednesday, June 26
The DeBarge home
Cameron, Louisiana

Tommy DeBarge held the steaming mug of coffee firmly in his gnarled hands. The old man noticed the headlines in the morning's newspaper and reached for his bifocals to better read the storm-related articles. After several minutes, he lowered the *American Press* and told his brother that this approaching storm had him worried. Tommy didn't think they would be safe in the old house, but Sidney refused to consider evacuating. He calmly dismissed his younger brother's concerns and continued buttering his toast.

Reaching for a coffee can above the stove, Tommy removed the lid, considering the thick wad of money inside. In the past, he never had much need for banks, but his concern for the hurricane made him rethink that position. With a new plan and a firm resolve, he turned to his brother once again.

"I'm going to put my money in the bank where it will be safe," he proclaimed and replaced the lid with a snap.

"Never trusted banks, myself," Sidney stated flatly, with a derisive snort. The old man was unrelenting in his skepticism of banks following the Great Depression. "Yep, a fool and his money are soon parted. You'll see; you'll see."

Just before lunch, Tommy DeBarge exited the Cameron State Bank and inserted a bank receipt into his worn leather billfold. He released the kickstand on his bike and pedaled off with a brown bag of groceries balancing in the wire basket that hung from the handlebars. Downtown businesses were taping up their windows and moving merchandise inside off the sidewalks. Tommy watched the activity, and the concern on the businessmen's faces, and felt reassured knowing that his money was safe inside the bank's sturdy vault.

Wednesday, June 26
The Cameron Parish Courthouse
Cameron, Louisiana

Throughout the day, the new Veteran's Affairs officer was beside himself with worry. He tried to focus on his work, but that soon became impossible. He phoned his wife to check on their son, who had recently broken his leg. Dr. Clark set the leg last week, and the heavy cast slowed the young boy down. There'd be no swimming at Rutherford Beach for five more weeks, but for a change his wife was able to keep up with the youngster. Everything seemed fine at home. His wife had packed two suitcases and boxed up some provisions for their evacuation tomorrow morning. In fact, the trunk of their car was almost full. They would need to bring an extra pillow, however, to prop beneath his son's cast while at the hotel in Lake Charles.

He paced the office and several times that afternoon walked up the basement stairs on the east side of the courthouse to check the summer sky outside. *What am I looking for anyway? A bolt of lightning to strike that church steeple?* He knew he must be worrying needlessly, but he had the worst feeling about this hurricane, this Audrey. He looked at the sky and gnawed on his fingernail while he smoked a cigarette in the cool breeze.

Is the breeze usually this cool on a hot summer afternoon? Maybe so . . . , he thought, trying to shake off this sense of foreboding, *then again, maybe not. This living along the coast is going to take a little getting used to.* He shook his head, laughing at himself. *This new job is great, so let's not blow it. I better get back to work.* One more drag and the officer dropped his cigarette, snuffing out the embers with his black, spit-shined shoe.

Wednesday, June 26
The Whitney Broussard home
Cameron, Louisiana

A mile away from the courthouse, Wednesday began as any other day for the Broussards. Whitney woke up, had coffee, and, after breakfast, went to his office at the motel, since his school was closed for summer vacation. Walking across the lawn, he tucked the newspaper under his arm.

I'll have plenty of time to read the Press *when there's a lull in activity at the office today,* he thought as he rounded the corner of Dan Street. As it turned out, Whitney's entire morning was busy. Quite a few pipeline engineers and roustabout workers from the offshore rigs checked into the motel.

"There's certainly a lot of traffic coming and going yesterday and today. What's happening on the rigs?" asked Whitney.

"All of the oil platforms in the gulf are being evacuated. In fact they should all be empty by now. It's the hurricane. Hurricane Audrey's supposed to hit sometime tomorrow afternoon."

Whitney realized he had missed the weather report last night and had not read the newspaper that morning. He handed the guest a room key, then reached for the newspaper beneath the counter. He removed the rubber band with a snap and quickly unrolled the paper.

HURRICANE AUDREY STILL AIMS FULL FORCE AT LAKE CHARLES. The headlines startled Broussard. Quickly, he scanned the lead article, which went into more detail regarding expected time of landfall. The Wednesday morning edition stated the winds would hit the coast "early Friday morning." Most of the motel guests were leaving for Lake Charles Thursday, tomorrow. He and Clara would need to make plans just in case they also had to evacuate Thursday. At least there was no immediate call for evacuation.

The hot summer day was a bit cooler under the shade of the pine trees in the Broussard yard as the children played outside. Despite the heat, the grass was cool and green in the shade. As on most any summer afternoon on the gulf coast, the salty air combined with the lush smell of clover to produce a humid, floral scent. When the bright midday sun shone directly overhead, the seats on the swing set became a bit hot for the energetic swingers. Clara opened the screen door and called the little ones in for their nap. At the shadow's edge beneath the pine boughs, Elaine and Ethel lay on their stomachs in the lush grass, looking for four-leaf clovers. The search unsuccessful, they eventually turned to making garlands from the white clover flowers. It was an undeclared contest between the sisters—the longer the garland, the better.

"Hey, here's a patch of flowers with longer stems!" exclaimed Elaine as she plopped down in the cool grass near the picnic-table legs. "It's too hard to tie those short stems together."

"Holy cow! I finally found one. I found a four-leaf clover!" Ethel yelled out as she crouched over, trying to break off the longest stem possible in the thick grass. "This one's going in my diary. I'll press it flat between the pages, and keep it forever." She proudly held up the kelly-green shamrock for Elaine to view.

Ethel was a typical teen and wrote in her diary each night. There were no secrets in the small leather-bound book, just private thoughts and girlish dreams. The diary's tiny brass key was carefully hidden in Ethel's jewelry box beneath the black-beaded rosary her grandmother had given her for her first Communion. For heaven's sake, if the key wasn't safe underneath her rosary, it wasn't safe anywhere.

Transport boats continued to arrive at the Magnolia docks hauling delicate equipment off the oil rigs, as the sweltering summer day wore on in Cameron. Late that afternoon, Whitney wrapped up his paperwork at the Broussard Motel and left the night clerk to handle the desk. After dinner that evening, he decided Clara might enjoy a change of scenery, a drive down to the beach. There was no need to hustle the children out to the car, because they, too, were eager for the outing, and ran ahead of their parents toward the garage. Heading east down the coast highway, Whitney soon turned due south onto Beach Road, which would continue for about a mile before reaching the coast.

Ethel and Elaine were giddy with excitement to play in the sand and look for seashells. They leaned their heads out of the backseat windows to get the first glimpse of the shoreline ahead.

"There it is! I see the waves!" Elaine proclaimed for the littler ones.

Her father pulled off the blacktop into a well-compacted parking area a safe distance from the shore. Four car doors opened at once, and the children bounded across the sand to the water's edge. Several of the clan waded in the shallows up to their ankles. As far as Elaine was concerned, that was far enough. None of the Broussard children knew how to swim. They had always held a parent's hand as they played in the waves of the gulf. As was often the case, swimming pools and swimming lessons were optional if you lived along the beach itself, as they did. Seagulls loudly cawed their presence above, and sand crabs scurried about the low dunes then retreated backward into their burrowed dwellings.

Whitney and Clara held hands as they always did on their impromptu dates. The conditions along the beach didn't seem very different this evening from other evenings. Bright skies still glared

Clara and Whitney Broussard, Sr., in front of their home on Dan Street in Cameron, Louisiana.

overhead, and a pleasantly cool breeze blew off the gulf. No signs of a hurricane were on the horizon, but the couple noticed that the surf was a bit rougher than usual.

Following at a distance behind their children, the couple shared the events of their day, still holding hands and enjoying the slow, unhurried pace. Whitney looked up and down the shoreline, not quite sure what he was expecting in the wind and waves but knowing he would recognize any significant change if there was one. The humidity caused the air to seem extra heavy, as if a person could reach out and touch the sea spray. He lowered himself down, resting on his haunches. Picking up a handful of sand, he slowly let the warm, white granules slip away through his fingers. The salty breeze blew through his dark hair.

Whitney stood up and dusted the sand off his hands, ready to head back home. He signaled his children to return from the water's edge. Shading his eyes with his hand, he glanced skyward, noticing a large flock of birds flying inland. A few other folks from town walked farther down along the unusually empty beach.

Wednesday, June 26
Home of Regina and Walter Phillips
Lake Charles, Louisiana

With news that the approaching hurricane was due to hit tomorrow afternoon, several relatives called Regina's home during the day asking about her mother.

"I'm so relieved to hear that Aunt Alice is already with you," a grateful Joe Cagle told his cousin Regina. Concern for his aunt's safety caused him to pause in a busy day at the Chevy dealership to check on her whereabouts. Alice took the phone from Regina, and soon was laughing with her nephew.

"Aunt Alice! What do you mean you're busy feeling pigs? What's that? Oh, you say you're *peeling* figs? Likely story, ma'am." His humor hid his concern, but the older lady got the message. She loved him too.

"Don't worry, Big Chief. I'm fine, and Brown will join me here tomorrow evening. Your mother called us today and said that she'd be spending Thursday with you and Mary Belle in town."

"Yes, we thought we'd hunker down tonight, however, so Mother wouldn't have to get out in rainy weather tomorrow afternoon. Quite a few of the family will be staying with us too, since we have a gas stove for cooking. If the electricity goes out, at least we can cook for a crowd in our kitchen. So, yes, we are having a huge slumber party here at 1717 Tenth Street. Kids will be sleeping in every nook and cranny. Want to come?" He chuckled. "Oh, if you come, bring some pigs—I mean figs."

"Bye, Joe. You're a good man to take such wonderful care of your mother. Your daddy would be proud."

Joe and Mary Belle Cagle on their honeymoon in 1945.

"Thanks, Aunt Alice. Goodbye."

He hung up the phone and slowly swiveled around in his leather chair. Joe was only thirty-eight, and the death of his father had come as such a shock to the whole family. Since his father's passing, Joe often took on the role of head of the family in matters such as this. When it came to a hurricane, he would rather be overly cautious in his planning, so he asked his sisters and brothers to arrive at his home well ahead of time. Mary Belle had stocked up on provisions, and there were plenty of toys for all the cousins to play with during their stay.

He reached for the black and white photograph of his parents on the built-in bookshelves behind his desk. It was his favorite picture of the two, taken only a few years before his father passed away in his sleep. His dad was wearing a suit, and a shy half-smile, a smile that Joe inherited.

He returned the photograph to its place on the shelf amid the many photos of his wife and eight children. Joe picked up the phone again and dialed the operator, trying to reach his friend Dudley Fawvor in Cameron. There was no answer. He'd try again later. He hadn't spoken to the Fawvor family in a while and he wanted to make sure Dudley had a safe place to stay in town tonight.

6:00 P.M., *Wednesday, June 26*
The Calcasieu Ship Channel
Cameron, Louisiana

Amid the noisy sounds of the seagulls and the harbor traffic, Capt. Louie Stoute was battening down the tugboat *George Hamilton* at the dock near LeBoeuf Road, as the small Monkey Island ferry ended its day. About a mile north of this road, the larger, self-propelled Cameron Ferry moved a full load of twenty cars across the ship channel to the west side, away from Cameron and toward the highway leading north to Hackberry, Louisiana.

In Oak Grove, Raymond Bartie and his oldest son, Eugene, finished up another long day in the fields, and moved the last of the equipment into the barns and sheds just as Johnny Meaux returned from his meeting at the courthouse. Another gust of unusually cool breeze flapped the frayed brim of Raymond's straw hat as he secured a final tarp over a load of field peas. Jumping down to the ground, the man tested the ropes to make sure his son tied them off securely.

"Good job, son," declared Raymond with a nod of his head to the teenager.

Taking in a deep breath of the cool air, Mr. Meaux unbuttoned his collar and removed his uncomfortable necktie. Johnny was a big man, and twenty-inch collars were hard to find. He smiled in relief as he walked over to join Raymond to chat about the crop, as well as the approaching hurricane that was expected to hit tomorrow afternoon.

"You're bringing in a good crop, Raymond. First thing in the morning, we'll secure the barn and the outbuildings, and then drive on up to Lake Charles after breakfast. Will that give you enough time to make ready before the storm hits?"

Mr. Meaux valued Raymond's opinion on all things farm related, and he genuinely cared for the Bartie family. They had worked side by side so often over the past decade that Raymond had become indispensable to the smooth operations of the farm. The Meauxs fondly watched all the Bartie babies grow up, and the children had free run of the property.

In turn, the Bartie family had grown to respect Johnny and his wife, Esther. For Raymond and Maybell, the farm had become more than just a job—it became their home, and a way of life. Mutual respect made all the difference.

Eugene slid the long, heavy beam across the wide doors of the barn into the metal braces. Both men were tired from the long day of work in the hot, blazing summer sun, and they welcomed the cool breeze. The father and son discussed the hurricane as they walked across the field toward their house. The field was quiet; no sound came from the grasshoppers as the pair made their way down the hard, earthen path to their home. Raymond threw his arm across the shoulders of his son, and Bartie's younger children rushed out to greet them.

"Daddy, Miss Esther said there's a big storm coming! Momma said it was going to rain cats and dogs. Is that true, Daddy? Can I have a cat?"

Wednesday, June 26
The DeBarge home
Cameron, Louisiana

Late Wednesday afternoon, lively strains of Cajun music on the radio spilled out of the screen door from the kitchen into the DeBarge garden. The elderly brothers finally found something they could agree upon—the need to harvest as many tomatoes as they could before the storm hit the next afternoon.

Holding a metal bucket full of tomatoes for his brother as the two walked between the fertile rows, Tommy reiterated his opinion that they should evacuate to Lake Charles. Sidney stated flatly that he was not leaving.

"Stubborn. You've always been stubborn," Tommy commented with a shake of his gray head.

"Worrywart," Sidney countered as he plucked off a big Beefsteak tomato.

He left several large green tomatoes on the vines, and reminded his brother once again that they had survived many, many storms right here in this house, and they will make it through this one, too. Their harvesting completed, the brothers headed indoors, each carrying a full bucket of vegetables to the kitchen sink.

The men enjoyed a simple supper of thick-sliced, vine-ripe tomatoes and chunks of mozzarella cheese. A loaf of fresh, crusty French bread and sugar-sweetened iced tea rounded out the meal. As the men wrapped up the day relaxing in their large Adirondack porch rockers, an unusually cool breeze came up from the south off the gulf.

Tommy decided to move his bicycle inside, off of the porch, but paused to watch several huge flocks of birds coming in from offshore. It seemed everyone was getting ready for the hurricane, even the animals. He was convinced that this storm would be a bad one. The birds continued their flight northward over Cameron Parish. Several miles inland, the gravel roads remained hot despite the cool breeze that had appeared from out of nowhere. Amid the tall, swaying cattails and low reeds of the roadside ditches, one crawfish—quickly followed by another—began to move, fleeing in advance of the hurricane. Animals have that elusive sixth sense, and it came into play that June evening. Soon the road was covered with hundreds of crawfish scurrying out of the ditches, oblivious to an approaching truck.

Inside the dusty cab of the truck, a young couple hummed along to the radio's lively Cajun music of "Jambalaya," but as they came upon the shifting mass of crawfish, their voices faded away. The driver slowed down, then slammed on the brakes, bringing the pickup to a complete stop. Amazed at the amount of crawfish on road, the two got out and each grabbed a shovel from the bed of the truck. They began scooping up the crawfish and tossing them into the back of the pickup as fast as they could shovel. Laughing out loud, the two made plans for a rather large crawfish boil as they reveled in their sudden good fortune. It was the perfect way to end a long day at work.

In Cameron, offices in town were closing for the day, with the understanding they would reopen for business once the storm system passed through the area. Some office workers had already left early that afternoon for Lake Charles.

At five o'clock, Geneva waited for Aunt Nona to lock the door of the Voter Registration Office. The two friends chatted about their busy day as they walked down the scuffed tile floors in the wide hallway. Exiting the heavy doors at the building entrance, they made their way down the courthouse steps to Nona's car. Instead of driving herself into work that morning, Geneva had caught a ride with her friend Shootsie Miller Theriot, knowing she would be able to get a ride home from D.W.'s aunt. Although she lived directly behind the courthouse, Nona welcomed the short drive to her nephew's home in Oak Grove that afternoon, but first she stopped at the nearby gas station and waited in the short line. The evacuation process in the morning might slow traffic along the highway to Lake Charles, and the always-organized lady felt safer having a full tank of gas.

Both women rolled down their car windows to catch the nice breeze while the attendant filled up the gas tank. Nona waved at her friend Alvin Dyson on the other side of the pump.

"Hey there, Alvin. Are you and Allie planning to leave in the morning?" she asked. Wynona Welch knew everyone in Cameron Parish. She was born and raised there and had held the office of registrar of voters for the past several decades. Much like Santa Claus, she knew when you voted and when you didn't. The middle-aged lady with deep auburn hair had never married. Some folks might call her an old maid or a spinster, but the people of Cameron Parish called her Miss Nona, a term of respect and affection.

Waving goodbye to her longtime friend, Nona paid the attendant and pulled out onto Marshall Street, the original name of the coast highway. Apprehension caused both women to look skyward, checking the evening skies for signs of the hurricane. As far as they could tell, the sudden and unusually cool breeze was the only notable change in the weather. To take advantage of this delight, Geneva rolled down her window even further as they began the drive to her home in Oak Grove along the edge of the gulf. Neither woman cared that her hair blew about in wild disarray. The intense heat from the past few weeks had finally eased, and the ladies took a simple delight in the sensation, knowing it would be short-lived at best.

Wednesday, June 26
The Griffith home
Oak Grove, Louisiana

D.W. was already home, high up on a ladder, busy hammering up plywood to cover the picture window of the dining room that faced the gulf. D.W.'s mother and father were also there. They were visiting from Port Arthur, having come over to pick figs at his uncle Buster's house.

Dora and Buster Welch's home had several huge fig trees on the property, and picking figs was an annual event for the family. One of their trees was said to be the oldest fig tree in the nation. Fig trees are not tall, compared to slender pines and majestic oaks, but because of its age, this fig tree was of course larger than most trees of its kind. While age and breadth are all well and good, this particular tree's value lay in the sweetness of its pink-tinged, pale-brown fruit borne on

The Griffith and Welch families gather in 1951. Geneva is on the far left; D.W. and Leslie, age five, are on the far right. Papa Griffith is on the back row, far right side, with Nannie Griffith to his right.

the wide-spreading, low-hanging branches. Nannie and Papa Griffith had been busy all day picking, cleaning, and making fig preserves. Even from outside, D.W. could smell the simmering, sweet fruit on the stove. He could almost taste a spoonful of fig preserves spread on a piece of hot buttered toast. It was a simple pleasure, and one he especially enjoyed.

Nona pulled her car into Geneva's driveway, put it in park, and let the engine idle as the two women got out of the car. As they walked toward D.W., both of them laughed and commented on the cool southern breeze coming in from the gulf, always a rare treat in the hot summer months.

"Hi, honey! Welcome home. Isn't this cool breeze divine?" Geneva exclaimed.

"I'll take this kind of weather any day!" remarked his aunt. "How are you, D.W.?"

From atop his ladder, D.W. turned around and chided them for not being more worried about the approaching storm. Shaking his hammer at the two, then pointing out to the gulf, his tone was serious.

"Listen, ladies, this storm could be a big problem . . . really big. This may be a cool breeze now, but we've got to batten down everything and get ready for hurricane winds that are coming tomorrow. Besides, this storm is different. The tides have been unusual, running crazy around the platforms, and I have no idea what's causing that." Looking out toward the breakers, D.W. paused, then remarked in a lower tone, "The tides and currents are different, and I don't like it."

"Well, you could be right," responded Geneva. "And just in case, I already stocked up on supplies and fresh batteries. We're set. Now get down here and let me welcome you home properly."

He couldn't help but smile. Turning back to the plywood, D.W. drove home the last nail, replaced the hammer in his tool belt, and backed down the ladder into his wife's waiting arms.

D.W. planted a kiss on Geneva and hugged his aunt Nona before she headed back to her car, waving goodbye. Cherie came bounding out of the house to greet her mom. Her tiny fingers were sticky from helping Nannie make the preserves. They made a sugary tangle in Geneva's hair when she threw her arms around her mother's neck.

"Bye, y'all," called Aunt Nona with a wave. "I've got to run along and finish preparations myself. I still have to pack before I can leave for Lake Charles in the morning."

No matter how you can them, figs are good stuff. On the morrow, however, several families in Cameron Parish would lose loved ones because it happened to be fig season, while yet another family would survive because of the fig trees.

Behind the house, Leslie and his grandfather walked across the backyard coming from the barn, deep in discussion about chicken eggs, the use of hay versus horse feed, and barnyard philosophy in general. Leslie looked up at Papa, hanging on his every word. Papa Griffith was not tall, but he was wiry and strong for a man in his seventies. He had once told his grandchildren not to worry about that bald spot on his head; there were still plenty of brains inside. The young boy thought grandfathers knew everything, plus they walked slower than most people.

Leslie's cocker spaniel, Bootsie, was happy just to sit in the shade of the house this day, watching all the commotion. Age-wise, Bootsie was like Papa Griffith. At eleven years old—seventy-seven in dog years—the family pet had been with Leslie since he was a baby. Bootsie was older now and moved much slower. Some days it was completely enjoyable to just sit—to do nothing at all. And today, the cool breeze felt good, especially to an old dog with a long fur coat. Life was good at the Griffith home.

On this evening, Nannie had already cooked dinner ahead of Geneva's arrival, and the meal was leisurely. Their two cars were gassed up, as well as the truck, ready to leave in the morning. All three vehicles were parked facing the road, ready for a quick exit if necessary. The cupboards were full, the kerosene lamps were filled, and fresh batteries were loaded in flashlights in case the electricity went out. Mason jars full of brown fig preserves cooled on the kitchen countertop, ready to box up that evening.

Cherie had been busy that day playing dress-up with a few odds and ends of frayed, feminine finery. In her bedroom, she managed to keep her balance in high heels, too large, but too cute for words. She dug around in an old cigar box full of trinkets and jewelry—her treasures. She chose the long Mardi Gras necklace with purple and gold plastic beads and placed it around her neck. Then she carefully lifted up her new accessory, a sparkly crown her grandmother had made for her that day.

The two had worked so hard on it. Nannie first drew the crown on stiff paper, making sure the pointy things were just right. Then Cherie had used her own little snub-nose scissors to cut along the lines. Nannie fitted it on Cherie's head and used scotch tape to secure the perfect size. The final touch had been several thin strips of aluminum foil to wrap around the crown. It wasn't junk jewelry—it was a work of art.

Cherie carefully placed the crown on her head, then pulled on the long white prom gloves her mom had given her. Now the five-year-old

A little man's best friend. This 1948 photograph shows Leslie Griffith, age three, with his dog, Bootsie, also age three, nine years before Hurricane Audrey.

was ready for her grand entrance. Clop, clop, clop—the battered high-heel shoes made such a clatter as she sashayed down the hallway. Dress-up was way more fun than trying to climb oak trees with her brother.

The earthy, equestrian smell of leather filled young Leslie's room. He worked at his sturdy wooden desk with several leather tools in easy reach. Tonight he was finishing a project—cutting, carving, and detailing a strip of leather. In time the tough strip would be pliable, but only after hours of softening with creamy leather polish. In one desk drawer, he kept a stack of catalogs for leather supplies and new tools. Before climbing into his bunk bed that evening, Leslie returned all his tools to their proper place, a habit he learned from his father. Without thinking, he methodically positioned each piece of leather-tooling equipment in its customary place in the desk drawers.

Moving from his desk chair, the young boy returned a small metal tool chest to its place in the closet. His dad had given him his own set of tools for his birthday several years ago. The red metal box was filled with a small hammer, a metal file, a small eight-inch saw with a wooden handle, a box of nails, and assorted guy stuff like string.

Oh, how he enjoyed these big-boy tools! In a matter of hours, however, these cherished items would be lost—seemingly forever.

Night had fallen in downtown Cameron. In the small business section, most stores were boarded up. Sheets of rough plywood covered the large glass windows in hopes of protecting the stores' contents from the driving rain and flying debris that always accompanied hurricanes. On other storefronts, masking tape had been applied to the glass windowpanes in crisscross patterns. Every little bit helps. Sidewalks were empty now. Streets were deserted. A lone vehicle from the sheriff's office patrolled the coast highway through town. The wind was sporadic, with intermittent gusts rustling the thick leaves on the oak trees that were so abundant in town. Rain began to fall, and the deputy turned on the wipers.

Geneva washed and dried the last of the dinner dishes and put them back in the cabinet. Her mother-in-law stacked several jars of fig preserves in the cupboard, a special treat for her son. The family had visited over steamy cups of coffee while listening to the six o'clock news on NBC's affiliate station, KPLC out of Lake Charles. In that evening's broadcast, the weather was the lead story and took center stage. Usually the evening weather report was last on the line-up, but not tonight. The local weatherman reported the details.

"It's staring right down our throats," he stated. "Hurricane Audrey is located about 300 miles due south of Lake Charles, packing winds over 100 miles per hour near its center. The latest advisory from New Orleans was issued at four o'clock this afternoon and indicated the center of the storm would reach the Louisiana coast late Thursday. Earlier today landfall had been expected to be early Friday morning, but those estimates have been revised because of the slight increase in forward movement from 7 miles per hour to the current speed of 10 miles per hour. Gale-force winds extend outward from the eye of the storm for 200 miles and are expected to be felt in the Lake Charles area tonight.

"The Weather Bureau bulletin also reported tides are rising and will reach five to eight feet along the Louisiana coast and over the Mississippi Sound by late Thursday. All persons in low exposed places should move to higher ground."

Later that evening, Geneva, D.W., and his parents listened to their short-wave radio, as was their routine, for the 10:00 P.M. weather report. D.W. adjusted the dial just a hair to clear up the bit of static noise. The marine operator in Galveston gave them the storm's wind speed, tide information, and coordinates.

"Hurricane Audrey has sustained winds of 100 miles per hour. The latest coordinates of latitude 27.0, and longitude 93.5, indicate the hurricane will make landfall Thursday afternoon."

The word "evacuate" was never mentioned.

The extended Griffith family went to bed peacefully, thinking they would have time to feed the animals before they left early the next morning.

Wednesday evening, June 26
Home of Dr. Cecil Clark
Cameron, Louisiana

All that day, Dr. Clark's office has been swamped with patients. However, the evening rounds at the small hospital went quickly for the doctor. On this summer night, there were only six bed patients in the clinic—a boy with a knee injury and two mothers and their newborn babies, which included a set of twins he had delivered early that morning. The patients were to be evacuated to the courthouse tomorrow morning, just in case. The night staff, Nurse Reyes and Nurse Porche, would contact him if there were an emergency, but the patients were recovering well, and he anticipated no midnight phone calls.

The Clarks had just finished building their new home five miles east of Cameron last October. Three months ago, Sybil had given birth to their third son, Jack. It was her good fortune to have found someone to help her with the two toddlers while she regained her strength and usual stamina. Zulmae Dubois was a Cajun godsend. While not from Cameron Parish, she had come highly recommended to the Clarks and had now been with them for almost two years. The older, gray-haired lady had a warm, motherly nature, which showed in the tender care she gave her five young charges. She and Sybil had become close friends. Zulmae helped out with housekeeping as well as baby-sitting, and the family just kept growing. The couple had designed their new four-bedroom home with a large family in mind. It was a good thing they did.

The white brick ranch-style house included a playroom for the five children where joyous noise was the norm. In the quiet evening hours, Cecil and Sybil retreated to their large bedroom, his favorite place—his comfort zone—where the two would sit and watch TV after the children had gone to bed. The Clark home was filled with toddler princesses, future cowboys, and a young couple with a bright future ahead of them.

A year from now, Dr. Clark would rebuild his home in the same place, but this time the house would be much smaller.

Sybil Clark was concerned about the hurricane out in the gulf—very concerned. She had already packed enough clothes for the five

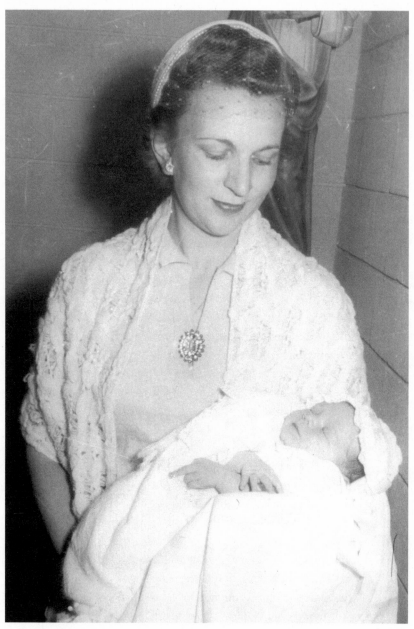

Sybil Baccigalopi Clark, wife of Dr. Cecil Clark, holds their newborn son Jack Benjamin Clark at his christening in May 1957, one month before Hurricane Audrey.

children into several suitcases for the trip to Lake Charles. One suit-case was filled with nothing but soft, white cotton diapers folded into neat triangles. They had loaded fresh batteries into flashlights, and the station wagon had a full tank of gas. Some of their neighbors had already left that Wednesday afternoon, but the Derouen, Nunez, and Mudd families were still at home.

It was the middle of summer and the days were at their longest. The Clarks enjoyed a late supper, but there was no thought of going to bed. Sybil changed from her uniform into a comfortable corduroy shirt and a pair of pedal pushers. Cecil, meanwhile, telephoned his mother to reconfirm tomorrow's evacuation plans and to check on his sons, who were staying another night with their grandparents.

The Rutherfords would drive the boys home early in the morning. By that time, Dr. Clark would have the hospital patients moved to safety, and he would be back at the house. The Clarks and the Rutherfords would then caravan their cars to Lake Charles as a group.

Sybil then spoke with John and Joe about their cattle roundup before wishing them a good night. After the phone call, the young couple went to the den and took turns rocking their infant son. The two toddlers played at their feet as rain began to fall outside. An hour or so after sundown, the children were all asleep, but the grownups' typical routine was shelved.

They were all on edge, so Zulmae and Dr. and Mrs. Clark stayed together to listen to the ten o'clock weather report on KPLC-TV out of Lake Charles. The hurricane was expected to hit Thursday after-noon. They would have plenty of time to evacuate the patients to the courthouse and then drive with the children to Lake Charles early in the morning.

Wednesday evening, June 26
Home of Regina and Walter Phillips
Lake Charles, Louisiana

Around dinnertime that evening, Alice placed a call to her hus-band to see if he had left for Lake Charles.

"Operator? Yes, I'd like to place a collect call to my home in Cameron," she began. If there was no answer, she could assume he had already locked up the house and was headed up the Creole highway to Lake Charles. He wouldn't go the other way, through the town of Cameron, because he would have to wait a bit for the ferry to cross the Calcasieu Ship Channel.

Sitting in front of the television, Brown Marshall struggled with the folding metal TV tray.

This was a mistake, he told himself, trying to balance his roast-beef sandwich with one hand while opening the tray legs with the other. When Alice was not at home, he ate casually and avoided the dining room for a quick bite in the den. Finally, everything was in place, but now the television was having a problem. High atop the two-story house, the large TV antennae tried to do its job in spite of the light rain that had started to fall. Strong cable wires secured the tall reception equipment to all four sides of the roof.

His day had been long and hard. All day the talk at the slaughterhouse had been about the hurricane. Tonight he just wanted to catch the evening news on TV to get the latest on Hurricane Audrey, except now he stared at the fuzzy reception on the screen. Setting aside his sandwich, Brown walked to the set and adjusted the tuning a bit. Things cleared up to almost normal just as the phone rang.

"Tootie? I'm surprised you're still at home. How was your day? Will you be leaving soon?"

"Hi, honey. Things have been hopping around here. All the preparations during the day took longer than I expected, though. People called about their livestock, and several came by to pick up their cattle in trucks for transport to Sulphur and Lake Charles until the storm passes. Other folks came by to get their fresh-cut meat from the freezers. They are worried the power will go out, and they'll lose their beef. I don't blame them. It sounds like we're going to get some high tide, possibly some water in the house since we are so close to the beach. I still have to secure the house before I can leave."

"But how long will that take? Are you still planning to drive here tonight?" asked Alice, concern evident in her voice.

"No, honey, I can't. I have just a few more things to take care of first thing in the morning, and then I'll meet you at Regina's. Okay? Remember, the hurricane isn't supposed to hit until late tomorrow afternoon. I'll be out in plenty of time."

Alice wasn't convinced, but she realized her husband wouldn't budge from the house until all was secure.

"Well, okay," she replied reluctantly. "Do you need any help? I could come home and help answer the phone. I need to pick my figs in the morning anyway."

"No, no, honey. You stay put. Stay with Regina and Walter until I get there. And don't worry. I'll be there long before the weather gets bad. Now go and enjoy those grandbabies. Did you can a lot of figs today? Don't let Walter eat them all before I get there, you hear?"

Brown was able to change the subject successfully for the moment, and Alice agreed to stay the course and spend the night with her daughter. She hung up the phone and returned to the kitchen to stir a large pot of preserves simmering on the stove. But her mind was far away, and she was deep in thought, worrying about her husband.

Regina was glad her mother had agreed to stay as planned. The kitchen was quiet now. The children were watching television, their job well done that afternoon. The family would have a light supper of sandwiches tonight since all the counter space in the kitchen was spoken for. Several dozen jars of preserves cooled on the counter, with at least that many more to be filled.

"Isn't this the best-smelling assembly line around?" asked Regina, beaming and taking in a deep whiff of the thick, steamy brew on the stove. Alice was lost in thought. Regina put her arm around her mother's shoulders and spoke softly, reassuringly. "Momma, try not to worry. Come on. Let's go listen to the news. The weather should be on soon."

The approaching hurricane had many of the locals worried, on edge. It was the lead story that night on both the national and Louisiana news. In the Phillips home, Alice listened intently to the statistics and landfall predictions. Thursday afternoon was the expected time of landfall.

"I'll have plenty of time to get there and back before the hurricane hits," thought Alice out loud.

"Mother, what are you saying?"

"Regina, I'm driving to Cameron tonight. I'm going home. I need to pick my figs in the morning and get a change of clothes while I'm at it. There are a few things I want to get from the house, too, just in case we get some flooding inside."

"Mother, please. I would worry. It's not worth the risk."

Amid her daughter's pleadings, Alice started gathering her things from the bedroom, making ready to depart. Alice's mind raced with worry. *My husband is alone, and I can't count on him to leave in time tomorrow.* She snapped shut the brass latches on her small suitcase and turned again to her daughter, who was becoming distraught.

"Momma, please don't do this. This is a hurricane—not some tropical storm!"

"I'll be fine, Regina. I'll be back before you know it. I promise." With that, she gave her daughter a hug and started down the hall to the front door.

Alice had a mind of her own, and in spite of the fun and carefree image she projected, she had opinions that her family valued. She had been a teacher in Longville, Louisiana for many years before moving to Lake Charles with her husband in the 1940s. Following the Great Depression, there were more job opportunities in the bigger, bustling port city. Several of her brothers had recently relocated there as well. At sixty-one, Alice had lived a busy, interesting life, and she told great stories about growing up in Merryville—stories almost as good as her nephew Joe told, but not quite.

Joe Cagle took top honors in storytelling, in holding his audience's attention. He had a gift for knowing just when to pause, arch an eyebrow, and slowly reposition the cigar in his mouth for a leisurely puff before continuing with the climax of his story. Yes, he was the best. It was an undisputed fact. There was a strong likelihood he learned the art from his aunt Alice.

Tonight Walter Phillips was worried about his mother-in-law and her hasty departure. As they walked out to her car, he tried to convince her to stay the night. Failing in that endeavor, he deposited her suitcase in the backseat of her car while Regina pointed out that the weather was getting bad.

"It's already starting to rain, Momma. I think you should reconsider. Please stay." Some gray clouds were moving into the area from the east, and indeed it had started to sprinkle.

"Now, Regina, I'll be back in no time. Don't worry. And Walter, my husband said not to eat all the preserves before he gets here tomorrow."

"Will you at least call me when you get there, Momma?" begged Regina, realizing that further protests would be useless.

"I will, sugar."

Alice tossed her purse onto the front seat of the car and turned to give Regina one last hug. All farewells said, Alice slid into the driver's seat and rolled down her window, waving to the couple as she backed out of the drive.

"Love you!" Alice yelled out the window as she shifted smoothly from reverse into first gear. Within moments her car had turned the corner and was out of sight, wisps of her gray hair gently fluttering in the wind.

Regina stood at the edge of the driveway. A terrible feeling settled in the pit of her stomach. A sudden gust of night breeze ruffled the soft cotton fabric of her dress and spun the dust along the edge of the sidewalk. Walter gently took his wife's elbow.

"Come on, Regina. Let's get back inside."

About ten minutes down Highway 27, Alice turned on the car's wipers and headlights. The outer feeder bands of the storm system had crossed the coastline. The few raindrops had turned into a steady drizzle, and she now needed the lights to see. Her old eyes weren't quite what they used to be, but she'd never admit to that. The Mills Brothers were on the radio singing "Opus One," and Alice felt forty again. *I'll just go a bit slower. There's very little traffic on the road tonight.*

Actually, quite a few cars were on the road, but they were all headed north, away from Cameron and toward Lake Charles. Alice noticed it, ignored it, and proceeded south anyway. It was dark by the time she slowed to cross the Gibbstown Pontoon Bridge. The rain was easing up and the roads were slick, but passable. Whenever she crossed the Intracoastal Canal, she always felt she was halfway home. Her spirits rose with each passing mile.

Several more miles down the Creole Highway, the rain had stopped for the moment, so Alice turned off the wipers. In the headlight beams, she thought she saw something in the road ahead. She was already going slowly enough to make out the movement—and to her surprise it appeared to be a herd of crawfish coming out of the ditch along the road.

"What in the Sam Hill is going on?" Alice uttered in amazement.

In all her years, she had never seen anything like it. Thousands of the tasty crustaceans were leaving the ditch for higher ground. It was impossible not to crush some of them as her tires made a swath through their ranks.

"Oh my gosh!" she whispered in the darkness. "Where's my Zatarain's when I really need it?"

Wednesday evening, June 26
The Marshall home
Daigle's Corner, Louisiana

An hour and a half after leaving Lake Charles, Alice turned off the coast highway and drove up the long, gently sloping driveway to the Marshall home. The rain had been intermittent, making the going much slower than usual. Alice had to admit that she was glad to be off the road and safely home.

Regina must have called the house, for Alice's tall husband stood silhouetted in the lamplight at the front window, waiting for her arrival. Brown came down the front steps carrying an umbrella just as Alice turned off the ignition.

"Brown, you won't believe what I just saw!" she told him excitedly once they were under the wide roof of the veranda. "It was a swarm of crawfish crawling across the road." She paused to give her husband a hug, then continued in a rush, "In all my born days I have never seen anything like it! I swear it was a caravan of crawfish étouffée on the move."

"I love you, Alice Cagle," Brown said shaking his head, while shaking out the umbrella.

"That's Alice Marshall to you, mister."

He kissed the top of her gray head. "Crawfish, huh? I don't know what to make of that." He opened the front door, holding it wide for his wife, but Alice paused to check out the clutter on the porch.

"What's all this? Oh, I see . . . are these boards for the windows?" There were several stacks of boards along with a few sheets of plywood placed on the porch against the wall. She could see that her husband meant business. "You've done this before, huh."

"Yeah, I didn't get to them this afternoon as planned, but I want to get them up first thing in the morning . . . while you pick your figs, madam." He tried to give her a stern look but failed miserably. "Regina called me, and she's very worried. Let's get inside and call her so she can rest easy."

Brown closed the heavy door behind them and turned out the porch light while Alice went to the phone to call her daughter.

"And by the way, Miss Scarlett, you're grounded."

"Fiddle-dee-dee."

Wednesday evening, June 26
The Whitney Broussard home
Cameron, Louisiana

After prayers that Wednesday evening, little Elaine removed several boxes of family photos from a shelf, sat down in a quiet corner of the den, and sorted through the photos, looking for pictures of her older brother. The phone call last night had reminded her just how much she missed Whit. She came across one of her favorite photos of the two of them together. He was pushing her on the swings. Elaine put the stack of photos back in the boxes but kept out the special one. Before going to bed, the little girl slipped the photo into the edge of the large framed mirror above her low dresser.

Elaine Broussard, age ten, at Cameron Elementary School, 1956-57.

Now I will think of him every night before I go to bed, Elaine reflected to herself as she pulled back the crisp white bed sheet. The rain outside sounded good, so she opened the window a bit more.

That night, the ten o'clock weather report said that Hurricane Audrey would hit Thursday afternoon, not Friday morning as previously thought. Unbeknownst to the Broussards, their neighbors, the Stines and the Fontenots, had already left for Lake Charles that evening. Clara and her husband decided to pack in the morning and head into Lake Charles to ride out the storm if necessary. Based on the weather report, there would be plenty of time to evacuate.

With the children asleep, the house was quiet and still. Clara turned out all the lights except one small one in the kitchen as she and Whitney headed to bed. In the middle of the night she would need that light to fix the baby a bottle.

In the girls' bedroom, Elaine's short brown locks ruffled in the stiff breeze that came through her open window. Normally the crickets, grasshoppers, and June bugs played a symphony of summer sounds, but tonight the neighborhood was devoid of any sounds except the steady rain that fell. The three oldest girls shared the roomy front bedroom, which seemed even larger during the school year with Mary Ann away at boarding school. The Marionite nuns managed St. Charles Academy and the adjoining Immaculate Conception School in Lake Charles. Attending the Catholic school was a family tradition. Now that Mary Ann was in high school, she boarded at the academy during the school year. Ethel, an eighth grader, just completed her first year there also.

As usual, Whitney and Clara made the rounds, making sure everyone was tucked in their bed. Whitney lowered Elaine's window to a one-inch opening because of the wet windowsill. It would be stuffy inside, but the rain would cool things off outside. The whole month of June had been oppressively hot. Anything that brought cooler temperatures would be a welcome relief. Or so he thought.

A mile away at the courthouse, Sheriff O. B. Carter had been occupied most of the day assembling a team of emergency management personnel and setting up short-wave radio operations on the second floor of the three-story building. Constructed in 1937 of concrete and steel, the courthouse was built nine feet above sea level—higher than the rest of the town's elevation by maybe four or five feet. It was the obvious choice of location for the Emergency Management Office.

When preparations were complete, the sheriff went home for the evening, knowing that tomorrow morning the evacuation of the parish would begin in earnest.

CHAPTER 4

Thursday—
The Lost Hours

Thursday, June 27, 1957
The Calcasieu Ship Channel
Cameron, Louisiana

The beam of the flashlight reflected dimly on the dark water of the ship channel. Midnight along this section of the Cameron docks typically proved to be a quiet time, and tonight seemed no different than many other evenings. Intermittent rain had been coming down for the past few hours, but for the moment, the downpour had stopped. Their shift would take them through the long night, and the two sheriff's deputies first wanted to check the tides for any change. The sheriff expected a phone call with an update on the conditions along the coast.

Standing at the water's edge, the deputies noted that at 12:15 A.M., no change was apparent in water level along the coast of Cameron Parish.

1:30 A.M., Thursday, June 27
Lake Charles Weather Bureau
Lake Charles, Louisiana

At the Chennault Air Base in Lake Charles, the clacking report of the teletype coming across the wire overshadowed the typical, mundane noises of the local Weather Bureau office. During a hurricane, all the staff remained energized, awaiting the latest reports. This report in particular would reveal to the meteorologists Audrey's new coordinates and wind speeds. Stunned upon reading the printout, the staff double-checked the report and realized that the storm had exploded in both intensity and forward movement.

The barometric pressure in the eye of the hurricane had dropped, and Hurricane Audrey had suddenly and viciously picked up wind speed. At ten o'clock the night before, Audrey was centered 235 miles south of Lake Charles, with winds clocked at 109 miles per hour. Now, three and a half hours later, the eye of the storm was boiling at its core just 150 miles south of the coast. The wind speed jumped to 132 miles per hour. Instead of continuing to move north at 10 miles per hour, Audrey now rushed due north toward the coast of Louisiana at 15 to 20 miles per hour.

The winds surrounding the eye wall continued to accelerate. Over the next three hours, Hurricane Audrey would continue to grow to mammoth strength and speed.

It was at this point in history that thousands of lives hung in the balance in Cameron and Vermilion parishes. There was no way to alert the sleeping towns along the coast by television—most TV stations were off the air at that late hour. But inaction could prove to be deadly.

One phone call could have made the difference—a call to notify authorities in the coastal communities of the sudden change—but no such call was placed to the Cameron Parish Sheriff's Office, or the Civil Defense command center in the Cameron Parish Courthouse, where a short-wave radio operator was on duty. No evacuation alert went out to the Calcasieu Parish Sheriff's Office, who in turn would have telephoned, or sent a short-wave radio message, or driven down to Cameron if necessary.

A Weather Bureau official reportedly tried to reach Mr. Joe W. Doxey, the secretary of the police jury in Cameron, but Doxey wasn't at home. At a minimum, if Sheriff O. B. Carter had been notified, he would have been able to use police cruisers with bullhorn loudspeakers to awaken the small, sleeping towns in his parish.

On the contrary—that Thursday morning, June 27, 1957, nothing of consequence was done to alert the towns along the southwest Louisiana coastline to the sudden and drastic change in the storm's intensity and, more importantly, its expected time of landfall. It was a colossal error in judgment, because before dawn the coastal communities would be trapped. It would be too late to evacuate by any means.

2:00 A.M. *Thursday, June 27*
Southwest Louisiana

Amid the sounds of the alligators, nutria, and other marsh creatures along the Intracoastal Waterway, a slight but definite rise in the water lifted the floating Gibbstown Pontoon Bridge a few inches above its usual level. The rain poured down steadily now, and the wind began to pick up speed, swirling a bit of trash along the dark roadside. The smell of an electrical storm filled the air. Halfway between the coast and Lake Charles, two cars traveled north along the highway at slower speeds than normal, crossing the bridge with a noticeable bump at the sloping access ramp. The two vehicles would be some of the last to make it out of Cameron Parish that night. Within the hour, the new pontoon bridge would be floating several feet above its intended design level, preventing traffic from accessing the bridge, and therefore cutting off the evacuation route.

In Creole, several miles south of the bridge, a single light glowed in the rectory window of the Sacred Heart Catholic Church, a welcoming sign on a stormy night. The streetlights gleamed softly in the heavy humid night air as the wind picked up speed and rain began to fall harder. A storefront sign on the Creole Pharmacy whipped back and forth, swinging in the strong wind coming from the east. Suddenly, as if by a single light switch, all the lights in Creole went dark, even the streetlights.

Fifteen minutes away in downtown Cameron, most offices in the courthouse were dark and quiet, except for the sheriff's office, and the Civil Defense Communication Center on the second floor, where a small crew was on duty near the short-wave radio. Downstairs, the three prisoners in the jail were sleeping soundly on the stiff cots in their cells.

2:00 A.M., *Thursday, June 27*
Home of Dr. Cecil Clark
Cameron, Louisiana

Sybil Clark couldn't sleep. On the den's deeply upholstered sofa, she sat near her husband listening to the sounds of the occasional gusts of wind and the rain outside the windows. She had given up all attempts to read, and concentrated on the radio weather reports. Several hours after midnight the phone rang, echoing through the dimly lit Clark home.

"Dr. Clark, water is seeping into the hospital from under the doors," reported the nurse, an anxious tone in her usually calm voice.

"We'll be right down."

Within minutes, both Dr. Clark and his wife were moving at a quick pace down the dark coast highway toward the clinic. The wind was only moderately strong, and the rain was intermittent. Back at the house, Zulmae stayed with the sleeping children.

Three blocks from the hospital, high water forced the Clarks to stop. They carefully turned the car around to return home through now-flooded streets. Gusts of strong wind buffeted the car. Sybil clutched the dashboard, straining to see through the rain on the windshield. Along Highway 82, a few cars were already heading east out of Cameron, fleeing ahead of the storm's rising waters. The coastal scene was eerie. It seemed to the Clarks that the wind was blowing the Gulf of Mexico into the town. The air, too, had a strange smell, like atmospheric smoke from an electrical storm.

The doctor realized he was going to need help in order to get to the patients. Help came in the form of his friend and neighbor, James Derouen, branch manager of the Calcasieu Marine National Bank. After a loud knock at the Derouen front door, Jimmy woke, dressed, and quickly joined Clark. Mr. Derouen wanted to go check on his bank building, too, which was near the clinic. Dr. Clark figured that he could let the truck lead the way, and he would follow as far as possible in his car. If his vehicle was near the hospital, Cecil could make it home to his family before the storm hit.

Sybil watched from the rain-spattered kitchen window as the two vehicles slowly drove down the flooded street and out of sight. She had decided to stay home with their children. Even in the darkness, it appeared that the weather conditions were deteriorating rapidly—and the remaining time to evacuate as well.

"I'll wake the children and get them dressed. We'll be ready to pick up the boys and then evacuate to Lake Charles the minute you return," Sybil had told her husband when he dropped her off at their home.

Both Cecil and Sybil had expected some flooding, but not this soon. Based on their failed attempt to reach the hospital, the Clarks agreed that the storm seemed worse to the west. They believed that, for the time being, John and Joe were in a safer place fifteen miles to the east with their grandparents.

"How could the hurricane have come so early?" she thought out loud, as Zulmae handed her a steaming cup of coffee.

Outside, the truck pushed through the water, slowly but surely. Clark honked the horn of his sedan, signaling his friend to stop along the way at the Frederick home. There he woke the family to the emergency weather conditions and made a quick phone call to the hospital. The doctor alerted the nurses of his situation and told them to prepare the patients for imminent transport to the courthouse. He hung up the phone, left the house, and struggled against the high wind back to his car. The two men resumed the journey toward the clinic.

As the two vehicles pulled out onto the highway, the streetlights flickered, blinked, and then went out. Next all the house lights in the neighborhoods went dark. Only the headlights beamed into the rain-streaked darkness. Soon, Dr. Clark abandoned his car and joined Mr. Derouen in the truck.

In spite of their determination, the water continued to rise, and the flooded street soon became impassable, even for the truck. The wind howled at near hurricane force. They turned the truck around and headed back to the doctor's car. Waving goodbye to his friend, Jimmy Derouen headed home, and Clark followed at a distance.

In the dark morning hour, the storm surge continued its push inland from the gulf. Strong winds began to move the water as if it were a river. A solid blanket of salty water soon covered all the roads, ditch-es, and front yards of the coastal neighborhoods. It gleamed like a giant wind-tossed lake in the doctor's headlights. Suddenly, the water rose with incredible speed.

Near the Phil Richard house, about halfway back to Clark's home, the storm surge forced the car off the road into a ditch. Dr. Clark opened the car door and jumped. Within moments the young doctor found himself in waist-deep water with no way to make it home to his wife and children. His first thought was to get to a phone. *I've got to tell Sybil to get out right away. I've got to call the hospital and tell the nurs-es to get help from the Sheriff's Department.* He realized he was now stranded midway between the hospital and his home.

Every step was a struggle to stay upright in the current, but he slowly made progress, traveling about the length of a football field. The wind was roaring now, and Clark realized he had to quickly take refuge inside the Richard home in front of him, even though there was no phone in the household. In the predawn darkness, as he fought his way through the waist-deep water, Dr. Clark could see the beginning of devastation along the coast. Wood-frame houses began to wash off their low foundations.

With only a few more feet to go, he battled the wind, making his way through the swirling water. The current was so strong now that it ripped the shoes off his feet. To his right, a rowboat appeared, headed in the same direction—toward the Richard house. A man was pulling the boat, unable to paddle in the wind. His family sat huddled in the small dinghy, his wife and three children clinging to the sides. Clark reached out to help, and the two men guided the boat up onto the porch of the house. The doctor held the boat steady while the man lifted his children one by one and carried them into the home. Having served its purpose, the rowboat was released to the wind and waves.

Dawn was breaking in spite of the storm. Waves had begun to dash against the walls of the house. Once everyone was inside, Clark closed the heavy front door. The young physician stood in the entranceway, dripping wet and barefoot. He leaned his forehead against the door and thought of his family. *Had there been time for Sybil to get them away to safety? The attic was so shallow, inaccessible.* The wind raged outside while water swirled about his feet as it seeped beneath the door, invading the structure. *The hospital . . . my patients.*

4:00 A.M., *Thursday, June 27*
The Griffith home
Oak Grove, Louisiana

Geneva woke at four o'clock feeling ill. She sat up slowly in the dark and swung her legs off the bed, searching with her toes for her slippers.

I'll get some pills from the medicine cabinet, she thought groggily.

Not wanting to wake D.W., she quietly opened the bedroom door and slipped out into the hallway. Geneva felt along the wall for the light switch. The light switch clicked, but nothing happened. She flipped the switch again. Nothing. The electricity was out.

She fumbled her way in the dark down the hall toward the kitchen, waking D.W. in the process. Concern about the hurricane had troubled his sleep, causing him to check the weather conditions twice during the night. Again he woke quickly, instantly alert. Sitting up, he reached for the lamp on the bedside table. Click. No power. D.W. reached for the flashlight he had placed near the lamp, powering up its beam. He quietly followed Geneva down the hall with the flashlight.

"I need to get some pills from the cabinet," she whispered, not wanting to wake the rest of the household.

"Okay," he said, shining the light to help her see in the darkness. Geneva stopped at the kitchen cabinet, and D.W. moved on past her to the front door. He came rushing back, all color drained from his face.

"My God, Geneva, we are trapped like rats. The water is already over the road—it's up to the rose garden. Get everyone up quick, and get them dressed."

In the short six hours since they had gone to bed the night before, the storm intensified rapidly. In the early morning hours on Thursday, June 27, the hurricane winds offshore pushed the gulf water ahead of them, slowly, quietly covering the beaches along the coast of southwest

Louisiana. Concealed in the dark of night, the storm surge inched upward, converged with the coastal marshes, and soon rose above the marsh grasses and low sand dunes along the coast highway. The Gulf of Mexico now stretched two miles inland, flooding all evacuation routes.

Within the next hour, Hurricane Audrey would slam into the coast with winds over 145 miles per hour, coupled with an unprecedented storm surge that moved 25 miles inland with numerous tornadoes. It was a killer storm, one that would deliver a lethal blow to the Griffith family.

Geneva hurried down the hall to wake her in-laws. D.W. dressed quickly in the dim glow of the flashlight, which he had tossed on the bed. Geneva next woke her two children from their deep sleep. She dressed Cherie warmly and laced up her daughter's sturdy shoes. By the time eleven-year-old Leslie had dressed in his cut-off jeans and T-shirt, D.W. was heading out the back door with a kerosene lantern.

The animals were restless in the barn, long ago sensing the change in weather. The chickens were already awake in their coop. There was no need for a rooster's crow on this day. Their squawking put the other animals on edge. D.W. opened the door to the coop, releasing the chickens. His muscles tightened as he swung open the heavy barn doors to release the livestock. He moved methodically in the dim light and hung the lantern on a prominent peg. At the stalls, he gave a loud *heeyah* and smacked one horse's backside, urging the group out into the darkness of the green fields beyond the barn.

At the back of the barn D.W. moved toward a fence. It was still dark outside, but he knew every inch of the barn and the cattle pen alongside it. The low bellowing of the herd had a nervous pitch that carried above the gusting wind. When he reached a heavy metal gate, he slid the latch and pushed the gate open wide, releasing the hundred or so head of cattle out into the open field.

Looks like we'll be having a long roundup after this storm, he thought, as the cattle nearest the gate moved out toward the pasture and the woods beyond.

D.W. cautiously retraced his steps back into the barn. Leslie's cocker spaniel, Bootsie, kept near the man, adeptly avoiding his heavy boots and rapid movements around the bales of hay and equipment.

Now slowing his pace, then coming to a halt in the vastness of the dark barn, D.W. paused and made the most important decision of his life. Many different tools and pieces of equipment hung on the beams and walls of the large barn, but D.W. grabbed only three items.

With Bootsie at his heels, D.W. retrieved his lantern, closed the barn doors, and carefully made his way across the yard, back to his home and his waiting family. He could hear the wind-whipped rustling of the leaves in the oak grove just out of sight in the darkness. It was beginning to rain again.

Geneva had joined Nannie and Papa near the front door of her home to take stock of the situation outside. Papa Griffith had lit two kerosene lamps, placing one in the kitchen and carrying one to the front door. The dim reflection off the dark water showed the vastness of the gulf ahead of them. Geneva turned away, her mind a jumble of thoughts and worry about her family. She knew there was no way they could leave now. Never before had the water risen so high over the road. D.W. had been right. This hurricane, Hurricane Audrey, was already different. The tides were extreme, and now the winds began to pick up speed around the house, whipping through the ancient oak trees in the early stages of dawn. They would have to come up with a plan to weather the storm.

Geneva was deep in thought as her husband returned through the back door. Bootsie rushed ahead to find Leslie in the front room. D.W. placed his tools on the kitchen counter and joined his family to wait for the hurricane's next move. He gathered Cherie in his arms and gave her a smile and a kiss as he came to stand near his wife. But Cherie wanted to look out the window with Leslie, so she wiggled back down to where the action was.

"I set the horses and cattle free, just in case. Since the power is out, we can't find out the latest information on the hurricane, of course, but this high water has cut us off from escaping to higher ground. I don't know exactly where Audrey's coming ashore, but it looks like we're in the thick of it. For now, all we can do is wait . . . and pray that the water doesn't rise any higher."

Standing in the dim kerosene lamplight inside their home, the Griffith family looked toward the gulf. They watched, they worried, and they waited. But they didn't have long to wait. Without pause, the water continued to inch upward through the front yard, rising to their doorstep. The water inched higher and higher and seeped under the doors into the house. The family went into action stuffing towels and sheets around the doors and windows.

D.W. realized he had to do more, and do it quickly. He rushed into the kitchen for his tools. From the three items on the counter—an ax, a saw, and a rope—the man reached for the long wooden handle of his ax.

"Kids, get back," instructed their father, as he returned to the front room with the heavy ax. Geneva and the children retreated to a corner near a window. D.W. had nailed up some plywood over the large picture window the day before, but the other windows remained vulnerable.

The wooden ax handle was well worn and smooth from years of use, and the blade was honed to a sharp edge. With a slow, sad swing, D.W. brought the heavy blade down upon a massive low credenza, shattering the furniture's smooth surface and the finish of the dark cherry wood grain. A few more whacks and the lovely piece of furniture broke in pieces. Papa Griffith lifted the longest, sturdiest piece of wood, and the two men began hammering up the planks across the front door. They broke up other pieces of furniture to nail the doors and windows shut. At one point, Geneva looked out through one of the remaining uncovered windows into the dawn light and watched the water come halfway up the glass pane.

This is just like being in a giant fishbowl, thought Geneva. It was all so strange, so foreign. She was terrified, frozen in the moment.

Once all the portals along the front of the home were boarded up and secure, the men set about trying to get some of the remaining furniture elevated above the water. Of main concern was Geneva's piano, which they were able to set atop two sturdy end tables. Geneva repositioned a crystal vase full of her roses. All the while, the water continued to seep under the door.

Amid the flurry of activity, Leslie left the group and went to his room. Like everyone else's in the house, his shoes were completely wet. He was glad he had put on cut-offs instead of long jeans. He began to place books, toys, and other items from his room on top of his lower bunk. Shoes from the closet floor were put up there, as well as his baseball bat and glove.

Forget the piano, he thought. *My stuff's not getting wet either.*

The situation looked hopeless. Geneva's chest heaved, and she fought back tears. Fear was becoming evident on all the faces in the room. Quietly Geneva took her daughter's small hand, and then her mother-in-law's. She led them both down the hall to her bedroom and closed the door. The wind had begun to howl, and the low undulating moan permeated the room. Geneva crossed the room and knelt down beside her bed. This was familiar territory.

"Come. Kneel beside me, and we will pray for God's help."

Cherie quickly moved to the bedside to kneel next to her mother, with Nannie close behind. Geneva was very comfortable in her prayers to her Lord, and she intended to ask God to lead them out of this awful predicament in which they found themselves. Cherie and her grand-mother folded their hands and closed their eyes. Geneva raised her eyes toward heaven, then slowly closed them and spoke softly, quaking.

"God, you promised us in the Bible that where two or more are gathered together in Your name, You would be with them—so here we are, three of us, and we are begging You to be with us and help us know what to do."

Geneva was strengthened now with a sense of confidence she lacked only a short time before. She nodded her head, believing in her heart that God would be with her family today and that He would give them the wisdom to know how to protect their family.

"Amen!" said Cherie, as she peeked from underneath one eyelid and realized that the prayer had finished.

"Amen," echoed Nannie softly.

The three generations of Griffith women held hands and returned down the hallway to the danger that awaited them all. In the horror of the days that were to follow, Geneva would come to realize that God would answer her prayers, but not in the manner she expected.

They returned to the kitchen, and to her shock, Geneva discovered that D.W. was standing on the kitchen breakfast bar chopping a hole in the ceiling with the ax. Water was now ankle deep in the house, with no signs of stopping.

Jolted into action, Geneva picked up her purse. She began stuffing it with tiny treasures from around her home, treasures that held so many memories. In her living room, the carpet squished like wet, gray Spanish moss underfoot. The drapes began to sag heavily as the rising water wicked its way upward in the fabric. The last item Geneva picked up was on top of her piano. It was the small photograph of her great-grandfather in his Civil War uniform. With a snap, she closed her purse and placed the strap securely on her arm.

Leslie reconsidered his own strategy and stole away to his bedroom once again. He quickly moved the items from his lower bunk up to the top bunk.

"There, that's better. They'll be fine up here." He turned about the room for a last look and reconsidered his desk and the leather tools inside. Just to be safe, he used the small hammer from his tool chest and nailed the drawers shut.

I can't believe there's water in the house . . . in my room! he thought as the last drawer was secured. Over the wind, Leslie heard his mother calling his name, and he returned to the kitchen in haste, causing waves to splash against the walls of the hallway with each hurried step he took. The water inched upward and soon covered the bottom mattress of the boy's bunk bed.

The hopelessness of it all weighed on Nannie Griffith as she looked around at all their fruitless effort to secure the doors and windows of the house.

Sometimes all the good work you do doesn't do you any good, mused Nannie. Now her son was compelled to chop a hole in the ceiling in a desperate attempt to provide an escape route from the storm surge.

The winds wailed outside, hissing through the cracks of the window frames. Water continued to seep in the house from the tiniest of openings in the doors and windows. Stuffed toys stacked on a chair in the corner of Cherie's bedroom began to float about her room.

Papa Griffith had lifted the children onto the countertop near the kitchen cabinets. Bootsie barked twice, and Leslie smoothed the dog's coat to calm himself as much as to calm her. The sound of sheetrock splitting under the force of the ax was more alarming than the sounds of the winds outside.

The water was now knee deep inside, and much, much deeper outside in the swirling currents. Thuds and deep thumps resonating from outside gave witness to the assault the house was taking from the elements and the debris. The storm surge was moving inland like a river. Leslie held tightly to his frightened dog.

The opening seemed large enough now to proceed to the next part of the plan. D.W. lowered the ax to his side and carefully placed it on the countertop. His father handed him the saw, and D.W. began anew to enlarge the opening with long, grating pushes and pulls of the serrated blade. Moving back and forth, the sharp teeth of the blade cut through the sheetrock, covering D.W. in chalky dust as he worked feverishly to complete this task.

All of the family waited anxiously in the kitchen, concentrating on D.W.'s efforts. Furniture was floating about the house now, and the wind had picked up speed dramatically. By the time D.W. cut a two-foot by two-foot hole large enough for them to crawl through into the attic, the storm surge stood waist deep in the kitchen. Geneva's skirt swirled about her hips in the salty water.

When the moment was right, Papa Griffith used a kitchen stool to climb up on the breakfast bar next to his son. Reaching down, he pulled a stool out of the water and placed it on the countertop. D.W. held the stool steady and helped his father up into the attic.

"Papa, have everyone stand on the beams, not the sheetrock ceiling." Nodding in affirmation, Papa reached down from the opening to help lift his wife, then his grandchildren, up into the attic, one by one.

In the front room, glass shattered in the windows facing the gulf. Water poured through the openings, forcing aside the boards and pieces of furniture they had nailed across the window frames. The churning tide of the gulf coursed rapidly through the house. The current swirled, pushed, and pulled at everything in its path. Household items tilted precariously, toppled awkwardly, then floated willy-nilly in every room. Yellow rose petals from the living room arrangement floated into the kitchen, out of place in the brown salt water. Geneva's piano struck a loud somber chord as it toppled off its unnatural perch on the end tables and sank beneath the water.

The family was quickly running out of time. D.W. reached down to help Geneva climb onto the counter. He steadied his wife's waist as she made the ascent into the narrow two-foot opening above.

The ax and the saw lay on the countertop alongside his two old saddle ropes. He gathered up the tools and passed them to his father above. D.W. climbed the stool and pulled himself up into the attic, just as the breakfast bar ripped away from the wall. The violent, fast-moving storm surge pushed the breakfast bar across the room and right out the shattered back window of their home.

Outside, Hurricane Audrey slammed into the Louisiana coast.

4:00 A.M., Thursday, June 27
Home of Dr. Cecil Clark
Cameron, Louisiana

The telephone rang again at four o'clock. Sybil dashed for the phone, hoping it was her husband with good news. It was indeed the hospital, but it wasn't her husband. The call came from Nealie Porche.

"Sybil, do you know what has delayed the doctor? He hasn't arrived at the clinic yet."

"No, I don't know what's happened. I'm worried. Water is beginning to come into the house here, too. You'd better get help from the courthouse for the patients."

The nurses sprang into action. Water was knee deep in the clinic and there was no time to lose. Within thirty minutes, two deputy sheriffs arrived in two flatboats to evacuate the hospital. The men worked their way through debris fields in the now three-foot-deep water, and carefully but quickly lifted each person into a waiting Jon-boat. The nurses had been ingenious in their preparations. They zipped each patient into plastic mattress covers up to their neck to protect them from the elements and possible infection. Supplies were also loaded into the boats, including flashlights, diapers, and baby formula.

Nurse Reyes stopped at the nurses' station to make one final call to report to her friend and supervisor, Sybil Clark. It was almost five o'clock. Dawn would be breaking soon.

"Yes, I think Cecil is lost," relayed Sybil softly. "The water is getting higher here. Good luck, Peggy." The two women choked back tears and ended their call. The nurse made haste through the rising water in the hospital corridor and reached the waiting boat at the emergency exit. Within minutes, phone service went dead in Cameron.

"We're trapped, Zulmae. This hurricane is moving onshore, and we're trapped. There's no way for us to get out of here." Sybil paused, her pulse quickening. "We have to ride out this storm right here. Let's get the children to the safest place in the house."

She and Zulmae gathered the three children in their arms. Together they splashed through the invading waters inside the home and took the children into the kitchen. Sybil put Jack in a bassinette and placed him on a shelf above the countertop. They lifted the girls onto the kitchen's long, six-foot dining bar and stood alongside, holding their hands. Water was knee deep inside the house now. Soon, Zulmae climbed up on the counter too, leaving only her feet to dangle in the water. There they waited. The increasing noise from the wind startled baby Jack, causing his tiny arms to jerk and flail about, but his little cries were no match for the din of the storm.

At the Richard house, Dr. Clark suggested they all move up into the attic to escape the rising water. The winds were screaming at 100 miles per hour, forming waves five feet tall on top of the storm surge. The waves uprooted trees, butane tanks, and buildings. Cars were tossed about like tin cans. They swirled in the water, floating for a moment, then disappeared rapidly to the bottom.

The Richard family rushed to gather a few supplies while the men pushed a chest of drawers beneath the opening into the attic. By now water was waist deep in the house, but the group managed to crawl into the attic without incident. From the relative safety amid the rafters, they could not escape the sounds of Hurricane Audrey's arrival. Windowpanes shattered, and soon the sheetrock peeled off the walls downstairs as the hurricane winds and high waves assaulted the structure.

Elizabeth Dianne Clark, age three, daughter of Cecil and Sybil Clark. This photograph was taken in June 1957, one week before Audrey. It was on a roll of film being processed in Lake Charles when the storm hit.

3:00 A.M., *Thursday, June 27*
The Whitney Broussard home
Cameron, Louisiana

Like clockwork, eighteen-month-old Helen woke up at three o'clock. After seven babies, Clara could make a bottle in her sleep if necessary. On this night she was awake just enough to notice that there was water standing in their yard, but Clara wasn't alarmed. Rain had fallen intermittently during the night, but there was no storm wind at the moment. The neighborhood was quiet. After the baby finished her bottle, Clara returned the toddler to her crib, and both mother and daughter fell back asleep.

The beginning sounds of the storm woke the Broussards before dawn. A dark, steamy pot of coffee was just what they needed to start this busy, stormy day. Soon they would have to wake the children, pack, and leave for Lake Charles.

Whitney rose from their bed and made his way to the kitchen, where Clara was putting a kettle of water on the stove to boil.

"That's strange," she murmured to herself. "I thought I left the light on in here." She flicked the switch again. "Uh oh. Whitney, the power is out."

Whitney went into the living room and flicked on the front porch light, which also failed to respond. He opened the heavy door and went out onto the screened porch. Clara had followed her husband and now paused at his side. The dim morning light reflected off a wide shiny surface.

Whitney's body froze as he took in the scene. His whole yard was covered in water. The whole neighborhood was covered in water. It was already up to the second step of the porch, over a foot deep. A sharp gust of wind increased in intensity, loudly whipping Whitney's pajamas about his legs. Audrey was coming ashore.

"Look at that! The whole neighborhood is flooded, Clara! What in the world? Something is dreadfully wrong." Rain had come through the screens surrounding the porch, making the floor slippery. *My children*, thought Whitney. *I've got to get my family out of here, and right now*. He turned to his petite wife, who strained to look through the damp screen. "Clara, if our yard is this flooded, the coast highway will be impassable. We've got to get out of here right now. The only place I can think of that will be above water is the courthouse. I'll have to go to the motel to rouse the guests immediately. Meanwhile, would you wake the children and get them dressed?"

Hurrying back inside, Whitney made his way to their bedroom. He dressed quickly but thoughtfully, choosing sturdy clothes and shoes. Clara, meanwhile, lit a kerosene lamp that she always kept in the pantry for emergencies. Leaving it on the kitchen counter, she entered the front bedroom where her three oldest daughters slept. She laid a hand on Mary Ann's shoulder, rousing her gently but firmly, and moved to wake Elaine and Ethel next. Clara explained to her daughters that floodwaters were in the yard, so they needed to get dressed.

"Your father is going for help and will be back very soon, so dress quickly."

The steam kettle whistled sharply on the kitchen's gas stove, but they would forego coffee this morning. Tucking his shirt into his waistband, Whitney tried to telephone his parents, who lived twenty minutes away in Creole, next to the Sacred Heart Catholic Church. He dialed the number and placed the heavy black receiver against his ear, but failed to connect. There was no dial tone, nothing. The phone lines were dead. He realized that several things were going to become critical within the next hour. Time was of the essence, beginning right now.

"Clara!" he called out. "I'm leaving to go rouse the men at the motel," Whitney told his wife, whose eyes now widened in concern as she paused in changing the baby. "I'll be back in fifteen minutes or so. Be ready to evacuate right away for the courthouse."

Not bothering with an umbrella, Broussard stepped off the porch steps into the water. *Oh heavenly Father, please protect my family. Give me strength in our time of need.* Whitney was a big man, and yet the water already reached his knees. His long legs moved powerfully through the water. In spite of his rapid pace, he felt a current pushing the water inland.

"That's odd," he said to himself, not breaking his stride. Reaching down, he cupped the floodwater in his hand and took a sip. "Salt water!" It was what he feared most when he and Clara first saw the light gleaming off the flooded yard. Rainwater didn't cause this flood. The gulf had moved onshore in the night hours, trapping them along the coast.

In five minutes' time he reached the motel. He was right. The two-foot-deep water made it impossible to evacuate by car. Several of the guests were already gathered near the office. To rouse the others, Broussard pounded on the doors of the motel rooms, alerting each sleeping guest to the impending danger outside. Soon all the men joined him at the office as he had instructed them to do. Whitney had need of these strangers. The water was rising so rapidly, he knew he could never get all of his family to safety without the help of these men.

"Men, you should all seek the safety of the courthouse. It's less than a mile away," he stated, pointing westward down the coast highway. "I will be taking my family there right now, but I need your help to carry my children. Will you do this for me?"

"Lead the way, Mr. Broussard." All of the men readily agreed to help.

By the time each child was awake and dressed, predawn light was breaking the dark sky.

"No bare feet today, little ones. No sandals either. Do you all have on sturdy shoes? Good. Did everybody go to the bathroom? Okay, we're ready." Despite her own worry and fear, Clara managed to remain outwardly calm as she stuffed the diaper bag full of neatly folded baby diapers and a few bottles of milk from the fridge.

"Let's go wait for your daddy by the door, okay? Mary Ann, would you carry the lantern, please?"

Rain pelted the windowpanes. At five o'clock, the eye of the hurricane moved rapidly toward the coast. The window of safety was closing quickly. Clara gathered her little chicks close by as they waited in the softly glowing light of the lantern. Ethel occasionally glanced at her mother for any indication of a crisis, but Clara calmly spoke in soothing tones to baby Helen and the boys. Clara was certain of one thing—if her husband said he would be right back, then he would be right back. Ethel relaxed, taking the cue from her mother's demeanor.

She moved to the window near Elaine for a closer look at the storm.

In the flooded parking lot outside the motel, Whitney's group started down Dan Street, and almost immediately encountered a boat heading toward them eastward from Cameron, from the direction of the courthouse.

"Look! Look there!" one of the hotel guests shouted, pointing toward the boat. Two deputy sheriffs rope-pulled a sturdy Jon-boat down the flooded highway, headed in their direction. The wide, flat-bottomed craft rode the water well and was a common fixture in Louisiana coastal communities.

"Over here! Help! Over here!" The men hailed the boat, waving as they shouted. The deputies waded toward Whitney, having recognized him immediately.

"Officers, I need your help. My house is just down the street here, and I've got six children that I must get to the courthouse," he pleaded over the wind. "Please take my children in your boat."

"I'm terribly sorry, Mr. Broussard. We can't. We're following orders," declared a deputy. "We just evacuated the hospital, and the patients will need their doctor with them at the courthouse, so we have to try to get to Dr. Clark's home immediately."

The deputies had briefly slowed their forward progress but now resumed their hurried pace, pulling the boat through the flowing brown water. The Broussard team turned in dismay and began to make their way up the short block to the Broussard home. In single file, the men moved northward, with the steady current aiding them. After several minutes, the house came into view. The glow of the lantern silhouetted his children in the window. Clara saw the men and smiled.

"Babies, your daddy is home, and he brought a rescue team to help us get to the courthouse."

The column of men opened the screen door and entered the house, closing the door behind them. Water lapped at the top step on the porch. Once inside, Whitney explained their plan. In thirty seconds, the men had their assignments.

One of the men bent down on one knee in front of Elaine. The tall stranger with wavy brown hair smiled and looked her in the eyes.

"Don't you worry, young lady. I'm going to help your daddy get you to safety. Are you ready for a piggy-back ride to the courthouse?"

Her eyes darted to her mother, then her father. If her parents were part of this outing, Elaine was all for it. She nodded and returned his smile; soon each man lifted a child into strong arms. Mary Ann walked next to her mother.

"Daddy, could we pretend this is a jungle safari?" When he wasn't playing truck driver, five-year-old David loved to pretend there were lions and tigers in his yard.

The group of twelve cautiously stepped off the porch into brown water, which now coursed stronger through the neighborhood. The roustabouts were strong from years of hard work on the oilrigs, and their muscles rippled as they stepped into the current following Mr. Broussard. With a firm hold, these strangers easily carried their precious cargo above the water. The water continued to rise, and their evacuation had only just begun.

Elaine had always been afraid of the water. The waves on the beach always seemed angry, and too rough for her to enjoy. Today the water was dark and just plain scary, but Elaine put on a brave face. She kept her eyes open and took in all her surroundings. The ten-year-old looked down at the huge arms that encircled her small self. Her arms were wrapped around a large, tanned neck she had never seen before. She was looking over the big man's shoulder, as he forged his way through the water that lapped at her feet and legs. Many parts of her own yard looked foreign to her. The swing set stood as though it was in a lake, and the seats were underwater.

"Our horses! What about Timmy and Pops?" Elaine yelled to her dad, but the wind erased her words.

Ethel was stunned into silence as she looked this way and that, trying to absorb all the strange and drastic changes in her familiar neighborhood. She, too, found it scary—but exciting, sort of like an adventure.

Clara exchanged looks with her husband walking alongside her, unable to hide her unspoken look of worry and fear. He smiled, reassuring his wife. Behind his parents, young David realized this was no safari. He had been wrong. He immediately began to change his game plan. This was definitely more like a Noah's Ark adventure than a safari. He looked again at the face of the big man holding him. There was some stubble on his face and chin—big dark hairs. Dad had that sometimes. Grampa, too. This stranger must be a good man.

"Hey, mister? I don't know how to swim yet, you know. So don't drop me, okay?" David rested his chin on the man's wide shoulder.

"I've got you, little man. Don't worry."

At that moment, a welcome sound carried above the wind. The whole group looked ahead in the mist toward the corner of the front yard. The sheriff's Jon-boat and the two deputies had returned.

"We can take your family now, Mr. Broussard. All of you, please get in the boat quickly." First the children, then Clara, one by one, were hoisted up into the craft. As the boat took on passengers, the deputies explained that they had never made it to Dr. Clark's house, because the current a bit down the road had been too strong as it moved inland from the gulf.

"We were forced to turn back just past the school, and not a moment too soon. Now, we need to hurry to make the courthouse before it's too late."

Mary Ann positioned herself up against the side of the boat. Her wet clothes dripped and chilled her uncomfortably in the wind, but she didn't care. These kind men had rescued them. The water continued to rise. It was now waist deep, with a stronger current moving inland from the gulf. For everyone, the view that they encountered seemed bizarre. Where there used to be ground, there was now water everywhere.

Mary Ann thought the water smelled different, too; not like rainwater from a flood but like the salt water at the beach. At that moment it hit her—this was no flood. They were fleeing from invading waters from the Gulf of Mexico. The realization startled the fifteen-year-old, but she kept quiet. There was no need to scare the little ones.

Each man seemed to adjust his grip on the boat ever so slightly, holding on just a little bit tighter. As a single-minded unit, the group heaved and pulled hard on the ropes, moving the Jon-boat down Dan Street against the current. One of the rescuers stood directly next to

Mary Ann in the water. Checking out her surroundings, the teenager noticed that the craft was wide, maybe five feet, and about fifteen feet long. The sides were deep—she guessed two, maybe three feet tall. *I'm sure we'll be okay. We'll be fine.*

The Broussard party angled through the neighborhood, going between houses to reach the coast road, Highway 82, which ran between the elementary school and the front of the motel. The winds howled and the murky water splashed and churned against the sides of the boat. A few cars were stalled along the narrow, two-lane highway ahead, their passengers long gone. Mary Ann lifted her hand and clutched the sleeve of the man beside her as he worked hard in the water to keep the boat on course. For the duration of the boat rescue, the fifteen-year-old kept a viselike grip on that shirtsleeve.

The men in the water struggled against the incoming tide, which constantly threatened to move the boat sideways. The going was slow, but the team was making steady progress. Clara held little Helen close to her chest and covered her ears from the noise of the wind. She said a silent prayer of thanks to God for their timely rescue and good fortune. The safe haven of the courthouse seemed within their reach.

Midway through the journey, the boat was hailed by a small group of people along the main road. Several times the boat stopped to take on more passengers. At one point, Ethel and Elaine recognized two classmates from school with their family, fighting hard to keep their footing in the current. Hattie and her little brother, Buddy Skidmore, were chin-deep in water.

Suddenly, the boy went under, slipping beneath the waves. His father pulled hard on his son's hand and brought him back to the surface. All forward momentum was lost as the parents simply tried to keep the children from drowning. The Skidmore family had only moments left before they might all be swept away in the storm surge.

Whitney quickly organized several men from the Jon-boat to form a human chain to reach his friends. Within a minute or two, these last passengers were safely aboard. Hattie sat near Ethel and Elaine, exhausted from her long struggle in the dangerous water.

"Buddy had already gone down two or three times. If y'all hadn't come by, I don't think we would have made it." Hattie's voice reverberated in the wind. She realized just how close they had come to drowning.

There was little if any room remaining in the boat now. The deputies realized that this would be their only pass through town before the storm hit with its full force, and clearly the courthouse was the safest place in Cameron.

The passengers made room for their friends, putting children on laps as best they could. The rim of the craft was perilously close to the surface of the water once everyone was on board. The two deputies, Mr. Broussard, and the men from the motel kept pushing, pulling, and steadying the boat. Debris began to be more prevalent as the gulf continued to push its way into town.

What normally was only a fifteen-minute walk from the Broussard home took an hour in today's storm waters. Fatigue was evident on the faces of the rescue team as the Sheriff's Department Jon-boat pulled alongside the east steps of the courthouse, just across the street from a small church. The craft grated against the concrete as the waves jarred the temporary mooring. Moving with haste into the building, the families were directed toward the stairway by the Civil Defense officers.

"The basement offices have already filled with water, so please move up to the top two floors. This way, please."

Clara and Whitney carefully climbed the stairway to the third floor with their six children. Their wet clothes chilled the band of refugees and dripped unceremoniously on the steps to join the puddles left by others who had preceded them. Elaine and Ethel clutched the stair rail so as not to slip. Along the wall of one of the upstairs courtrooms, a long wooden bench offered a few seats, a place of rest for Clara and the little ones. She staked her claim, placing the diaper bag nearby on the bench. Toddlers Helen and Richard squirmed for a chance to play on the floor at their mother's feet. Five-year-old David stayed close by his father. The rising sound of the wind was indescribable, and David was old enough to know this wasn't normal. It unnerved him, and he covered his ears with his tiny hands.

The wind was well past hurricane strength when the Broussard family and friends found safety in the strong concrete building. Soon after that moment, the avenue of refuge was cut off to others striving to make it to safety. As the wind increased in intensity, so did the size of the waves around the neighborhood. The eye wall of Hurricane Audrey was just offshore, packing 145 mile-per-hour winds.

Although the courthouse sat on the highest elevation point in town, the Gulf of Mexico quickly rose to its top steps. Salt water poured into the side entrance where the Broussard family had entered the building only minutes before, spilling down the basement stairs like a rushing waterfall. Within minutes, Geneva's basement office flooded to the ceiling, with the muddy, brown water toppling the water cooler. The heavy wooden desks floated half-submerged, while the metal file cabinets' paper contents became a sodden mass. Swept off Geneva's desk, the framed photographs of her children sank to the floor.

4:00 A.M., Thursday, June 27
The Marshall home
Daigle's Corner, Louisiana

Alice Marshall woke early to the sounds of howling winds. The screen on the window of their second-floor bedroom made a racket, banging and clapping against the frame. In spite of the slow rain, Alice had left the window ajar last night, as she always did, to catch the cool night breeze coming in from the gulf. She opened her eyes in the dark room and immediately wondered why the stairway light was out. She always kept it on during the night just in case she had to move about in the darkness. Alice reached for the bedside lamp switch. The low howl outside increased with a sudden, stronger gust of wind. It whipped the drapes at the window, which knocked over the lamp on the nightstand, startling Alice. The glass lamp base shattered on the hardwood floor.

"Careful, honey. Watch the glass. Stay put while I get a light on," Brown cautioned groggily as he leaned over toward his bedside table. Click. Click. Click. Nothing. No light. Their power was out. Alice sat up in the lovely antique four-poster bed and brushed the sleep from her eyes.

"What in the world?" wondered Brown out loud. He reached for the wind-up alarm clock beside the lamp.

"Alice, it's not quite four o'clock, but it seems like we've lost our electricity. The power's out." He returned the Big Ben to the night-stand and swung his legs out of bed, his toes easily finding his slippers. Carefully, the man made his way to the window nearest his side of the room. Alice could see his silhouette in the darkness, and she scooted to his side of the bed and followed him.

The window was on the front side of the house and faced south, looking out over the front yard and the row of tall ancient oak trees standing between the house and the coast highway. They both peered out through the glass and were stunned by what they saw. Alice couldn't trust her eyes on the view before her, for it appeared that water covered their yard.

"Brown, what is that? What do you see?" she asked, pointing to the ground below. The windowpane rattled with the force of the wind.

"It's hard to see very well through the screen," Brown replied. "Let's go downstairs." He wasn't about to tell her what he thought he saw, because it didn't make sense. It was too soon for the hurricane to hit.

"Okay. We can get some candles from the kitchen." Alice definitely wanted some light in the house.

"I also put the kerosene lamp on the counter last night. It's ready to light. Hold my shoulder, honey." Brown cautiously moved down the staircase with Alice's hand on his shoulder. She gripped the fabric of his nightshirt with one hand and the stair rail with the other. The large house was creaking in the wind. It was an eerie sound in the darkness. At the base of the stairs, Alice flicked on the light switch, hoping against hope. Their eyes were now beginning to adjust to the dark, and they could see much better. The pair made their way through the living room and dining room without a misstep, finally reaching the kitchen. Brown knew every inch of the house, having lived there for decades. He kept a rack of matches on the wall near the stove, and now he lit the lamp's wick with a steady hand. Soon the kitchen was awash in flickering lamplight.

With a reliable light source now successfully established in the house, Brown walked to the kitchen's back door, opened it, and stepped out onto the back porch. Alice literally bumped into his back when he halted abruptly.

"Oh, my God," Brown let out in stunned disbelief. "This storm is upon us, Alice!"

Water covered the yard as far as they could see into the darkness. *It moves like a river*, thought Brown. He bent down on the porch steps, brought up a handful of the water, and tasted it.

"This is not from the rain. This is salty. This is the gulf water," he told Alice above the gusts.

The storm surge looked to be about a half-foot deep, because it hadn't come over the bottom step. It rippled darkly in the wind. Brown knew that it would be deeper out on the road, however. The two returned to the kitchen and closed the back door. Alice was quiet. Her eyes were wide as she looked up at her husband.

"How can this be happening, Tootie? The weather report said the hurricane wouldn't hit until the afternoon—not for another ten or twelve hours! How can this be?"

Brown took a deep breath to regain his calm so as not to alarm his wife. He reached out, putting both hands on her shoulders and grabbing her full attention.

"Alice, we've got to get out of here quickly. We have no time to spare, so let's get dressed and leave within five minutes. Do you understand?"

"Yes. Yes." She nodded her head without blinking. Brown released her shoulders and picked up the lantern. The couple retraced their steps through the parlor and back up the stairs in the foyer.

They dressed with care, but with haste. Alice donned a blouse and a matching skirt. There was no time to select a belt today. Foregoing her usual stockings, she chose anklet socks and Keds, sensible tennis shoes that laced up. Brown decided against cowboy boots and was just lacing the ties of his work boots when Alice returned to the closet one last time. Reaching to the shelf above, she pulled down a large purse, similar to a beach bag. Moving to the dresser, she poured the contents of her smaller straw purse from yesterday into the larger leather bag, making sure her wallet was there.

"The coast highway is flooded," stated Brown as he tied the laces in a sturdy knot, "but if we can make it out of the driveway to the cross-roads at Daigle's Corner, and then head north through Creole, I think we will make it out of this mess. The Creole highway is our only way out, Alice." He stood and moved to get his wallet from his bureau top.

"Ready?" Brown asked.

"One more thing," Alice said, with her back still to him. She opened a drawer in her jewelry box and removed a velvet drawstring pouch. She slipped the pouch with its glittering contents into her purse. *Just in case*, she thought to herself. "Ready!"

With the handle of the lantern held securely in his hand, Brown led his wife downstairs at a deliberate pace, then through the house toward the back porch. As they passed through the living room, Alice removed a photo album from a shelf and tucked it under her arm. In a small room off the kitchen, Brown went to an old wooden desk and pulled out several folders from the file drawer. Watching her husband from the doorway, Alice thought of another keepsake she wanted to take with them—her cookbook. Moving across the kitchen, she opened a cupboard and selected one book off the crowded shelf.

"Okay, let's go," directed Brown as he turned on a flashlight. He collected the truck keys from the wall hook, extinguished the kerosene lamp, and closed the back door behind them. The rain had eased for the moment, but that wouldn't hold for long. The two made their way down the porch steps into the backyard alongside the pecan orchard. Even in the darkness, it was obvious that the water had risen considerably in the last five or ten minutes. Alice followed her husband into the dark current—the water rose up to her knees. Brown aimed the flashlight on the truck, parked about twenty feet north of the house.

The current was moving at a steady pace but luckily was pushing them toward the truck. Brown opened the driver's-side door and helped Alice into the cab. Tossing her purse inside first, she slid across easily on the vinyl-covered seats. Brown climbed in behind her just as the rain came down in earnest once again.

The heavy-duty Chevy engine started smoothly, and Brown revved it up just a notch. When he turned on the headlights, the beams highlighted the yard to the tree line. It was too dark to see beyond the fig trees in the backyard. There was no sign of life around the neighborhood. No lights shone from the homes in the distance. He hoped they had gotten out earlier ahead of the rising tide.

Brown realized that the gentle downward slope of the long driveway meant the truck would be entering deeper water, but driving through a flooded street was something he had done many times before. For now, the floorboard was above the water. He eased the truck into first gear and drove slowly out of the backyard, then alongside the house, passing Alice's sedan in the driveway. Another couple hundred feet and they would reach the main road, the coast highway.

The truck was pushing against the current, against the invading storm surge, so Brown kept it at a crawl. Even then, water began to splash over the grille and onto the hood. Alice felt water on the floorboard. It seeped under the doors as the truck inched deeper in the floodwaters. The wind was blowing harder now, and the water continued to rise. Alice clutched her bag against her chest and prayed. With a jolt, the fast-moving current of the storm surge swept the truck off its intended path and off the driveway. Alice screamed and grabbed the door strap.

The motor sputtered and Marshall struggled with the steering wheel, but it was to no avail. The engine flooded with salt water and the fan belt came to a complete stop. Brown tried several times to restart but eventually gave up his attempts.

"It's no use, Alice. We've got to make it back to the house and quickly!"

The truck had been pushed to the side of the driveway that positioned Alice's door on the leeward side of the storm surge. Within the confines of the large cab of the truck, Brown switched places with Alice and pushed open the passenger-side door. Water swirled deeper into the truck as Brown stepped down into the current.

"Stay close to me, honey," he yelled over the sound of the wind.

Alice looped the strap of her leather purse over her shoulder, kept one hand on the door handle, and stepped off the running board into her husband's outstretched arms.

The couple abandoned the truck in the front yard at the edge of the driveway and struggled to keep their footing in the fast-moving current. The storm surge pushed them northward back up the front yard toward the wide front steps of the veranda. Alice's skirt swirled in the water, which now reached almost to her hips. She was struck by just how forceful it was, so much like the summer tides along the beach. The rain came down in icy sheets, and the unrelenting wind dropped the temperatures rapidly. In a few minutes, the two were able to make it up the submerged veranda steps and finally onto the porch. The house stood on low piers, and the water moved beneath the structure, splashing up onto the porch in its relentless push inland.

Brown opened the heavy front door and ushered Alice inside, leaning heavily to close the door solidly behind him. He turned to his wife, who was visibly shaken and on the verge of tears. She stood in the dark foyer in a dripping puddle from her own wet clothes. Raising her chin, Alice produced a brave smile, and the two went to the kitchen and relit the kerosene lamp. Brown took a second lamp down from the pantry shelf and positioned the wick a bit higher before lighting it also.

"Alice, honey, it appears we are in a bad fix. I've got to secure the house and try to keep the water from getting inside. I'm going to get the boards and toolbox from the front porch and nail the wood over the windows like I had planned to do. Why don't you change into some dry clothes and get warm. I'll just be on the porch for a few minutes."

"All right," agreed Alice, frightened and cold. They retraced their steps, each carrying a lantern to the front room. Alice stopped at the niche in the wall and picked up the telephone receiver. *Regina. Let me call Regina. She'll be so worried.* No dial tone. She pressed the black button twice but to no avail. Nothing. Alice slowly hung up the phone, then turned and proceeded up the stairs. Brown placed his lamp on a table near the front windows, providing a bit of light onto the front porch.

Brown was deeply concerned about the suddenness of the storm's arrival. *The highway is way too flooded. It's useless now. No one will be able to get out!* He realized that there was little time left to nail the shutters closed on the front porch and get the remaining pieces of lumber moved inside the house. When Alice had almost reached the top of the stairs, he turned the knob on the front door, and the wind blew the door open, thumping it loudly against the wall of the foyer. The storm winds blew through the front rooms until Brown moved onto the porch, closing the door behind him with a firm tug.

Water was coming onto the porch now, and the man moved quickly to complete his first task. Grabbing the hammer and some long nails from the wooden Remington box on the porch, he closed the green storm shutters on the four large front windows, and nailed a board across each for added protection.

Next, he moved the toolbox into the house and returned to the porch for the other boards. After several trips, all the material was in the house. He leaned against the front door and turned the brass lock firmly into place.

By that time, Alice came downstairs with a dry towel for her husband thrown across her arm. She had stripped off her own wet clothes and dropped them into the bathtub upstairs. After changing into a pair of pants and a warm shirt, she toweled up the water from the polished oak floors of the bedroom and returned downstairs to help her husband.

Brown pushed the damp brown hair from his forehead and took several deep breaths after he placed the last two boards on the floor of the adjoining dining room.

"I've laid out some dry clothes for you. Let's get you warm and dry upstairs."

It was then that they noticed the water seeping under the front door, coming into the house.

"Here, let me have that towel," he said urgently. Pushing it against the door, he stopped the seepage for the moment.

"Oh, Brown! How deep is this flood going to get?" blurted Alice. The wind shrieked through the columns on the veranda and rattled the window frames in the dim light of the living room.

"Honey, reach into that box and get a handful of nails, would you please? I've got to make sure this door stays closed," Brown said as he selected a shorter board from the stack in the center of the room. Taking the hammer from the loop on his workpants, he soon had several boards nailed across the doorframe.

For the next hour, Alice and Brown worked feverishly to secure the downstairs windows with plywood already cut to their size. Adrenaline, fueled by worry, coursed through their veins, and their task progressed at a steady pace.

"I never thought I'd be hanging this plywood over the windows from *inside* the house," Brown remarked with a shake of his head, "but if the glass breaks during the hurricane, the wood will help keep the rain out. Every little bit helps."

Daylight was just breaking through the few uncovered windows. The storm surge continued to rise, and the hurricane winds rapidly increased to a constant undulating moan, punctuated by shrieks that rattled the windowpanes. Water was almost knee deep inside the house and seemed to be rising. By the time the plywood covered most of the windows on the first floor, Alice was near frantic.

"Enough, Brown! Let's get upstairs. Let's get upstairs now!"

"Okay, but let's grab some food and water and bring it upstairs with us. No telling how long this will last."

Alice selected a basket from the pantry and began placing items inside it to last out the day upstairs, including bread, some canned goods, and a jar of apple butter. Wading through the water in the kitchen, she opened several drawers to get the can opener, a few utensils, and a box of matches. The tap water was a gray color, so they settled for a large can of fruit juice.

The tall cattleman carried the heavy basket for his wife, his height keeping it well out of reach of the water. The couple sloshed their way through the living room and to the foyer. A low, delicate end table toppled and floated in the parlor, its white lace doily floating momentarily on the brown water as they waded past. The deep burgundy velvet of the Victorian sofa was becoming a sodden piece of finery in the once lovely parlor. None of that mattered now—all they cared about was surviving the storm.

The wind was so loud that little else could be heard as they made their way up the stairs. From the top of the landing, the couple looked back downstairs to see water defiantly filling the home in spite of their efforts.

Alice rounded the corner of the stair rail and went down the short hall to their bedroom, which faced the beach. Brown placed the food basket on the low dresser and joined his wife at the window. In their bedroom, two southern-exposure windows faced the gulf and another window graced the west wall. The view that confronted them was inconceivable. It took their breath away as though someone had hit them in the gut.

From their bedroom on the second floor the neighborhood came into full view. Alice gasped and covered her mouth with her hand as the full impact of the scene hit her. In the gray dawn light, the couple was horrified to witness the vast expanse of water that covered the land as far as the eye could see. Long rows of white-crested waves moved inland, invading the neighborhood. The undulating pitch of the screeching wind seemed to be the voice of the huge waves.

Brown could just make out the few head of cattle that remained in the holding pen. He had released most of them to open range the night before. If the water level held to its current depth, the herd would survive the storm.

The row of tall, ancient oaks with massive trunks and limbs was all that stood between the house and what used to be the beach. The thick branches writhed and shook in the face of the hurricane wind. Leaves ripped away from the limbs and blew against the bedroom's windows. Below in the front yard, the white truck stood in the dark water as a silent reminder of their failed evacuation attempt. The hood was under water, and waves splashed over the roof of the cab.

The rising tide that had crept ashore silently in the early morning hours had robbed the coastal towns of valuable hours—and was now driving inland at great speed like a rushing river.

Alice looked out the westward-facing window toward the town of Cameron about five miles away. The treetops hid most everything from view, as did the sheets of rain, but the homes of their closest neighbors were visible here and there through the oak grove. There was no sign of human activity anywhere.

Brown slowly stripped off his wet clothes as he thought hard to devise a plan of action. Toweling off the dampness, he changed into dry khaki pants and shirt and slipped the hammer into the loop of his pants. He took extra cash from the dresser drawer, slid the bills into his wallet, and returned the billfold to his back pocket. Marshall dried his thick hair with the damp towel, noticing once again the unusual chill in the air.

Alice, meanwhile, threw the pile of wet items into the large, claw-footed bathtub, then used her husband's towel to quickly dry the floor. As she passed the bathroom window, a horrifying sight froze her to the spot.

A tornado snaked its way down from the sky about a mile east of their house, moving inland toward Creole. The long, dark funnel writhed and twisted menacingly above the oak grove, a stark contrast to the gray skies.

"Brown, come quickly!" she yelled without taking her eyes off the tornado. He joined her in a rush, and his eyes followed her pointing finger to the funnel cloud. They stared at the twister as it bounced and dipped to the ground below. In a matter of seconds it was beyond their view, hidden by a sudden sheet of rain.

"Let's check the backyard." Brown took his wife's hand and they went down the hall toward the north-facing back bedrooms. From there they had a different take on the storm conditions. The garage and its attached tool shed stood about thirty feet north of the house. The building gave them a good perspective of the flooded neighborhood because they could clearly see how deep the murky water was around the garage.

"It's getting deeper by the minute," Alice remarked after only a few moments at the window. "How deep do you think it is?"

"Hmmm . . . four, maybe five feet. Our house is on piers a foot and a half tall, topped by eight-inch flooring. And with the water that seeped into the downstairs, I'm guessing about five feet." Even as they stood there, the Marshalls watched the storm surge rise continuously. Occasionally, Alice turned her head and looked into his reassuring eyes.

"Alice, honey, try not to worry. The house is well built. It's strong. I've had water inside this house before."

In the foyer, water continued to inch up the stairs. The minutes clicked past rapidly. The clock above the mantel chimed once at 6:30 A.M. but could not be heard over the noise. Outside, the wind increased to 125 miles per hour, blowing east to west as the eye of the hurricane approached the coast. Waves formed on the top of the storm surge and slammed into the house. Glass broke in one of the boarded-up windows in the living room, and then in another. The shutters held, but the storm surge pushed water between the slats like water from a fire hose.

"Look!" Alice cried, pointing to the floor below. The couple watched from the landing at the top of the stairs as water began to pour into the house and fill the downstairs rooms. The brown gulf water invaded the home, pushing furniture around the parlor. The dining-room chairs floated and toppled. All the while, the wind maintained a deafening shriek.

7:00 A.M., Thursday, June 27
The Marshall home
Daigle's Corner, Louisiana

In the bottom floor of the home, the water rose steadily step by step up the stairs. Alice turned from the second-floor railing to rush to the safety of their bedroom. Brown stood transfixed, but jumped back reflexively when the water below him suddenly surged to a height of five or six feet, slapping against the walls of the wide stairwell. He heard Alice scream and felt the thud of another large wave against the house as he ran down the hall to their bedroom.

From the window, Alice watched a neighbor's home slide off its foundation and float for a moment, twisting in the wind and waves. She could discern the family clinging to the attic window, just above the water. The rain came in sheets, sideways now, but Alice could see the waves crashing against the neighbor's roof. With agonizing slowness, a wing of the house ripped away from the main portion, leaving a gaping hole in the structure. Soon the rest of the house broke apart in large chunks. The screams of the family went unheard, lost in the howling wind as the roof collapsed on top of them.

Alice's own sobs racked her short frame. They knew the family well. Brown held her close beside him with an arm about her shoulder. For a brief moment they saw some of the family floating on parts of the roof, but they were quickly pushed out into the woods beyond the property. One of the older children, the nine-year-old boy, struggled in the waves and grabbed for the branches of a nearby tree. He looked so small climbing up the trunk to higher boughs. Finally, the lad halted his ascent and held on tightly.

Hurricane Audrey had arrived with a vengeance. The eye of the storm came ashore with wind speeds of 145 miles per hour. Alice and Brown had run out of time.

Over the sound of the screaming wind, Alice and her husband heard a deep, rumbling sound building up as if boulders were tumbling toward them. They looked out the windows toward the gulf to see a long wall of water, a huge wind-blown wave, coming their way. Never in all the years surviving hurricanes from the gulf had Brown Marshall seen anything like this massive wall of water approaching the coast, heading toward their home.

Brown took Alice's arm without a word and rushed down the hall toward the rear bedrooms of the second floor. Hopefully the row of stalwart oaks in the front yard could afford their home some bit of protection from the oncoming tidal wave. But this wave was much taller than the trees.

Passing the stairway, the two hurried into the back bedroom, slamming the door behind them. Alice stood pressed against the wall beside the door, too afraid to get near the windows. She looked into her husband's eyes as she had done so often before in their time together. Brown embraced his wife against his broad chest, holding her close. The house literally shook from the noise. Alice felt her husband's grip tighten ever so slightly. They held each other, suspended in the moment, as the noise of the approaching tidal wave became deafening, thunderous.

"God help us," he whispered against her soft curls.

In a matter of heartbeats, the massive wave crashed into the house, easily topping the roof. Once ashore on the beach, the tidal wave rapidly dispersed to lower levels, blended with the already present storm surge that was topped by ten-foot waves, and pushed inland.

Few people who saw the actual tidal wave lived to tell. Those who did survive it never forgot it.

The house lurched off its foundation, rammed by the force of the wave. The water lowered slightly, pulled back, formed another wave twenty feet tall, then slammed against the slow-moving, floating home. With shrieks and moans, the wooden structure suffered greatly under the onslaught.

The Marshall house broke apart in a matter of moments. All the upper-floor windows shattered as the frame of the house bent at strange angles. The stairs broke away from the wall in the stairwell. The north wall opened up at the corner, tilting the upper floors dangerously. Audrey's hurricane winds roared through the fractured structure. With great difficulty in standing, Brown pulled Alice away from the wall and moved her toward the nearby window.

With a deep, wooden groan, the bedroom floor tore away from the far wall. Alice's screams rent the air. The couple lost their footing and slipped down the tilting, wet floor into the raging waters below. Furniture followed their path down the slippery slope. The heavy porcelain bathtub ripped from its plumbing and sank immediately beneath the water. As a final insult, the roof collapsed onto the floor where the couple had just stood.

Thrown into the waves, Brown surfaced quickly near the edge of the collapsed roof. The couple had linked arms, but Alice had become separated from his grasp underwater.

"Alice, my God, Alice!" The sea spray stung his eyes as he searched the surrounding water for his wife. "Alice! Alice," he called out again.

A wave thrust a large section of the roof against his shoulder, and he instinctively grabbed for it and held on. A few seconds later, he spotted his wife.

Alice surfaced with a gasp for air within a few feet of her frantic husband. Brown reached out and pulled her toward him and the roof. As the eave dipped in and out of the water, the two managed to climb onto the rough, shingled surface. They crawled on their stomachs toward the middle, hunkering down against the hurricane winds. Luckily, the section was wide, about twenty feet across.

Pieces of their home bobbed to the surface and floated all around them, suspended atop the storm surge. Their new Westinghouse refrigerator bumped against the stairs, which floated nearby. Larger portions of the walls and floors slowly rose from the depths and began to break apart in the waves. Boards, timbers, cabinets, furniture, clothes—household items of every imaginable sort were borne along in the fast-moving current. This debris field surrounded Alice and Brown in an eerie coexistence for a time. As family heirlooms and jagged pieces of their home swirled about the desperate couple, they became surrounded by the remnants of their own lives. The deadly scene developed into a darkly reflecting mirror of their life together—solid and firmly connected one moment, then torn asunder the next. It was also a harbinger of things to come.

The wind and waves propelled the roof through the water like a huge water ski. It swiped across treetops and bumped into telephone poles. Each jolt scraped Alice's elbows and hands along the shingles as the couple lay flat on their stomachs. She tried to keep her eyes open as much as possible despite the sting of the salt water.

There's nothing but water everywhere! she thought, stunned by the scene that surrounded them. She could tell they were moving quickly through the woods beyond their house. *My God, it's blowing us all the way to town!* she thought in amazement, then paused as she realized that both Creole and Cameron must be submerged beneath the storm surge.

Brown looked around and took stock of their situation. Alice was beside him, their shoulders touching. The hurricane screamed in their ears. Rising and falling between the waves, their large section of roof somehow held together. As the waves thrust them across the chenier, other pieces of homes and destroyed structures came within their view. Their raft tilted perilously in the water, as the waves crested high then plunged downward. It scraped and thudded against pieces of other buildings in its path. At one point the roof glanced off a tall pine, then another tree, coming to a temporary halt in an oak as it lodged within the massive tree.

Alice reached out and grabbed hold of a tree limb stretched out above the roof, near her shoulder. The oak was part of the earth, the land, and Alice wanted to be connected to the land, not the invading waters of the gulf. Suddenly, she froze in her movements. A man's body hung limp in the branches nearby. Alice locked eyes with his own vacant, open eyes, but the awkward drape of the human limbs among the tree limbs left little doubt that the man had met his end. This close-up view of death dispelled any disbelief she might have of his fate. With the roar of the hurricane sounding in her ears, Alice closed her eyes in a vain attempt to block out the horror of the vision.

There was no chance to make a decision to climb into the tree, for the next wave sent the roof spinning off at dizzying speeds. Several times Alice was swept near the edge, but Brown held a firm grip on her forearms. As if in a fog, they unconsciously focused on staying as close to the middle of the roof as possible, and repositioned themselves time and again.

Debris blew through the air, hitting the roof with solid thumps before bouncing off and slipping beneath the dark water. A large section of metal roofing twisted and disappeared overhead as if sucked upward in a funnel draft. Waves deposited timbers and branches on top of their raft, but more waves would sweep away the debris.

At one point, Brown discerned a piece of floor, or possibly a wall, in the water about thirty feet off to their right. It was a much smaller piece of debris, but six people clung to the timbers. The wooden piece was too small to support their total weight, so the people were forced to cling to the sides, their shoulders just above water. The two groups stared at each other in shared anguish. Brown lost sight of the group when a wave crashed upon his own raft. When the wave cleared, he again caught sight of the other party, but only three people were left gripping the boards. One man swam desperately back toward his group in the water, but he was too far from the object to regain his hold. The wind howled and pushed against any headway he made. After another series of waves, the man was gone. All that remained clinging to the boards were a man and a woman with a small child. The woman gripped the toddler against her shoulder with one arm and held the raft with the other.

Alice and Brown watched helplessly as a jagged board came flying out of nowhere and struck the woman in the head. The man reached across the small raft for her arm, but she slid beneath the waves as if in slow motion, still holding her child. He dove in after her, but never resurfaced.

The hurricane continued to rage against the coast, and in time the Marshalls' roof floated in an area devoid of tall trees. Brown realized that meant the storm must have blown them out of the chenier and into the marsh north of Cameron and Creole. An hour had passed, but it seemed like days.

Livestock from the Creole ranches converged in the Marshalls' windblown path. He realized his own herd of cattle was probably in the mix. Alice and Brown could see the animals struggling in the deep waves. The longhorns were big animals with powerful legs and they fought hard to stay afloat, but it was a losing battle. The salt water stung their eyes, making the cattle angry, confused, and dangerous.

The storm surge pushed several head of cattle alongside the roof. Instinctively seizing the chance to get out of the water, one frightened animal thrust out his front hooves and tilted the roof edge below water as he tried to claw his way on board. Brown grabbed a piece of lumber that had been deposited on the roof and rose to a kneeling position. He pushed hard against the animal's head, directly between the long-horns. Brown's thick hair blew wildly about in the wind as he kept pushing. He was able to stop the steer from getting his hind legs on the roof, but the animal would not give up his tenuous position. In desperation, Brown swung the long board out then brought it back hard against the animal's skull. Both the man and the steer were thrown off balance. Brown fell on his side, still gripping the board. The animal slipped back into the raging current and was soon swept away.

I better hang on to this board, he thought, and slowly crawled on his knees back to Alice's side. The hammer in his pants loop was the only other tool he had. *Without nails, I don't see what good a fourteen-inch hammer will be,* he mused. Brown lay down and placed the board beside him, as Alice reached out to hold his hand. He was no longer a young man with unlimited energy, and the battle had sapped his strength.

For a while, he concentrated on just breathing without getting any water in his mouth. He closed his eyes, and the wind continued to scream in his ears.

Rain pelted down in sheets, like needles of ice. Both Alice and her husband shivered with cold. With the roof once again buoyant, the couple tried to regain their strength for the long day ahead of them. There were times when the wind blew so hard it was difficult to breathe. The wind literally took their breath away.

Alice lowered her head onto her arm. Once again she sent up a silent prayer for God's help. She had seen so much death in the few hours since Audrey hit unexpectedly before dawn. It was too much to accept, and she closed her eyes against the burning salt water.

How could the storm have gotten here so soon? she wondered over and over. *We should have had ten or twelve more hours before it struck, plenty of time to evacuate! How could this have happened? How?*

Brown had also watched in horror as the other group perished within sight of their roof. He thanked God their own raft was larger, which gave them a better chance in the rough water. The husband and wife struggled in the hurricane winds to stay on their roof all morning while Audrey pushed the Marshalls from the marsh north of their home into the vast expanse of Calcasieu Lake.

The roof of their former home would serve as their life raft for the next eighteen hours, but neither Alice nor Brown could have known that their worst trials lay but a few hours ahead.

Survivors—black and white, young and old, those who could swim and those who could not—all fought for their lives in those harrowing hours. Anything that floated—doors, mattresses, pieces of lumber—became a life raft. Alice and her husband witnessed many people struggling to stay afloat that morning. Had these people been able to swim through the storm surge successfully, some could have reached the safety of the Marshalls' roof, but that was not the case.

When the hurricane made landfall, people were not choosy by any means. Once they were thrown into the water they grabbed for anything that floated. The animals did the same. Bobcats and raccoons, rats and mice, nutria and snakes—all sought higher, drier ground. The animals of the coastal terrain and freshwater marshes were angry. The salt water stung their eyes and blinded many. Some, like the snakes, became very dangerous under these conditions.

Brown first caught the slithering movement off to the left out of the corner of his eye. He knew at a glance that the large black snake was a water moccasin. While the moccasins preferred to live near marshes, ponds, and even smaller bodies of water, Brown had killed several on his property over the years. Locals who lived near ponds knew to also check the branches of trees near the water. Snakes are born climbers, and a water moccasin was nothing but a long, powerful muscle with two deadly fangs on one end.

Alice hated snakes.

Each time the water invaded its space, the snake moved from the edge of the roof, inching closer to Brown. Without alerting Alice, he reached for the piece of lumber beside him, but it was gone. He leaned up on his elbows to check the rooftop for its location. Brown looked in all four directions, but to no avail. The board was definitely gone. There was no telling when it had washed off the roof. The wind alone could have blown it away in a single gust.

All Brown knew was that he had to keep the snake away from them. That single thought was all that occupied his mind. If a wave came at the wrong moment, the wrong angle, the snake could be pushed against him and Alice. The minutes dragged on, but he kept his eyes on the snake's movements and prayed for a board or even a stick to come his way. Nothing materialized.

Alice, meanwhile, began to stir and turned in Brown's direction. It was inevitable that she would see the cottonmouth, and her scream cut the air, carrying above the wind.

"Brown! A snake!" She grabbed her husband's arm, pointing in horror.

He nodded his head in acknowledgment.

"Where's that board? Push it off with the board!"

"I can't," he admitted, keeping his eyes on the snake. "It washed away." The serpent moved a foot closer, and Alice screamed again in fright.

It was then that Brown remembered the hammer in the loop of his pants. Rolling on his side, he slid the hammer from the loop. The handle wasn't as long as he would have liked by any means, but it would have to do if the man was to attempt a preemptive strike. By now the snake was close, about eight feet from the couple. Brown shifted to a kneeling position and moved a foot toward the moccasin, then another foot. When the pitch of the roof slowed between waves, Brown rose slowly to a crouched position. He then lifted his arm high and swung the hammer down with all his might. He struck the head dead center, killing the snake. It writhed in reflexive death throes atop the roof. Marshall backed off for a few moments; then, using the tool once again, he pushed the snake farther away. Waves eventually washed it from the roof and out of sight.

Although it was brief, Alice and Brown both experienced a moment of respite in the storm as the immediate danger ended, and the eye of the hurricane began to move over the lake.

5:00 A.M., *Thursday, June 27*
The Johnny Meaux farm
Oak Grove, Louisiana

Just a few doors down the road from the Griffith home in Oak Grove, the storm surge had also crept across the fields of Johnny Meaux's farmland. Under the cover of darkness, the gulf waters rose above the dried stalks of the harvested crops. A thick field of corn that was top heavy with green ears not quite ready to yield struggled against the rising wind and invading tide. Atop each husk, yellow corn silk fluttered like thin, satin ribbons in the sudden gusts.

Nothing woke D.W.'s uncle Johnny, who slept soundly through the night. Over several decades, his wife, Esther, had grown accustomed to his deep snores, and she too was oblivious to the sounds of the approaching hurricane.

Across the field from the Meaux farmhouse, noise from the storm woke two-year-old Walter Bartie and his parents. Looking outside in the predawn light, Raymond and Maybell found that rising water had covered the yard and the fields surrounding their home. The rest of the family rose, dressed, and waited in the dark to see just how high the water would get.

"Raymond, we've got to get to the Meauxs' house!" his wife implored.

When the storm surge covered their front porch that morning, Raymond and Maybell gathered the children about them and started the hazardous journey across the field to the larger, sturdier Meaux house. The wind howled a deep moan above the trees along the ridge of the chenier. Carrying his youngest son, Ray led his family in a single line where he knew to find the submerged but well-worn path that crossed the field.

By now, the knee-deep water pushed inland with a steady current, and the children held hands tightly to keep their footing. There were six children, all under the age of fifteen, and one slip could cause the others to fall. But fortune was kind for a brief moment, and the group of eight traversed the field without mishap.

Still holding little Walter, Raymond pounded on the Meauxs' back door, trying frantically to wake the household. Water continued to inch upward. Eight-year-old Ray Jr. was almost swept away in the current that swirled under and around the house. Water washed over the steps and into the back screened porch.

"Mr. Johnny! You've got to get up, Mr. Johnny! There's water in the house!" yelled the desperate man.

Johnny Meaux finally awakened to Mr. Bartie's yells. He swung his legs off the bed and was shocked to be standing in water. Once inside the kitchen, the Bartie family found a moment of rest, and a safe haven—but not for long. There was barely time for the Meauxs and their houseguest, Mrs. Stewart, to get dressed before the storm surge rose dramatically, ripping away the porch from the single-story structure.

Raymond's mind focused on a single thought—to get his family to a higher place, out of the floodwaters. He instructed his children to follow him down the hall into the pantry, where he lifted them up onto the sturdy wooden shelves. He told the older ones to climb toward a small opening in the ceiling, which led to the attic.

Springing into action, Eugene climbed to the top shelf and pushed the wooden ceiling panel open. The teen helped each child into the attic one by one as the water continued to rise. Within moments, the salty water from the gulf surged waist deep inside the farmhouse, separating the group from Maybell at the opposite end of the house. Raymond called out to his wife, knowing he could not leave the children even for a moment, then he too climbed into the attic.

Maybell struggled to reach her family in the pantry, but the fast-moving water made that impossible as it pushed her down the hall. Household items and furniture floated throughout the farmhouse, crashing into the walls and further separating the mother from her family.

Reaching high above his tall shoulders, Mr. Meaux grasped the cord attached to the pull-down attic stairs in the hallway. At six foot two, the barrel-chested man stood his ground in the fast-moving water to help the three ladies up the stairs and into the dark confines of the attic.

All the people on the Meaux farm climbed to safety in the rafters that morning, but the two groups ended up in separate wings of the house—and in separates attics. Neither group could see nor hear the other. Worry and fear for her children overwhelmed Maybell Bartie, and she pressed her dark curls against a rough wooden beam. With Audrey's winds screaming through the rafters, the sounds of the hurricane completely absorbed the mother's cries of anguish.

In a short time, the farmhouse broke apart under the assault of the waves. The roof collapsed on top of the dismembered walls of the frame home. Maybell's group sank beneath the waves and surfaced amid the horrifying elements of the storm. Huge waves of debris-filled water swept the four out of the yard. Grabbing hold of floating pieces of wood and timbers from the house, the four were blown several miles out into the submerged town of Oak Grove, where the waves eventually pushed them into a thick stand of trees.

Bruised and battered, the group desperately clung to the tree limbs for survival. A random toss of the waves had deposited the four adults at varying levels among the branches of a sturdy oak, with Mr. Meaux at the lowest point, only about twenty feet up in the tree. Propelled by

140-mile-per-hour winds, pieces of the farmhouse, the large barn, and numerous outbuildings became assault weapons, sailing through the air and water. One such board slammed into Johnny Meaux, leaving a large rusty nail deeply imbedded in his leg near the knee. Injured by the flying debris, he was unable to climb any higher. Throughout the long day he managed to survive in the lower branches, but was hit by more waves than the three ladies above him. Eventually the force of the waves and fast-moving current tore off his clothes and shoes. The stinging rain pelted the four like needles of ice.

When the roof collapsed on top of the other wing of the house, Mr. Bartie and the children clung to each other and bobbed to the surface quickly. Almost immediately they grabbed hold of a large floating portion of the roof. The determined father managed to get all six of his children on top of the shingled roof, but the strength of the wind and the force of the waves constantly threatened to wash them into the turbulent water. For several minutes they rode the raft atop the waves as if on a speeding boat. Raymond stretched his arms protectively over the little ones, but with a sudden jolt the family's raft knocked up against a tree, pushing them closer toward the edge of the roof.

Raymond realized that his children could be thrown off the roof at any time and that they stood a much better chance of survival in a firmly rooted, supple tree. With little time to spare before the next wave rolled over them, he lifted each child into the limbs of the tree, all the while holding little Walter close against his shoulder. Each child got a firm hold on a tree branch.

There was no defense against the next wave that crashed over them, however, and the wall of water wrenched the two-year-old out of his father's arms. Although Raymond frantically searched the water for his son, the fast-moving current swept the child away. Little Walter was lost to the storm.

For the next four hours, both groups fought to survive the unending assault from the huge waves from the gulf, the freezing cold rain, and the flying debris. Raymond constantly encouraged his five children to hold tightly to the branches and to hold their breath when yet another towering wave approached.

Off in the other stand of trees, Maybell worried constantly about the unknown—for the safety of her missing children and husband. It wasn't long into the morning when a jagged piece of timber hit her thigh, opening a long, deep gash in her flesh. She maintained her grip on the oak limb despite the injury to her leg and tried to focus on that monumental effort alone—that and prayer. As the day wore on, however, Maybell found herself finding reassurance in a rather unexpected and unusual source.

Although the Meauxs and Mrs. Stewart were in the tree, her nearest companion turned out to be a large blackbird seeking shelter from the storm amid the leaves and branches. The big bird dug its sharp claws into the bark of the oak and stayed close to Maybell for the entire day. The black bird and the black lady became kindred spirits and, in a surprising way, brought comfort to each other. Both the bird and the lady had limited resources with which to battle the elements, and they were both small compared to Audrey's strength, but both had a strong grip on the branches of the oak tree, and both had a strong determination to survive. As far as the bird was concerned, for the duration of the storm Mother Nature was the enemy, not this human.

If that blackbird can hang on, so can I, Maybell reckoned with determination.

Both the lady and the bird closed their dark eyes against the water's irritating salt spray, and rode out the storm together in the oak grove.

Thursday, June 27
The Austin Davis home
East of the Cameron Parish Courthouse
Cameron, Louisiana

D.W.'s aunt Nona felt safe in her current surroundings. Last evening, after she had dropped Geneva off at home and visited with her relatives a bit, she accepted an invitation from her cousin, Tad Davis, to spend the night with the Davis family. A warm camaraderie always filled the home, and the cousins stayed up late chatting over a pot of coffee.

Despite the sounds of the rain on the windowpanes, it was easy to feel safe in the strong, pre-Civil War mansion. The Davis house, built in 1844, survived many hurricanes and floods over the past century. Nona took comfort in that thought. A few hours after midnight, however, the household woke to the sounds of the advancing hurricane.

Before dawn that morning, several families seeking a safe haven tried to reach the courthouse but failed in the attempt. They took refuge with the Davis family when their cars and trucks flooded out in the street near the Davises' front yard. As people abandoned their vehicles along the road, the swift current caused many to lose their footing. Around daylight, Mr. Davis organized a human chain of men to rescue those who found themselves in such dire straits. Those who were fortunate enough to be swept into the Davis yard were "netted" by the strong men who linked arms, their chain stretching from a tree to the Davises' front porch. The men kept at it as long as possible, but eventually the current became too strong and they had to return to the house themselves.

The Davis family offered food and comfort to their guests, who arrived wet but safe inside the home. Knowing that it might be a long time before they had a good hot meal after the hurricane passed through the area, Mr. Davis had instructed his wife to cook everything perishable, then open canned goods from the pantry as needed. Nona lent a helping hand in the kitchen she knew so well.

When the rising water entered the house, Mr. Davis got all the people, including about 50 children, upstairs to safety. Alone downstairs, he then prepared the structure itself for the hurricane's assault. He turned off the gas, and opened all the windows and doors so the house would not wash off its foundation. Wading through knee-deep water in his home, Mr. Davis took one last look around from the base of the stairs, and then turned to make his way up to the second floor to his family and friends. At the top of the stairs, he embraced his wife, and led her away from the landing. In the two upstairs bedrooms of the Austin Davis home, over 150 people crowded together, strangely quiet as Audrey's hurricane winds began to bear down on the town.

Surrounded by neighbors and townspeople she'd known all her life, Miss Nona worried about her relatives down the road in Oak Grove.

She hoped they had time to make it to higher ground. Rather than stare at the seventy-five worried faces pressed shoulder to shoulder in the room with her, Nona closed her eyes. That move only heightened her sense of hearing. Outside, Hurricane Audrey's winds shrieked and raged against the dormer windows of the Davis home.

5:15 A.M., Thursday, June 27
The Calcasieu Ship Channel
Cameron, Louisiana

After ensuring the safety of his family inside the Austin Davis house, the tugboat captain drove the large truck through the dark, flooded streets of Cameron. Caught off guard by the early arrival of the storm, Mr. Stoute wanted to tie additional mooring ropes to his tugboat, the *George Hamilton*. The water continued to rise as he sought to reach his tug moored near the smaller Monkey Island ferry, and eventually he was forced to abandon the truck and finish the watery journey on foot. The going was so difficult, and the water so deep, that Captain Stoute sadly realized it would be impossible to make it back to his family without some sort of alternative transportation—such as his boat.

When Stoute reached his tugboat, he turned back to look toward the town. He saw the water rising at an incredible rate, now surging over the ridge where the courthouse stood. He couldn't believe the rate at which the water continued to rise and push inland. Stoute, like most residents of Cameron and Vermilion parishes, never expected this powerful a storm, nor this high a water level. Returning to his family was foremost in his mind, and he knew there was only one way to accomplish that now—on the *George Hamilton*.

From the dock, he jumped on board his tug, untied the lines connecting it to the ferry, and readied the wheelhouse. While he worked quickly at his task, he couldn't help but wonder how the other, larger Cameron Ferry was managing the waters in its berth a mile or so north of this smaller ferry. He understood why no one in town would want to use the Monkey Island ferry today. Who would want to be on the island during a hurricane? But Stoute knew that townspeople would be desperate to cross the ship channel to safety on the main ferry at the highway crossing.

Battening down the hatches and securing the door, the captain started the powerful engine. By this time the turbulent waters in the ship channel were well over the banks, and the strong little tug pushed northward right along with the incoming gulf waves, making its way through the streets of downtown Cameron. Jutting above the treetops, the top of the courthouse came into view.

5:00 A.M., *Thursday, June 27*
The DeBarge home
Cameron, Louisiana

When the water began coming up the steps of the DeBarge house early that morning, eighty-five-year-old Sidney relented to his brother's pleadings. In the dim predawn light, the two elderly men had watched the wind launch the green tomatoes as if they were baseballs, sailing them through the air out of the raised vegetable garden, which now lay submerged beneath the brown water. Sidney reluctantly agreed with Tommy that they needed to leave. But first Sidney wanted to make some coffee. By the time the pot of coffee had dripped, gulf water was creeping into the kitchen, too deep outside for them to make it to the courthouse. Their window of opportunity had closed.

Sidney had never learned to swim, and for the first time that day fear mingled with his confusion as he looked about for a means of escape from the encroaching water and deafening wind. For an hour the two sat on the rarely used stairs in the hall, while the water continued to rise. When the storm surge rose to nearly four feet inside, waves began to pound the house. Tommy told his brother to climb up into the attic.

"My legs are strong, and I will swim for help and maybe find a boat," Tommy offered.

Sidney carefully climbed the attic stairs, the water swirling at his feet as it rose relentlessly within the house. When he reached the top and entered the attic, he steadied himself by holding the rafters. With the door wide open, the wind shrieked through the confines of the long, narrow attic. Cautiously Sidney turned back around to look down at his eighty-four-year-old younger brother.

In the dim light their eyes said it all. A look of trust, friendship, and kinship passed between the two old gentlemen. Raising one arm, Sidney gave one slow nod of his head. Tommy raised his arm in response, and let the waist-deep current carry him out of the house.

In the turbulent waters outside, the winds were fierce. The waves were even stronger. Tommy was startled by their ferocity, but his path was chosen, and it was too late to turn back now. He kicked his legs confidently in the strong current, trying to go with the flow.

Over the sounds of the hurricane winds, Tommy heard a loud cracking noise and, looking back, saw their house breaking apart. A huge, fast-moving wave ripped the walls from the frame of the structure. Another wave tore the roof apart in sections. Tommy watched as the house disappeared under the surge of water. He knew his brother was dead.

The waves continued their advance inland and seemed to grab the old man, tossing him about like a cork. Trees, homes, and debris followed his tumbling course through the water. He finally was able to grab onto a board, and hung on for his life. Fortunately he was blown to the side of a metal warehouse, where he was able to take refuge in the upper floor. From a small upstairs window, he watched other people struggling in the huge waves. Some swept past rapidly—others disappeared suddenly amid the debris and whitecaps, as if pulled below by a menacing hand.

All the while, the deafening wind seemed like a conductor orchestrating each instrument of the storm into an explosive, angry symphony punctuated by deadly crescendos. Rain came down in sheets, but Tommy could occasionally discern nearby rooftops, with people clinging desperately to air conditioners and vent pipes. Dipping from the dark clouds overhead, a tornado bore down on several homes along one street, exploding each like a bomb. Cars were tossed like matchsticks in the waves, crashing into structures and sending the people on those rooftops into the water below.

For eight hours, the elderly man rode out the storm alone in the metal structure, which rattled and shook but remained bolted together. A jumble of thoughts—memories of his life and his brother—filled his head. Tommy DeBarge had indeed lived a long, full life, and much of it flashed before his eyes during the worst hours of Hurricane Audrey.

6:30 A.M., *Thursday, June 27*
The Griffith home
Oak Grove, Louisiana

Once in the attic, D.W. looked around at his family huddled together in the dim light. There was only a four-foot rise in the roofline, so everyone was bent over, crouched on the rafters. They were forced to avoid standing on the sheetrock ceiling of the kitchen, since the material was not strong enough to hold any weight. It was the rafters or nothing. Cherie clung to her mother's wet skirt. Geneva smoothed her daughter's dark hair, murmuring words of comfort. Leslie held his frightened dog. Bootsie had stopped barking but moved her head nervously, straining to locate all her family members. Papa's shoulders drooped as he tried to remain calm under the extreme conditions. He had to be strong for Nannie.

If D.W. had been able to read the wind speed indicators on the offshore oilrigs, he would have been horrified to find that the winds had increased to 145 miles per hour. By 6:30 A.M., the full force of Hurricane Audrey's winds had slammed into the coast.

The family had been able to escape immediate danger from the storm surge as it coursed through their home, but the seriousness of their current situation was obvious to D.W. The wind was raging now at a fever pitch. Looking down into what remained of their kitchen below, the young father made another critical decision. He reached again for his ax.

D.W. moved a safe distance from the group and slowly but deliberately began to chop a hole in the leeward side of the roof. Wood chips from the boards of the roof flew into the air with each restricted swing of the ax. There was little room to swing, but finally, several good whacks opened a sizeable chunk, large enough for the saw to complete the work. A strong cross wind now whipped from the opening in the kitchen ceiling out through the opening in the roof. Geneva's long, brown hair lashed about her face. Outside, the fierce gusts ripped off some of the roof shingles, sending them sailing high into the air like deadly scythes.

Papa Griffith became concerned over these new developments. He caught hold of D.W.'s arm and said, "Son, please don't do this. You will weaken your house. This is a strong house and it will stand this storm. I know, because I built it with plenty of nails."

D.W. lowered the ax and reached for the wooden handle of his saw. "Dad, I have to do this. I have to try to save my family."

Without pause, D.W. moved the saw into action, pushing and pulling against the thick plywood of the roof. As he continued to enlarge the hole, D.W. could hear the wind raging outside, shrieking and moaning. In time his task was completed, and he slowly bent to rest on his haunches. He set the saw aside and slung the coiled saddle ropes over his shoulder, hoping to anticipate the storm's next move.

The family waited nervously as dawn's light pierced through the escape hatch in the roof. They had no way of knowing that the deadliest part of the hurricane winds, the circular edge of the eye wall, was just offshore.

Beneath the attic in the Griffith house, the water continued to rise higher and higher. Previously the storm surge had moved like a river through the structure. Now huge waves pounded the flooded home, the sound reverberating into the attic as the house shuddered under each assault. The boardwalks from oil wells in the marsh became battering rams against the structure. First the sheetrock, then the timbers from the home's walls began breaking away, falling into the water. Every piece of furniture, every appliance was thrust from the home. Even the bathtub was pushed out of the house by the forceful currents. The house groaned as the frame and remaining walls twisted and struggled to stay intact. Soon the sheetrock of the ceiling began to give way.

The ceiling is melting! thought Leslie, in shock. Below, the water rose to the ceiling of the house, and indeed the sheetrock crumbled, dissolved as they watched.

The Griffiths stood only on rafters, looking down at the swirling water below. The roar of the hurricane wind was deafening. Their grip on the rafters above was tenuous at best. The hopelessness of their situation reflected in their eyes as they exchanged wordless glances.

D.W. and Geneva were both consumed with thoughts of how to save their two children in the short time they most likely had remaining above the deadly current below. He extended his hand to Geneva's cheek, and the young couple locked eyes.

"I want you to crawl out onto the roof first," yelled D.W. over the wind. "Then I'll hand the children to you."

With trusting hazel eyes, Geneva gave a firm, understanding nod of her head. She first reached into her purse, stuffed her wallet into her brassiere, then crawled out onto the roof. She clung to the opening while D.W.'s hands circled his daughter's tiny waist and he lifted Cherie to Geneva. Leslie crawled out behind his sister.

Before he lay down on the rough grainy shingles, Leslie wanted to see the storm. He had always wanted to go out in the gulf on a big boat like his dad, but so far that event had not happened in his short life. Today, he wanted to see the Gulf of Mexico in his yard. From the somewhat protected leeward side, the boy slowly crawled forward a few feet, then raised his head to look over the peak of the roof. Through the mist and the near-blinding wind, Leslie satisfied his curiosity. There lay the huge expanse of the gulf, stretching as far as the eye could see. It covered the landscape, and not with a scenic view as he had envisioned. This view assaulted his senses so overwhelmingly that he couldn't fully absorb the scene before him. This wasn't the beach; this wasn't the gulf. This was danger's doorstep. The view was terrifying and exciting at the same time. He found it hard to tear his eyes away from the unreal scene.

A few moments later, Leslie inched backward and lay down on the rough, grainy shingles. He positioned himself to get a better grip with one hand on the edge of the escape hatch, and the other on his dog.

The wind tore at his pale blonde hair, and at Bootsie's coat. If she was barking now, Leslie couldn't hear.

D.W. climbed out next and, crouching low, took little Cherie into his arms. Nannie, then Papa, followed the others out onto the roof. There was not enough space around the opening for all the family to secure a hold, however, so Geneva and Papa moved over toward the leeward edge of the gabled roof, where they could hopefully get a good grip against the strong wind.

In the eerily gray morning light, Geneva was stunned at the sight that met her eyes. The storm had moved ashore and the Gulf of Mexico now covered the land as far as the eye could see in all directions. The once blue waters of the gulf had been churned by wave after wave. Now the murky brown storm surge covered their green pastures. The barn was gone, and the livestock was nowhere to be seen in the deep water. Only the tops of trees and telephone poles were visible above the water.

Waves began crashing over the roof. D.W. held Cherie in the safety of one strong arm, while clinging to the roof opening with the other. Leslie struggled beside him to maintain a good hold on his dog.

It was then that the house collapsed. The 145-mile-per-hour wind, the storm surge, and the debris all combined to shatter and splinter the wood frame. With a final groan, the timbers gave way. Geneva and her family landed in the water—their roof had suddenly become their raft. They renewed their grip as best they could and sailed off on the roof through the raging black water.

Thus began the Griffiths' longest journey together.

Propelled by the huge waves, the roof bashed into a large oak tree northwest of where their house once stood. Geneva had just enough time to duck her head as they crashed against the trunk of the tree, under an overhanging limb. Unfortunately, she couldn't avoid her ankle being crushed between the roof and the tree. She cried out as she felt, and heard, the bones crush.

D.W. tossed a piece of rope to Geneva. Fighting off the pain, she followed his instructions. She tied one end around her waist and the other around Cherie's, desperate to keep her child close. D.W. busily tied Leslie onto the limb they had just crashed under, telling him to lie down on the limb and hug it. In the back of his mind, however, D.W. heard a warning voice, and he stopped tying the rope. He thought better of his plan and started unleashing his son from the tree.

"Geneva, untie Cherie!" he called out.

D.W. and Leslie got back onto the roof with the others, abandoning the tree for now. Call it fate, or call it divine intervention. The warning voice in the back of D.W.'s mind must surely have been the Lord watching out over them, because that limb was later to go completely and rapidly under the water.

After battering against the large oak tree for some time, the roof became dislodged by the constant wind and wave action. The family clung to their raft as it spun around and was rapidly swept away into the woods behind the Griffith home, where it slammed into another oak tree. Lacking a good handhold, Geneva and her father-in-law were thrown into the turbulent water. They were able to grab hold of a toothache tree, much smaller than the oak and with only two limbs to cling to. They were only about ten feet away from the rest of their group. There they clung, Papa's back to the gulf and Geneva facing the storm.

D.W. began to move his mother and the children up into the limbs of the tall oak.

"Son, climb as high as you can, so there will be room for the others," he yelled over the wind. "Put Bootsie down, and climb quickly."

Leslie looked at the trusting dog squirming slightly in his arms. He had found it almost impossible to hang on to the roof while clutching his dog as well, but he had never released his hold. At this point, with only seconds to act, he knew his daddy was right. Leslie buried his face in Bootsie's coat, then crouched down to set the dog onto the roof beside his feet. He knew that the family would see to it that the dog got safely into the tree with them.

"Hurry, son. Careful now!"

D.W. stood on the lower limbs near the top of the roof and guided his son to a good spot in the tree. With both hands free and the wind at his back, the young boy climbed—quickly at first, but then a bit slower as he crawled higher. Leslie climbed with the confidence an experienced eleven-year-old boy would have. This was his tree, after all. Soon he leveled out and lay down on a thick limb about eight inches in diameter with a gentle but distinct upward slope. Circling his arms around the limb in a viselike grip, he inched his way forward until his legs stretched out completely. The rope that his father had recently tied around his waist dangled below and whipped about in the wind. Leaves blew past his face, and the icy rain pelted against his exposed skin like sharp needles.

When he came to a stop, the young boy looked down at his father, who was now positioning Cherie on the tree limb just below Leslie. Despite the rain, Leslie quickly spotted his dog at his father's feet. While the human activity moved at a desperate pace around Bootsie, the cocker spaniel made a sudden and startling move. Leslie watched in disbelief as the old dog—his best friend—turned to face the water's edge and unexpectedly jumped off the safety of the roof into the dark water.

"Bootsie! Bootsie!" he yelled out to his dog. "Here, girl. Come back!"

He turned his face away from the wind to follow Bootsie's movements. The family watched in shock as their pet swam off with the current toward the woods and soon moved out of sight. Leslie called out again and again in distress, even though he realized there was no way his dog could make it back to his side. His salty tears mingled with the brine of the sea spray on his ruddy cheeks. Bewildered and frightened, he lowered his gaze in silent resignation, and looked toward his mother and grandfather struggling to hold their own in the strong current.

D.W., meanwhile, kept moving without pause to get his family to safety. Once his tiny daughter was secure, D.W. positioned himself on a limb directly below her. Nannie was last to abandon the roof, and she and D.W. stood on that lower limb just out of the water, their shoulders level with Cherie and her strong limb of the oak.

The storm's surge on the Front Ridge was now over ten feet deep, topped by tall, ten-foot waves that crashed over everything in their path. The waves' action seemed to have a deathly, relentless rhythm, as if they were pursuing prey. A wave would crash against the roof and the oak tree, forcing the family to hold their breath till the wave passed over them.

Then, just as it happens along the beach, the water was sucked back slowly as it built up another long column of water, hundreds of feet long. But unlike a normal ebb and flow, these swells—these long rows—were massive. Some waves were bigger than others. These columns rose upward and formed a ten- to fifteen-foot wave on top of the existing storm surge. Audrey's 145-mile-per-hour winds then pushed each column forward with a horrifying, vibrating roar. The huge wave would arch then crash over its prey.

Papa Griffith locked his arm over the limb and kept his back to the storm. Geneva tried to keep her gaze on her children. Facing the storm, she often lost her grip on the limb of the smaller tree as the waves crashed down upon them. Each time the waves began to wash her toward the marsh, she would have to swim back to the tree, as the water pulled back to form yet another wave. Geneva was young, and strong, and determined—but she was tiring quickly. Each time she lost her grip on the tree limb, D.W.'s heart sank and his anxiety rose to unbearable heights, until once again his Geneva would surface, gasping for breath.

Cherie's petrified, high-pitched screams pierced the air, calling for her mother.

Depending on how rapidly the waves moved upon them, D.W. would try to coach his children when a wave approached. "Get ready. Hold on tight. *Hold tight.* Take a deep breath *now* . . . and *hold* it!" he would yell.

Cherie and Leslie would fill their tiny lungs with as much air as they could. Everyone waited, eyes tightly closed against the burning salt water. The wave's roar would turn into a deep, bubbling thud as the wave covered and submerged the victims.

The height of the oak tree afforded the children more refuge than the others. Papa and Geneva were not so fortunate. At water level, they had to hold their breath much, much longer.

At one point between the onslaught of the waves, Papa looked at

Geneva clinging less than a foot away from his own branch. His last words to his beloved daughter-in-law were, "Geneva, you must hang on so you can live to raise your children."

"Papa, I don't know if I can or not. I am so tired."

"You have *got* to—don't you hear Cherie crying for you?"

She realized she had to do something to keep from drowning, to survive. She remembered something D.W. had told her once before about the gulf—how there were usually three big waves and then a smaller one. Holding the tree trunk, Geneva held her breath and went under the water as the first three waves crashed overhead, coming up for air on the fourth. She found that she had managed to surface closer to the tree this time and decided to stick with this pattern of resistance as long as she could hold out. After repeating the process over and over, Geneva began to lose all sense of time, for the waves and the struggle seemed to go on forever. She was fighting for her life, and she was losing.

Oh, God, please give me strength, she prayed silently.

At one point when she surfaced, she saw Papa hanging limp in the branches, his head lowered onto his chest. The next wave swept his body from the tree. Using her last bit of strength, Geneva gripped her branch tightly and wrapped her legs about his body. In the turbulence, she soon lost her hold on the tree limb. Desperately she stroked against the current and was able to make it back to the tree. There she clung against the waves, her fingers gripping the branch, her legs locked around her father-in-law's lifeless body.

Only ten feet away from her husband, Nannie watched in horror. "Oh God. Oh dear God," she moaned beside her son.

Within minutes, Geneva was once again washed away from her tree, and she felt Papa's body wrenched from her by the swirling current. Exhausted, she tried to catch him again but couldn't maintain a grip with her broken ankle and dangling foot. Finally, his limp body washed out into the marsh behind their property. Hurricane Audrey had struck a lethal blow against the Griffiths.

"Goodbye, Papa. I'm not far behind you," murmured Geneva as she watched him float away.

Higher up in the oak tree, young Leslie watched his grandfather's body sink into the water. He could see Papa's head just below the dark surface. The vision seemed unreal, haunting. He had seen his grandfather die, and yet he couldn't wrap his mind completely around the fast-moving events. In actuality, the young boy just didn't want to believe what he was witnessing. It was too much, too much.

Papa, Papa. Oh, Papa! This can't be happening. Papa can't die—he just can't! his mind screamed. The bald spot on Papa's head was visible through the murky water, and his hair was still floating on top. In a few moments, Leslie saw his grandfather's body surface briefly, bobbing to the top once or twice, then finally sink deep below the dark waves.

Adrift in the storm, Geneva turned to look at her family through the wind and mist. Her brave son held so tightly to the tree limb. She could hear the screams of her young daughter, calling for her over the sound of the howling winds. Cherie, too, had seen her grandpa disappear beneath the water. Nannie Griffith had just witnessed the death of her husband, and was suspended in horrified agony.

Geneva raised her arm and waved goodbye. D.W. saw his wife say, "Goodbye. I love all of you."

He frantically started pointing to a rope hanging over the limb of the toothache tree to which his Papa had been holding. D.W. had noticed the rope a few minutes before when he saw that it was still tied to Leslie's waist. The loose end was just within D.W.'s grasp, so he yelled to his son to untie the rope from his waist.

Maintaining his hold on the tree with one arm, Leslie loosened the knot and worked the rope free. D.W. then secured one end of the rope to the oak tree and threw the other end toward Geneva. It was too late to save his father, but if Geneva could just reach the rope in time, there might be hope for her.

Geneva realized that this was her last chance. She would not last five more minutes in the turbulent gulf waters. The rope was just a few feet away, but she was so tired, so very tired. The rope was it—her final hope of reaching her family, and the safety of the oak tree.

The vision of her family, the cries of her daughter, and the desperate situation all combined to summon what remaining energy Geneva had left. From somewhere deep inside she found the strength to kick her legs once more in spite of the pain in her broken ankle. A few powerful kicks and she stretched toward the branch and grabbed the rope—her lifeline. She held on for dear life, knowing this was not a rehearsal; there was no second chance with the rope.

D.W. pulled the rope with a focused, single-minded purpose. His mind raced with thoughts of saving his wife: *Not too fast, or I'll lose her. Steady, steady now. Come on, Geneva. Hang on.*

Between the trough of the last wave and the crest of the next wave, he managed to pull his wife toward him slowly, surely. Soon, Geneva was beside the oak tree, but D.W. was unable to pull her up completely. Her skirt had become tangled in a bramble bush beneath the water. She was so close to her family, but now found herself wedged under the tree limbs. Refusing to let go of the rope, she tugged at her skirt, pulling the fabric from the long thorns until the skirt tore free. At long last, D.W. pulled Geneva up into the oak tree. She was exhausted, but in a better place now.

6:00 A.M., Thursday, June 27
Home of Dr. Cecil Clark
Cameron, Louisiana

Sybil Clark had been right to worry. She had seen enough storms along the coast in her life to realize that this was a bad one. The early morning light was dim, but she could see that the water had continued to rise even after she and Zulmae placed the children on top of the kitchen counter. It had been almost two hours since her husband had left in his second attempt to reach the hospital. The power had gone out in the house, and the phone lines were dead. The hurricane winds topped 140 miles per hour, pushing the storm surge higher and higher.

Water had begun hours ago to seep into the house beneath the doors. Sybil closed all the windows of the house, but it couldn't stop the pressure. Outside the winds were tearing through the trees. Branches were snapping off, stripped of their leaves. Huge limbs cracked like lightning as they tore away from the tree trunks. Debris from the neighborhood began to fly through the air. Shingles from nearby roofs blew dangerously close to the windows of the Clark home. Waves were forming on top of the rushing water as it pushed inland, inundating the neighborhood and spilling into the marsh just beyond the coastal town.

She thought of her sons and her inability to reach them by phone.

"Thank goodness Joe and John are safe at their grandparents'," she confided in Zulmae.

Waves began to pound the house with dull ominous thuds. The wind howled a demonic roar that penetrated the walls of the home, rattling the windows. The structure was taking a beating—and the water continued to rise. Out of the kitchen's picture window, they could see huge waves pushing uprooted trees, refrigerators, baby cribs, and pieces of houses through the neighborhood. The water inched upward. In desperation, Sybil locked the back door, then pushed a bed-room chest of drawers against the door that led to the living room, try-ing to keep the knee-deep water in the kitchen from getting any higher.

The heavy chest now stood flush against the door, but it was to no avail. The strong, dark water easily pressed through the edges of the doorway, rapidly filling the kitchen to a depth of almost four feet. Sybil joined the others on top of the dining bar. Reaching out for her two smallest children, she cradled them against her chest. Three-year-old Elizabeth wrapped her arms around Zulmae's neck. The five of them huddled together.

Outside, the wind speed increased to a fever pitch of 145 miles per hour. The house groaned. The white brick walls cracked as the mortar gave way under the pressure. With a grating, shattering splinter, the picture window exploded. Hurricane wind tore through the house. Pieces of plywood began peeling off the walls. The built-in oven popped out of the wall, and the refrigerator was thrust into the middle of the kitchen, swirling about with the water current. The walls began to break apart, and the heavy back door ripped off its hinges, floating into the kitchen. The kitchen no longer offered a safe haven. There was danger in each piece of falling debris.

"Zulmae, we might stand a better chance of surviving outside," yelled Sybil above the noise of the wind.

Sybil suggested that the heavy door might make a good raft, so they tried to make their way to it. Zulmae eased into the water carrying Elizabeth, while Mrs. Clark lunged for the door with little Jack, and Celia. The two women clutched the children tightly. As they waded through debris in the kitchen, the house exploded like a bomb. There was a loud, jarring sound, and in an instant, the ceiling and roof collapsed on top of them. Water came up to Sybil's chest, and falling ceiling debris hit her head.

When she regained consciousness, Sybil was sinking under the water. *Wake up. Swim . . . swim.* She struggled to shake off the fog that enveloped her brain. *Swim.*

She began to kick, slowly at first, but increasing in strength. When Sybil broke the surface of the dark water, she gasped for air. As she filled her lungs with deep breaths amid the howling wind and waves, she looked about franticly for her children. Neither the children nor Zulmae were anywhere in sight. Panic gripped Sybil like a vise that tightened with each passing second.

She was faced with a scene the likes of which she had never before witnessed. The house was gone. Water covered everything. *Am I in the Gulf of Mexico?* Debris choked the water around her. Timbers, branches, and household items floated everywhere. She fought her way through the debris searching for her three children. Several times she was pulled underwater by the turbulence, and each time she would fight her way back to the surface. A board drifted past and Sybil swam toward it. When it was within her grasp, she hung on for her life.

It was near eight o'clock when the Clark home was destroyed and Sybil was thrown into the water. The winds now pushed and tossed the board toward the Nunez home, a neighbor's house in the distance that was damaged but still standing. A huge hole had been ripped in the side of the house, and several people were visible in the attic. She noticed the empty expanse of water between herself and the Nunez home where two houses had stood only moments before. They were now demolished by Hurricane Audrey—the Jimmy Derouen home and the Vaughan home.

Eighteen homes had made up the Garber subdivision, where the Clarks lived. Thirty-two people from those homes would not survive Hurricane Audrey's wrath.

Still clinging to her board, Sybil was pushed rapidly by the current toward the Nunez house. From her vantage point in the rafters, Mrs. Nunez spotted Sybil struggling in the waves and motioned to her to swim to the attic. Plum Nunez was an elderly, frail, white-haired lady, but her glasses helped keep her eyesight sharp enough. The tiny Frenchwoman yelled out encouragement but the words were lost in the hurricane winds. When she thought she was close enough, Sybil abandoned her raft and kicked strongly through the rough gulf waters, each arm stroke bringing her closer to the attic opening.

Out of breath, but safe now in the Nunez rafters, Sybil received a warm welcome from the four elderly storm victims.

"You're Mrs. Clark, aren't you, dear?" asked Plum above the noise of the hurricane. "This is my husband, Eulice, and our friends the Mudds."

In the middle of this raging hurricane, there occurred many moments of genteel politeness and Cajun camaraderie. Toward the end of this longest of days, however, the survivors would also experience despair, exhaustion, and the deepest sadness the community would ever know.

During the next hour, Sybil sat on the wooden floor of the expansive attic. Lost in grief, she regained her strength, but her mind was numb. The relative safety of the loft was short-lived, however, as an hour later the wind, waves, and strong current combined to shove the house off its foundation. Floating now, the structure began to rock and sway in the deep water. The roof creaked with each jolt and jerk. Looking up, Sybil was reminded of her own roof's sudden collapse upon her children.

"I'm going out on the roof," she announced and promptly crawled out through the gaping hole in the wall. In a short time, the other four followed her. The wind tore at their clothes and hair, but the group held steadfast to the gently sloping roof, which soon broke away from the twisting and turning house.

During the intensity of the storm, the roof's loose antenna wire whipped back and forth, posing an additional threat to those on the roof. Eventually the wire tore loose, lashing about Sybil's neck like a bullwhip, nearly choking her. As she worked frantically to untangle the wire, a wave swept the young woman off the roof and back into the water. Sybil held her breath underwater while her fingers worked feverishly to loosen the wire from around her throat. Finally free, she struggled against the lesser current on that leeward side of the house and was able to crawl back onto the floating roof with her neighbors.

Water tore at the remaining structure, breaking the pitched roof apart into large, flat pieces, which in some ways afforded a safer ride. The morning wore on in agonizing slowness. The unrelenting waves pushed the roof out into the marsh on the northern edge of Cameron, then onward into the vast Calcasieu Lake.

5:30 A.M., Thursday, June 27
The Calcasieu Ship Channel
Cameron, Louisiana

Earlier that morning, dawn had broken against the dark, rainy ship channel where the Cameron Ferry struggled in the rising winds. Moored by six heavy ropes since eleven o'clock the night before, the wide, flat ferry rode the waves, trying desperately to stay afloat. Well stocked with fuel, the ferry's twin GM engines ran at full speed against the wind, simply to keep the ferry in place. Captain Primeaux knew that it was imperative for the ferry to survive the storm, so that the highway would be accessible when the storm passed. Preparing for the worst-case scenario, the captain had chosen to tie the ferry off about thirty feet from all sides of its U-shaped berth, just in case the hurricane arrived early.

The wisdom of Captain Primeaux's decision became apparent as conditions deteriorated rapidly. The surf pounded the berthing dock of the ferry, which would have torn the craft apart had the captain moored adjacent to the loading area as usual.

Unfortunately, a line of twenty vehicles on the Gulf Highway realized too late that the ferry could not take them across. At dawn, the column of traffic stalled in knee-deep water at the Cameron Ferry crossing. A few hopeful passengers stood near their cars, frantically trying to hail the ferry. Honking car horns competed with the sound of the roaring wind. The water continued to rise, rushing across the road as it moved inland from the gulf. Some people returned to their cars;

others abandoned the vehicles and tried to make their way to the court-house about a mile back east along the highway. Those who hesitated to seek safer surroundings were soon trapped as water rose inside the cars up to the dashboards. Waves began to wash over the hoods of the cars.

For the people in the cars there was no hope—no hope of evacuat-ing on the ferry, no hope of surviving the rising storm surge and waves. Parents desperately held their children close as they watched the water rise above the car windows. Light dimmed inside the automo-biles. Screams of the trapped families filled the pockets of air as water continued to seep into the interiors. With a thunderous jolt, a large wave slammed into the line of stalled traffic, pushing and tumbling the cars off the highway and submerging everything in its path.

Suspended offshore, Captain Primeaux and his engineer, John Rutherford, braced for the massive wave to hit the ferry. The captain looped one forearm through the spokes of the ferry's steering wheel and gripped the rungs with his other hand, steering all the while to keep the craft facing into the wind. The wide, flat vessel met the larger wave head on, and two of the thick mooring ropes snapped under the force of the wall of water. Like a cork on the end of a fishing line, the ferry dipped briefly beneath the wave, but after a few harrowing moments righted itself above the water's surface. Four of the six mooring ropes held intact. Below deck, the cylinders of the twin GM engines never missed a stroke. Mr. Rutherford's routine maintenance operations also paid off tenfold, as the watertight seals on the deck hatches kept the craft buoyant throughout the long morning hours of Hurricane Audrey. The two men hunkered down and rode out the storm.

Thursday morning, June 27
The Griffith family
Oak Grove, Louisiana

Up in the tree with her family, Geneva stood on her broken ankle on the stump of a limb. She carefully turned around, maintaining a firm grip on a branch above, and faced north toward the marsh, the wind now at her back. The view she encountered, however, was a nightmare. Geneva stared directly into the eyes of a water moccasin slithering in a fork of the tree two or three yards ahead of her. Her first thoughts were of her children's safety from this new threat.

Cherie was closer to her parents and could be protected if need be. From his prone position, Leslie now faced the storm to better gauge when the next wave would hit. That way he knew when to hold his breath. He had no idea that the deadly snake was in the tree with them. His tennis shoes had long ago been torn away by the storm's fury, and his feet were left bare against the rough bark.

Geneva signaled to D.W., pointing to the snake. His eyes widened in alarm, but he remained silent. D.W. put his finger to his lips and cautioned her to keep quiet about the snake, so as not to frighten the children and possibly cause them to fall into the raging waters below.

The long black tail of the snake was coiled around a tree limb. The salt water burned the serpent's eyes and almost blinded it to the surroundings. Geneva's eyes searched the tree for any other snakes or immediate danger they might have to face.

She spied a necklace, a string of orange beads, that had snagged on the next higher limb. The beads swung in the stiff wind. So far, there was just the one snake, but that was danger enough.

Amazingly, the water still rose. As it inched higher up the tree, the snake continued to slither about the branch. Geneva tried to formulate a plan of action, but surviving the hurricane itself took all of her strength. Throughout the day, Geneva kept her eye either on that snake or on the rhythmic swing of the orange beads.

For hours the family endured the agony of the raging storm. Their wet clothes offered no protection from the elements as the wind blasted their bodies. Never had they been so cold. Little Cherie's skin was gray and she was shivering, but her momma was with her now. And her daddy would keep them all up in the tree. Cherie's long curly black hair was wet and tangled and blew about in the wind. The rough bark of the oak scratched her cheek, and the salty foam stung her eyes. The five-year-old was a fragile figure, but she held her breath as the waves rolled over them—and she never, ever let go of her tree limb.

As Hurricane Audrey pushed its way due north, Lake Charles was taking a beating. The many and varied bands of the storm system still wrapped Cameron Parish in a death grip, circling around the coastal area like the rings on a target. Along the coast, the water depth and wind speed varied from mile to mile within the bands that circled the eye of the hurricane. In the Oak Grove and Creole area, the storm surge rose highest, a solid wall of water rising almost fourteen feet, topped with waves that sometimes were themselves ten to fifteen feet high.

The one critical factor in the development of a storm surge is the wind. Another important ingredient is the geography of the land—the coastline. Hurricane Audrey's 145-mile-per-hour, Category 4 winds combined with the extended, shallow offshore coastline of Cameron Parish to produce the deadly storm surge that struck the southwest Louisiana coast. It was the storm surge, not the wind, that killed so many along the coast.

To make matters worse, Hurricane Audrey hit dead on—perpendicular to the coast—not at an angle glancing along a coastline. It moved slowly due north, never once changing course, the only hurricane on record to do that. Then in the final ten hours at sea, Audrey exploded and bolted forward at an alarming rate, slamming into the coast like a head-on collision. The result was not just a single tidal wave—the wave was coupled with a killer storm surge of massive proportions that continued to move inland for twenty-five miles, flooding much of the parish for days afterward.

With the pain in her ankle, and the mind-numbing onslaught of the hurricane, Geneva never realized when she herself was bitten on the leg by a snake sometime during that day. Her ankle developed into a source of constant pain, but having to concentrate on surviving the hurricane took her mind off anything else. She continued to battle the waves, timing her breathing for air instead of water.

Geneva watched and prayed for rescue planes. She hoped they would be saved and asked her husband if he thought help would come soon. D.W. told her, "I don't think so, because I don't believe anyone knows. I think everyone is dead but us."

By this time, she had a raging fever and was speaking almost incoherently. Her thoughts were jumbled, bouncing feverishly from hope to despair then back again: *This must be what the end of the world is like. Is this the end of the world? No. No, maybe not. I remember that when God had ended the world with the Great Flood and only Noah and his family were saved, God had promised that this would never happen again. Never. Oh, God, give me strength. God should be sending our rescue plane soon.*

Thursday morning, June 27
The Cameron Parish Courthouse
Cameron, Louisiana

Several government employees had the same idea early Thursday morning—take shelter at the courthouse—and they now stood with their families at the upper-floor windows near their desks. It proved to be a wise choice. They would never forget the sights that met their eyes.

In the early morning light, several people at the windows pointed in awe at the sight of a tugboat making its way across the main street of Cameron into the nearby neighborhood of Henry Street. Capt. Louie Stoute piloted the tugboat *George Hamilton*, struggling against the wind and waves, in a last desperate attempt to rescue his family and 150 others stranded at the Austin Davis home, about a quarter-mile east of the courthouse.

Unhooking the tugboat from its berth near the Monkey Island ferry, Captain Stoute had pushed northward with the storm surge up LeBoeuf Road. When he crossed the coast highway, Stoute steered northeast of the courthouse. As he coursed through the water past the old Henry home, the vessel came to a sudden, jolting stop. The tugboat's powerful propellers had become entangled in a mass of barbed-wire fencing. Despite his brave rescue attempt, Stoute spent the remainder of the hurricane inside an attic on Henry Street.

Life and death situations unfolded in the immediate area surrounding the courthouse. In the quiet community of 3,000, about one-third of the population sought and found refuge within the walls of the courthouse before the wind and waves closed all avenues of escape.

After seven o'clock that morning, the water was too deep, the current too strong, for anyone to get out of the area. Time had run out. From the safety of the upper-floor windows, the refugees watched the desperate struggle of the people stranded outside.

Many families who sought refuge could see the courthouse through the trees, but the gulf water eventually became too deep for them to approach. They were so close, but not close enough. Adrift in the storm surge, they were pushed by the wind and waves past the building, onward through the small neighborhood, and out into the waters of the marsh north of town.

Clara Broussard warned her children to stay away from the windows, but Mary Ann already stood with a throng of people watching the water below. Homes began to wash off their foundations and float past the courthouse. People screamed in horror watching as victims clung to boards in the rough surf but quickly lost their grip, sinking beneath the waves, which were now about ten feet tall. The lucky few who managed to swim to trees around the building crawled as high as they could in the branches. One man with his dog in tow found a safe berth in a sturdy oak tree.

From the safety of the top floor, people watched in horror as children floated past. Separated from their parents, they stood little chance in the fast-moving storm surge. Debris of all kinds began to fill the water, remnants of warehouses and stores in the business district. The debris became weapons of Audrey, striking and killing many victims in the storm surge.

Sometime around 7:30 A.M., the sound of the wind changed from a shrieking howl to a rumbling, deeply vibrant sound. Those at the south-facing front of the courthouse noticed something else—the roaring sound wasn't just the wind. A solid wall of gulf water ten feet above the storm surge came barreling over the town toward the courthouse.

By the time it reached the building, this wall of water had reduced in height to about five or six feet, and it moved past the concrete structure with a soft thud. Within a few seconds, everyone realized that the courthouse had stood its ground. It was impossible for them to imagine the size of the larger wave that hit the beach itself.

In the wooded area around the courthouse, many of the people clinging to trees were washed away by this sudden rise in the storm surge. From the rear windows of the building, however, several people spotted a small group, possibly a family, still clinging to a tall pecan tree. After the water rose suddenly in downtown Cameron, it stayed at that higher level for quite some time. All the while, wind-blown waves rolled in from the Gulf of Mexico, one after another.

Had the courthouse been closer to the beach it would have been hit with the full force of a fifty-foot tidal wave, instead of this quickly lowering ten-footer, which blended into and raised the level of the storm surge that already surrounded the building. Once on land, this killer wave caused many deaths in the homes nearest the beach east of Cameron at Daigle's Corner. For most of those victims who were situated a mile or two inland, it was the constant, unrelenting storm surge—not the shoreline's lone tidal wave—that took their lives.

As she stood at the window Mary Ann also came to realize some-

This graphic overlay indicates the depth of the water along the coast of Cameron. The Cameron Parish Courthouse sits at the highest point in the parish, nine feet above sea level. Water levels were much deeper in all lower elevations. (Courtesy of the Cameron Parish Public Library Historical Archive Collection)

thing profound in her young life. She now fully comprehended that they had reached the courthouse just in time.

"God is indeed with us this morning," she whispered to herself. For a teenager, this was a revelation. She made her way to her father's side, for a dose of temporal reassurance.

From another window, Ethel and Elaine watched the hurricane's destructive force along the side street, where wave after wave slammed a small church near the courthouse. Wrenched off its foundation, the church lurched and slowly spun around in the storm surge, bumping into nearby buildings and submerged vehicles in the parking lot. The wind tore through the cross-topped belfry. Somehow the church doors remained closed, and the building floated like a massive cork on the waves. The water rotated the church in place slowly, until it finally came to rest in almost the exact spot on which it stood before the storm began.

Less fortunate were the people floating past on parts of buildings. Some attempted to steer their "rafts" with boards, but the current and wind overpowered their efforts. A small house floated past like a boat. A woman desperately clung to an open front door.

Inside the courthouse, throughout the storm people of all faiths gathered in groups large and small to pray. Others sat alone with bowed heads in a private plea. Mary Ann looked around at the crowded room, noticing that many of her good friends had also made it to the safety of the courthouse, but so many others had not. Whitney and Clara, meanwhile, worried desperately about his parents, who lived down the coast in Creole.

From the submerged basement floor, toilets began to back up and overflow into the bathrooms of the upper floors in the courthouse, effectively bringing sanitary conditions to an end.

A mile away, the elementary school and the stand of pine trees along Dan Street helped to protect the Broussard home from the destructive force of the waves, but the storm surge pushed through the coastal neighborhood just the same. Shortly after the Broussards escaped in the boat, water crept into the house and rose to a height of eight or nine feet in the yard. In Clara's dining room the heavy china cabinet floated perilously in the muddy brown water, which now reached as far up as the light switch. Water seeped into the glass-paned doors of the cabinet, and the crystal goblets rose slowly off their shelf. In the felt-lined drawers, the soft patina of the sterling silver flatware soon became covered with brown silt from the gulf water.

On the bookshelves, damage was instantaneous. Wedding pictures, childhood memories, school photos—all were ruined. The family Bible, which recorded the Broussard births and deaths, also fell victim to the invading salt water from the gulf.

About fifteen miles east in Creole, Whitney's parents, Numa and Helen Broussard, had also been awakened by sounds of the storm early that morning. Joined by their two daughters and a son-in-law, the five family members had little time to wait for the hurricane to worsen. A deep rumbling sound began to swell from the south, the coast, and shook the house. Strangely, the sound of hooves overpowered the sound of the wind. Along the road in front of their home, and through the dense trees of the grove, a large herd of cattle stampeded north in their direction, trying desperately to outrun a massive wall of water almost fifteen feet high. The cattle pounded the pavement and bellowed their plaintive cries as they charged through the already flooded neighborhood. The stragglers and the calves were the first to be overtaken by the surge of gulf water, and they quickly disappeared from sight.

Alerted by the cattle's plight, the family pulled down their attic stairs and climbed up as water invaded the house. The last person into the attic turned to close the door as water completely filled the rooms below. Earlier, when the elderly couple realized there was little likelihood of avoiding the storm surge, Mr. Broussard had his son-in-law shut off the propane gas supply to the house. He then opened the front and back doors, allowing the house to fill with water if need be before it would float off the pilings.

Crouched in the attic, Whitney's parents and his siblings rode out the storm in safety, despite bouts of terror. The house shuddered and groaned in the hurricane winds, but the structure held in place. In the Creole area, the storm surge rose thirteen feet, pushing the water level in the house to the ceilings. It also floated the piano, which pounded against the ceiling for hours on end, directly below the Broussards huddled in the attic. The fractured ivory keys produced a terrifying hammered refrain, a backdrop theme to the deadly scene below.

Hurricane Audrey continued her destructive assault on the coast of southwest Louisiana. The torrential rains came down in sheets for hours on end. Pushing northward toward Lake Charles, the eye of the hurricane eventually passed over the Cameron Parish Courthouse around midday, bringing a temporary lull in the assault. When the backside of the eye wall crossed the parish, the winds shifted to the opposite direction in full force.

As the day wore on, all the Broussard children became hungry. There was very little food in the crowded courthouse. None of the residents of Cameron Parish had been aware of the overnight explosion in the hurricane's intensity, and as a result few families had brought with them enough food for an extended stay. Civil Defense personnel made available a supply of emergency rations kept at the courthouse. Those families with food shared what they had with as many children as possible. Their immediate needs taken care of, Whitney and Clara occupied the little ones in play as best they could.

CHAPTER 5
Thursday—
The Eye Moves Ashore

Noon, Thursday, June 27, 1957
The Calcasieu Ship Channel
Cameron, Louisiana

During the morning hours of Hurricane Audrey, the two-man crew aboard the Cameron Ferry battled wind and waves to stay afloat. Four of the six rope-lines connecting the ferry to its onshore berth had snapped during the storm that morning. However, the weather granted the ferry a brief reprieve, for around noon, the eye of the hurricane moved over the Texas-Louisiana line, passing directly over the town of Cameron.

Realizing he only had a short time, possibly a few minutes, to secure the ferry before the backside of the hurricane moved ashore, the captain quickly devised a plan. Captain Primeaux knew that the sudden calm was but a temporary lull, and he could not leave the controls, but his engineer, John Rutherford, grabbed the one tool they had left at their disposal—a long, heavy anchor chain.

The water in the ship channel lay flat and calm compared to the raging waves of the morning hours, and Rutherford used it to their advantage. Tying a lifeline rope around his waist, the man crawled over the floating pile of debris and dead cattle lodged between the ferry and the dock, all the while dragging one end of the heavy chain. Once on the dock, he worked at a fast pace to secure the chain in place, then crawled back over the dangerous debris to the deck of the ferry, just as the most powerful winds—those surrounding the eye

159

wall—slammed onto the coast. Audrey's eye provided only fifteen minutes of calm, but it was a desperately needed window of opportunity to save the ferry.

Noon, Thursday, June 27
The Griffith family
Oak Grove, Louisiana

In the forest of Oak Grove, the Griffith family had suffered throughout the long morning. Sometime around midday, when the eye of the hurricane moved through Cameron, Oak Grove, and Creole, the wind and the waves calmed. In some pockets of the community, the east-west hurricane winds stopped completely, and the sun shone brightly, but only for a few minutes.

As the eye of the hurricane passed over the Griffith family, the area became eerily quiet. The rains stopped; the roar of the winds was now totally gone. What a welcome relief from the hours of torture they had endured. Geneva looked into the sky above, still searching for a rescue plane. Her fever raged.

D.W. cautioned them not to loosen their hold on the tree just yet. Sure enough, the eye continued on its path, pushing north toward Lake Charles. It wasn't long before the backside of the storm hit. The winds roared from west to east now, in total reverse from the direction on the front side of the eye. To Geneva, it seemed less fierce than the first part, but she was numb and conscious of little. The snakebite was taking its toll. For the next four hours, the family endured the storm's wind and waves in the strong, supple oak tree.

Noon, Thursday, June 27
The Johnny Meaux farm
Oak Grove, Louisiana

When the eye of the hurricane passed over the Griffith family in

Oak Grove, it also passed over the Bartie family trapped less than a mile away in the same forest. Raymond's five surviving children thought that the sudden calm heralded the end of the storm, but their father cautioned them not to drop their guard just yet. For the first time that day, he was able to talk to his children without the sound of the wind stifling his words.

"How are y'all holding up? Is everyone okay? I don't know how long this break will last, but y'all did good staying in this tree. Is everyone in a good spot? If anybody wants to climb higher or change positions, now is the time to do it."

"I'm so tired, Daddy," breathed his thirteen-year-old daughter, Leda Mae, as one of the younger children began to cry.

They slumped over their branches, tuckered out and scared. Raymond tried to reassure each of them, but they all thought of their little brother, and they cried.

Except for the treetops, water covered everything as far as the eye could see. The vast expanse of the flood didn't offer much hope, but somehow he had to save his children. The brown water beneath them seemed well over ten feet deep, but they had managed to find strong limbs and joints along the trunk of the tree. He knew it would take a miracle for all five to hang on for a longer length of time.

The children shifted positions, finding limbs they could straddle while facing and holding on to the trunk. Seated in the forks of the tree, the Bartie children now had a better chance of surviving the second half of the hurricane, as the winds began to hammer Oak Grove once again.

Thursday afternoon, June 27
The Griffith family
Oak Grove, Louisiana

A mile away in the forest, God may not have sent Geneva her rescue plane, but He had given her strength. She firmly believed that God had also given her children strength, for it was a miracle in itself that her two young children had been able to cling to that tree for hours.

Around 4:30 that afternoon the winds began to subside to bearable speeds. Toward the end of that longest of days, the water also started to recede. First the Griffiths saw a fence post poking through the water. Then the high point of the Front Ridge emerged—a bit west on the same ridge where their house and barn had once stood.

D.W. pointed to the high spot and said, "I am coming back, and will build my house on that piece of land."

Geneva looked at him as if he had gone mad.

"Well, *I'm* not. If I ever get out of this tree, I am going to put miles between me and Cameron Parish."

The supple oak tree had survived everything the hurricane threw at it. As the water receded further, their home's roof settled at a forty-five-degree angle to the tree trunk. The family climbed out of the tree and back onto the roof. A wide, fresh scar now marred an expanse of the bark on the tree trunk where the roof had grated against it repeatedly with each rise and fall of the waves during that long day. The fury of the wind was gone now, but the remnants of the last outer bands of the storm system blowing in from the gulf sent the temperatures dropping still.

With help from his dad, Leslie was the last to crawl out of the tree from his high perch. His entire body ached from the long hours in the tree, but his mind was so curious he couldn't rest just yet. Before he sat down on the roof he peered through the trees in every direction. He knew they were in the woods not far from his house, but nothing looked familiar yet. He was trying to get his bearings again, but his house was gone. So was the big green barn.

His mother reached up and grasped his hand from where she sat on the roof. Leslie turned, looked down, and noticed her ankle. There was a red gash on it, and it looked swollen. Fatigue overcame curiosity, and Leslie plopped down on the roof next to his mother, as she kissed his fingers. *I'm so cold . . . so cold,* he thought. His short-sleeved T-shirt offered little protection. His whole body was shaking. His youthful energy was spent. Soon his mind became as numb as his limbs.

Nannie sat unmoving on the roof in quiet despair, all spark gone from her eyes. Cherie huddled in her mother's lap, shivering—but oh, what a joy to be in Momma's arms once again. Her face was snuggled against her mother's chest, and her tiny fingers gripped Geneva's blouse, with no intention of ever letting go. Cherie closed her eyes against the world and slipped off in brief slumber. Geneva's fever from the snakebite and broken ankle had dulled her senses, but for now, the best medicine was cradled in her arms. Her children had survived.

Thank you, God. Thank you for my children.

D.W. collapsed beside his wife and children, relieved to give his legs and arms a much needed rest. He looked at his little girl, so tiny in her mother's arms. At five years old, Cherie was still his baby. There was a lump in his throat now. D.W. watched his wife gather a sleeping Cherie closer against her chest, smoothing back the long dark curls. Tears rolled down Geneva's cheek as she bent to kiss Cherie's scratched forehead.

D.W. put his arm around his son's shoulders, pulling him close against his side. The man's red-rimmed eyes ached from the salt water. He closed them slowly and let his body relax, his head lowered, his shoulders slumped. His breathing became slower, calmer, deeper, now that he knew he no longer would have to hold his breath as he had to so many times that day.

His mind could find no relief, however, and was filled with many thoughts that pushed aside rest—visions of his father as he drowned, and thoughts of where his body might be now. He thought of his mother and the despair she must be feeling at this very moment. When a person suddenly loses a parent, the ache is so intense, as if you were once again a child. His mother was with him, though, and he reached out to hold her hand. Her countenance remained dazed, but she slightly squeezed her son's hand in response.

D.W. sat up and tried to focus, to clear his mind. He had much to do.

Geneva looked through her fever-fuzzy eyes to see D.W. moving to the edge of the roof. He was reaching out from the roof down into the water. She watched as D.W. pulled up a heavy, cumbersome object. It was a piece of their living-room carpet. Though it was wet, he hoped it would afford his family some bit of protection from the elements. They were far from safe, with no shelter or food in sight.

Geneva glanced at her watch to check the time and saw that it had droplets of water under the glass. Tapping the case, she discovered that the watch had stopped at eight o'clock that morning, the time she must have fallen off the roof and into the water.

Looking around this once beautiful land, D.W. saw unimaginable destruction, and its debris now cluttered the scene. A centuries-old oak tree lay toppled, its gnarled, widespread roots piercing the air. Pine trees were uprooted and snapped in two by Audrey's force. Snakes were about, and danger still lurked beneath the water. Their ordeal was far from over, and he had to save his family.

For an hour, the Griffiths huddled under that piece of carpet as the water continued to slowly recede from the woods.

I have never, ever been this cold, Geneva thought as she was racked with chills. Cherie, too, had come down with fever, and their combined body warmth couldn't shake away the cold. D.W. held his son near as he scanned the vista before him. Water was everywhere, and nightfall was only two or three hours away. The water was only about three feet deep on the ridge now, and maybe, just maybe, relief was in sight.

Noon, Thursday, June 27
Calcasieu Lake

Sometime around midday, the hurricane winds in the lake began to lessen in intensity as the eye of the hurricane passed over the area near the Marshalls. The rain began to ease up somewhat, and within minutes, the lake was calm. The sun shone brightly overhead.

"Oh, thank God. It's over," Alice marveled. "It *is* over, don't you think?" Alice asked her husband as she pushed up on her hands and tried to sit up on the roof for the first time. Her elbows were scraped and raw, as were her chin and hands. She was exhausted and cold.

"I don't know, honey. There are storm clouds on all sides of us," remarked Brown as he too sat up, regrouping in the sudden, unexpected calm. The couple sat still for a moment, both taking in their surroundings.

"Alice, I think we are in the eye of the hurricane."

Alice was already nodding in agreement, as she too grasped the reality of the situation. His comment had been void of emotion—happiness from the temporary relief they were experiencing at the moment was tempered by the realization that their ordeal was only half over.

Brown looked around in all directions but could not figure out their position in the lake. There was no discerning north from south because of all the twists and turns the roof took during the storm. Besides, it was hard to think clearly in the cold. The two lay down again and huddled together for warmth. Alice cried softly against her husband's chest. She cried from blessed relief and sheer exhaustion. She had never been so tired, or so cold. Every muscle ached from four hours of constant exertion during the storm. Afraid to rest, she drifted into only a fitful sleep.

In the sudden calm, marsh animals that had somehow managed to stay alive that morning desperately sought firm, dry ground. A large raccoon and several nutrias began to crawl on the Marshalls' roof, looking like large half-drowned rats. While most of the animals were not hostile, Marshall wanted to protect his turf from invasion and used the hammer to frighten and push the nutria back into the water. The raccoon snarled and hissed, showing its claws, but once again the hammer won the battle. For the moment, the unlikely soldier had successfully defended their fragile position of safety. Brown collapsed next to Alice and closed his eyes.

Their rest would be brief, however. With the eye of the hurricane passing directly overhead, the sudden calm would be short-lived. Hurricane Audrey was massive in size—300 miles wide. The calm, inner eye of the hurricane had once been 50 miles in diameter, and while it pushed across Cameron Parish, those who struggled to survive had only a short time to prepare for the backside of the storm to hit. And hit it did.

Hurricane Audrey continued to roar onto the coast along the Texas-Louisiana line. The center of the storm pushed northward, moving past Cameron Parish toward Lake Charles and Sulphur. The calm eye of the hurricane soon completed its passage over the lake and the Marshalls' raft. Without warning, the winds shifted directions, now coming from west to east, as the backside of the hurricane began its assault on Cameron. In the calm of Calcasieu Lake, a wave formed, pushed by the deadly, most intense winds surrounding the eye wall. The 145-mile-per-hour winds on the backside of the eye set in motion a series of waves ten to twenty feet tall, and the horror began again.

For the next four hours the Marshalls found themselves battling hurricane winds and waves as they had that morning. In many ways it was worse than the front side of the storm, because their strength, already sapped, became fully depleted. It was all they could do to stay on their raft. Alice and Brown suffered greatly from exposure and bits of flying debris. They soon lost all sense of time and place. All they knew was the rough surface of the shingles, as they slid back and forth along the roof. Never once did Brown release his hold on his wife.

When the eye of the hurricane passed overhead, the lull also granted Sybil Clark and her group a time to relax their hold and breathe without sea spray and waves washing over them. The winds calmed; the water on the huge lake flattened out in brief repose. For as far as she could see, there was nothing but water. The five neighbors closed their eyes and dozed from sheer exhaustion, but the break in the storm lasted only a matter of minutes.

The backside of Hurricane Audrey silently advanced, and the calm of the lake was shattered in an instant. The wind began to scream, howling at a deafening pitch once again. Abruptly, the roof lifted into the air and exploded, boards flying in every direction.

Sybil soared high in the air, landed hard in the water, and sank deep beneath the waves. When she surfaced, waves almost ten feet high bore down upon her again and again. Each time she surfaced, she clawed the water for a board or anything else on which to cling. Finally, a piece of the roof floated nearby and she grabbed it. This portion looked like a ladder made of two long two-by-fours. The rungs between the planks afforded Sybil a sturdy raft, albeit smaller than the roof the five of them had shared.

Where are the others? worried Sybil.

Nearby, Plum Nunez struggled in the water, gasping for air. She had lived a long life, but she had never learned to swim. As fate would have it, the next wave propelled Sybil's ladder directly into Plum's path just as the elderly lady began to go under once again. Sybil reached out and pulled her onto the ladder. Plum gripped the wood beams with surprising strength. She knew this was her last hope.

Throughout the afternoon, the two women somehow managed to stay afloat on their raft. Debris of all kinds cluttered the water and bumped against them. Trees, furniture, and boards of all sizes posed a danger in the raging water. Clumps of gulf seaweed and dislodged marsh turf threatened to entangle the ladder and sink it with the added weight. Sybil and Plum both pushed the obstacles away, hour after hour. Their arms and hands took a beating.

Exhaustion made them numb. To make matters worse, each cross-piece between the long two-by-fours had a sharp, exposed nail protruding from both sides. The women were bruised and bloodied, and eventually when debris would hit them, they felt no pain.

All the while, Hurricane Audrey roared northward. The strong winds surrounding the eye wall of the storm system now hammered Lake Charles. By late afternoon, the winds relented. The gusts lessened considerably, and then finally stopped, as Hurricane Audrey pushed north out of Cameron Parish. Out in Calcasieu Lake, the waves eventually subsided to more rounded, controlled swells.

A deep sense of loneliness crept into Sybil's wounded emotions. As she looked about her surroundings, she felt as though everything had been destroyed and everyone in Cameron had been killed. She tried in vain not to think about her three babies, for that was the worst pain of all.

Plum's husband and the Mudds drowned in the lake that day, but Mrs. Clark and Mrs. Nunez had survived. Their constant struggle had consumed Sybil's conscious mind for eight hours, but now she and Plum were faced with new dangers—from the creatures of the marsh.

Many people who had survived the early hours of the hurricane perished in the final hours. Many of these bodies were washed out into the lakes, the marsh, and the Gulf of Mexico, and would forever be on a list of the "missing."

Thursday, June 27
The Richard house
Cameron, Louisiana

Along the coast highway in town, Sybil's husband rode out the storm in the attic of the Richard home all through that long, terrible day. The small band of storm victims—Dr. Clark, the Richards, the other family, and their cat—huddled together for warmth, and for comfort. From the attic opening in the ceiling, they could see the house break apart slowly beneath them. At the height of the storm, the 145-mile-per-hour winds shook the structure mercilessly. The group clung to the rafters. Miraculously, the main frame and the roof somehow held together.

Clark closed his eyes and took several deep breaths, trying to free his mind of the numbing agony that plagued his every thought. He sat there helpless, knowing there was nothing he could do to save his family. Myriad images of what they must be going through played over and over in his mind. He knew that Sybil was young and strong, but he knew that Audrey was deadly and much, much stronger. Dr. Clark slowly opened his eyes. He took another deep breath and shook his head in an attempt to banish the invading thoughts.

Maybe Sybil will make it because she can swim, he told himself. *Our oldest boys are with Mother in Oak Grove. Surely the storm will not be so bad there, and they will be safe. Focus on that. Focus on that.*

The attic shook, pummeled by wave after wave. Fearful of being trapped, one of the men wanted to chop an opening in the roof. He used the Richards' sledgehammer against the boards to make a small opening, large enough for several of them to poke their heads through.

At one point during the morning, Dr. Clark stood up to stretch his legs and ventured a look outside through the hole in the roof. What he saw assailed his senses. He witnessed a neighbor's house cracking apart, quickly becoming a pile of timbers dispersed by the tall waves. Furniture and heavy appliances were set in motion amid the storm surge. The debris rammed against another nearby home, belonging to the Doxey family, and broke it apart. The young doctor watched people clinging to the roof of the shattered structure as it flipped and toppled over in the next huge wave, sending the family beneath the dark water. Some of the group emerged from the depths and grabbed for trees or any piece of floating debris they could reach.

Soon the small group in the Richard attic began to pray, reciting the Lord's Prayer for God's help. Dr. Clark silently moved his lips in unison. His prayer was for his wife, for his babies. In years to come, he would recall the devout prayers said by this desperate gathering in the Richard attic. To his way of thinking, there never was a more religious group.

Below them, the storm surge was but a few inches beneath the ceiling. Waves slammed the Richards' furniture up through the sheetrock, shattering the group's false sense of safety. With each passing hour they waited, knowing that the house could go at any moment. By two o'clock that afternoon the roof began ripping loose, but somehow most of it managed to stay in place. By four o'clock, the winds began to die down. Soon the waters calmed as the last bands of the hurricane moved northward to finish their assault on Lake Charles. For eight hours the group endured Hurricane Audrey's fury. By 5:00 P.M. that Thursday, the Richards' guests climbed down from their haven in the attic and faced the devastation outside.

The first thing Dr. Clark noted upon leaving the Richard home was the bareness of the landscape. Where many homes had once stood, there was nothing save for a few bricks peeking up from the flooded neighborhood. Where lush landscapes had once enveloped the community, there was barren terrain—no bushes, no small trees, no flowerbeds. The water was retreating back into the gulf at a steady pace.

A family slowly emerged from the marshland behind the neighborhood. They had survived the collapse of their home by clinging to a sturdy oak tree at the edge of the marsh. Other survivors straggled in too, congregating in the yard of the Richard home. All were numb with shock at their experiences during that long day, and told of the destruction they had seen, the homes they had lost. They were drained both mentally and physically.

One weathered, middle-aged man who came from the direction of the courthouse spoke of how the county building had withstood the storm, saving hundreds of townspeople who had taken refuge within its walls. Meanwhile, Dr. Clark turned to begin his walk home.

The man called out, "Hey, Doc, we just passed by a lot of people who are now heading toward the courthouse, carrying their injured. Many of them need medical treatment. They need your help bad."

The doctor stopped and slowly turned back toward them. A member of his group spoke up quickly.

"The doctor needs to get home first. He has to find his family and make sure they're safe," he interjected. "He got stranded here while trying to reach his patients at the hospital."

"Well, I saw those people, and they need his help *now*, not later," countered the other man.

"Leave him be, I said."

Others in the group started voicing their opinions, but the conversation was halted quickly by one calm, firm voice.

"Let's break it up," stated Dr. Clark.

He turned away and began walking alone across the muddy, littered yard, now heading in the opposite direction—westward toward the courthouse. Barefoot, he stepped through piles of debris and brush where a road used to be. He focused on where he placed his feet instead of on his inner pain. He was three miles from the courthouse, and two miles from his home and family. *I took an oath. . . .*

4:00 P.M., Thursday, June 27
The Cameron Parish Courthouse
Cameron, Louisiana

Toward late afternoon, the rain stopped and a deep chill settled over Cameron Parish, leaving behind an unusually cold breeze. Water levels began a slow but steady descent in these waning hours of the storm and now stood at about three feet around the courthouse.

The mood inside the building also changed noticeably. Fear was soon replaced by hope—hope that some people outside might have survived. Those inside the courthouse began sending rescue parties out into the surrounding neighborhood. People climbed down from trees, roofs, and attics. In hip-deep water, a slow steady stream of hardy survivors all headed in one direction—to the safety of the courthouse. Many of these people carried their young and their injured and were directed to the section of the building set aside as a makeshift clinic by two nurses from Dr. Clark's hospital. Others, like a small six-year-old boy who sat alone on his roof, were unable to move. Rescuers lowered him, overcome by shock and exhaustion, into the waiting arms of people below. From late afternoon through late evening, survivors mounted the steps of the courthouse and were met by Sheriff Carter's emergency management team.

The storm surge continued to recede from the lake and the marsh north of Cameron and Creole. As the floodwater returned to the gulf, it retraced its path across the swamp and the ancient, wooded ridges of the cheniers. The retreating waters flowed slowly through the small towns, carrying marsh animals and bodies of the dead, depositing them at random.

Outside the courthouse, oil and gasoline floated on the surface of the water from hundreds of vehicles that had been submerged nearby. The oily residue clung to the basement walls inside and the concrete walls outside.

In the early evening, Hattie Skidmore's thoughts returned to her little dog, Ginger. Night would be falling soon, and if Ginger were alive, she would be hungry.

"I'm worried about my dog," Hattie remarked as she looked out at the flooded neighborhood surrounding the courthouse.

She told Mary Ann and Ethel Broussard that yesterday had been their laundry day, and she had spent an hour ironing her clothes with her dog waiting patiently on her bed. At long last, all the blouses and cotton dresses were crisply starched and pressed, hanging neatly in her closet.

When the storm woke them early this morning, the muddy water was already invading their home and was ankle deep in her bedroom. While she quickly dressed, Hattie noticed that the water threatened the lower rack of clothes in the closet. She removed her freshly pressed clothes from the rod and placed them very carefully on top of her tall mattress, high above any possible water damage.

"I didn't want all that hard work to be for nothing. I didn't want the water to mess up my dresses," the teen explained. Her parents called her to evacuate and told her to leave the dog behind. With no choice, Hattie lifted fluffy Ginger, kissed her head, and placed her little dog on top of the clothes.

"Stay, Ginger. I want you to stay right here until I come back for you tomorrow," she had instructed her dog. Ginger barked once, lay down on a crisp white blouse, and folded her tiny paws.

Mary Ann Broussard followed her friend's thoughts. They stood at the window together, and each recalled just how high the water rose during the storm. The two exchanged glances but didn't express their thoughts on the dog's chances for survival. Dusk fell outside the packed building, and the girls returned to their respective families.

An hour later, the Civil Defense personnel received good news about the Cameron Ferry. At six o'clock that evening, Captain Primeaux shut down the twin engines of the ferry after nineteen hours of grueling, nonstop operation. He and John Rutherford successfully manned the craft throughout the hurricane. The anchor chain had done its job as a makeshift cable, stretching across to the dock and securing the craft in place during the final hours of the storm. It would take some hours to clear away the debris from the boat slip, but the craft itself was intact. The Cameron Ferry would soon be able to take part in its most critical mission on the morrow.

Earlier, when the hurricane winds began to ease noticeably around his warehouse refuge, Tommy DeBarge knew that the storm would soon move out of the area. With that thought in mind, the elderly man was able to lower his guard somewhat, and he closed his eyes for much needed rest. It was a fitful sleep, interrupted by visions of his brother waving goodbye from the top of the attic stairs.

When dusk began to fall a few hours later, the water had gone down considerably. Tommy headed in the only logical direction and approached what appeared to be Smith Circle, the horseshoe-shaped road that surrounded the courthouse. Debris stood in mounds ten and twenty feet tall. In his mid-eighties, the man might have lost a tad of his hearing, but not one bit of his sense of smell. The cold gusts of wind could not erase the foreign smell that permeated the streets. Several boats and a large tanker stretched across Marshall Street, the coast highway, looking so out of place on land. Mud oozed beneath his shoeless, cut feet as he crossed the still-flooded downtown area. In the cloud-covered dusk, he saw his goal just ahead.

The man paused in the knee-deep water to tuck in his tattered khaki shirt with gnarled and shaking hands. He squared his lean shoulders, held his head up high, and carefully walked up the courthouse's muddy, slippery steps and into the mighty concrete structure. Tommy DeBarge had overcome wind, waves, and old age—and had emerged as a survivor of Hurricane Audrey.

Thursday, June 27
The lone journey of Dr. Cecil Clark

Two miles from the courthouse, the young doctor tried to remain focused on his journey, and on his surroundings. The scene was horrific. The stark whiteness of large home appliances seemed out of place amid the ravaged neighborhood. Bathtubs, washers, and dryers were dumped unceremoniously hither and yon by the hurricane, far away from where the homes once stood. Pilings and piers stood empty. The structures they once supported were now broken apart and carried away by the storm surge into the marsh beyond town. An automobile rested on its side against a large tree, mud oozing from its shattered windows. Deep pools of brown water covered every low spot, every ditch, as the invading tide retreated toward the gulf from whence it came.

Along the way, Cecil Clark saw people materialize from damaged homes. Neighbors embraced. There was little conversation. Pockets of people picked their way through rubble, everyone heading in the same direction—westward toward the courthouse. The closer he got to downtown, the more he wanted to turn around and go home.

At the edge of town, Dr. Clark heard a familiar voice calling out. Sheriff O. B. Carter approached from a stand of trees. The sheriff had escaped to his attic, but his house had been swept out into the marsh. Now, he too was heading for town.

"I was fortunate, Doc, but my neighbor's house, the LeBleus', was blown flat. Conway used his saddle rope to tie Vergie and several other neighbors high up in a tree to survive the storm. He had them strung together like Christmas tree lights, and he saved lots of lives."

The two men—one young, one middle aged—walked together, talking as they neared the remains of the severely damaged Cameron Elementary School. Everywhere Clark looked he saw reminders of children and his family. He paused for a moment in front of his sons' school.

"I don't know if Sybil and the children got out in time. I don't know if they made it." Clark paused, and his eyes wandered off. Hazy images of the LeBleu home came to mind. The sheriff said it had been "blown flat." Clark knew the LeBleu home well. It had been built at the same time as his home, and it too had been of sturdy white brick.

A small group of survivors approached the men, hailing the sheriff. The doctor returned to the task at hand and continued his journey alone. As he walked carefully through the debris down Marshall Street, he looked northward up the remnants of Dan Street and thought of his dear friends, Whitney and Clara Broussard. Their home was hidden from view by numerous trees. *I delivered some of those precious children.*

At this point, the doctor was within a mile of the courthouse, just a fifteen-minute walk on a normal summer day. But this day was anything but normal, and portions of the coast highway itself reflected the damage caused by Hurricane Audrey. During the first two miles of his journey, Clark had come across a section where a huge chunk of the highway was gone, as if some massive creature had taken a bite out of the roadway. In other spots, the receding waters had undercut the roadbed, and the surface of the highway had cracked and fallen into the resulting gully. Audrey caused massive damage both coming and going.

As the young doctor did so many times during his trek, he worried again about the hospital patients and the twins he had delivered in the wee hours of Wednesday morning. The surrounding countryside was so demolished that he had no idea where the normal landmarks used to be, and he had lost track of where he was along the coastal neighborhoods. Since exiting the Richard attic, he had clearly witnessed the destruction to his community, and could easily see how many survivors could have suffered severe injury. He could only guess at the number that would be waiting now at the courthouse.

Even in the less flooded parts of the road, he was slowed by piles of sodden debris. He waded through ditches filled with the murky brown water that had so recently covered the town. Everything smelled of mud and swamp water as the storm surge continued to empty back into the gulf. His bare feet took the brunt of the passage. Cuts and abrasions began to show on his feet, and stone bruises were unavoidable, but he was determined to make it to the courthouse before nightfall. The wind had calmed to almost normal, but cold gusts blew against his damp clothes. Moisture from the storm system had literally refrigerated the air.

It was impossible to push from his mind his worry and fear about his family. That was his greatest pain. *Had Oak Grove been hit this bad? Surely not—it couldn't be. How could any town have been hit as hard as this? The boys will be okay with Momma and Joe. But Sybil. Sybil and the babies could not have survived the huge waves. I need to go home . . . I want to go home.*

But Dr. Cecil Clark had taken an oath, and he knew he must keep to his chosen path. For him, there was no alternative. Soon he became anesthetized by the grief, and continued to place one foot in front of the other.

6:30 P.M., Thursday, June 27
The Cameron Parish Courthouse
Cameron, Louisiana

The nurse stared out of a second-floor window in the courthouse. If

Dr. Clark was alive, she knew he would come here. She had been his nurse since day one, and she knew the character of the man. She and Peggy both admired and respected the physician. Nealie Porche and Peggy Reyes were sharp and intuitive, and over the past five years they could often anticipate his next move, anticipate what assistance to provide. That was their job, and they did it well.

Together with his wife, Sybil, the nurses stood by the doctor's side every day treating patients. Sybil also directed the daily operations of the hospital, and kept the supply room well stocked with every medicine and medical item the doctor might require. Today that was to be a godsend.

Two hours ago, when the water had begun to go down outside the courthouse, the two nurses left the safety of the building and headed for the hospital. If the structure had survived the storm, it could be a source of much needed medical supplies. They pushed through floating debris. They crawled over wrecked vehicles and clawed their way through piles of sodden rubble. They saw a cottonmouth and avoided the snake's path. Both women suffered from lack of sleep, but the chill in the air, and the hope of retrieving supplies, spurred them on and renewed their energy. In time they had reached the hospital from which they had evacuated over twelve hours ago.

There it stood. The Cameron Medical Center had survived the storm in shattered dignity. The structure was damaged but portions were still standing. The nurses had a single purpose, and they quickly set about their business. Pushing aside scattered timbers from around the door, the two women entered the clinic. What they saw was disheartening. Large pieces of delicate medical equipment lay ruined throughout the hospital, strewn about like undignified pieces of metal instead of the lifesaving tools that they had been the day before. The storm surge had left its offensive mark on the once-sterile walls and floors as well.

"Oh, Peggy, this is awful. Everything is destroyed." Her voice trailed off as she sloshed through the receding water in the hall, peering into each room. The floors were muddy and slippery, so they braced their outstretched arms against the walls as they neared the closed door of the storeroom. The door opened with a creak, its progress hampered by items on the floor inside. In the dim confines of the room they took stock of the damage inside. Water had obviously come under the door during the storm, and had risen almost to the ceiling. Most of the shelf items lay ruined. Bandages and sterile gauze lay in a sodden pile on the floor with most of the other medical supplies—except for those on the very top shelf. Those remained unscathed, untouched by the storm surge.

The two nurses worked quickly to retrieve sterile suture sets and preparation trays from the top shelf. They also carefully picked up usable bottles of penicillin and several other types of medication, adding them to their limited stockpile. When the women had exhausted all the resources of the storeroom, they expanded their search to other areas. They passed the file room and realized that the drawers full of medical records would probably be a total loss.

Inside Dr. Clark's office they found the doctor's medical bag, which must have floated on the rising water inside the room. As she turned to leave the disheveled office, Nurse Porche noticed the framed photograph of Dr. Clark's family, wrinkled and blurred, lying flat on the shelf. The large custom-framed LSU diploma hung nearby, water-marked and askew on the wall.

"Nealie, do you realize just how close we all came to riding out the hurricane in this building?" It was a rhetorical question, and Peggy continued, not waiting for a reply. "Do you think the Clarks survived? I'm so worried, I can hardly think." The two had avoided talking about it all day in front of the patients, but now in his office, the question was unavoidable.

"I am sure of only one thing. If Dr. Clark made it safely through the storm, he will find his way to his patients. He knows we were taking them to the courthouse."

The two friends fought back tears as they left the hospital carrying the precious cargo of medical supplies. They spoke little as they viewed the destruction of their town along the way. As they approached the courthouse, they were both thinking how fortunate they were to have escaped safely with their patients before dawn that morning. And they also knew they had a long, busy night ahead of them.

Counting down the tasks before her, the nurse dried her clean hands and put the medical supplies away in their makeshift clinic in the courthouse. It seemed as though several hundred people had arrived while they had been gone. The two nurses began treating the injured as best they could. Next, they worked quickly to get the medical supplies organized. Then they were busy attending to the newborns and the two mothers.

One nurse paused and peered out the glass window, leaning forward for a better view. She thought she saw a person with a familiar gait about a half a block away. At almost seven o'clock in the summer months it was still daylight, but the banded storm clouds simulated a false dusk. She set aside the medical tray she held and looked again. There he was.

"I think I see Dr. Clark!" she called out, still facing the window. She turned, and the two weary nurses shared their first smile of the day. The injured were going to be taken care of now.

At seven o'clock that evening, Dr. Cecil Clark climbed the steps of the Cameron Parish Courthouse, all the while being briefed by one of his nurses on the current caseloads and the number of injured storm victims. He entered the building and went directly to his obstetrical patients housed in the sheriff's office. The transformation was immediate—the weary storm victim became the physician once again.

6:00 P.M., *Thursday, June 27*
The Griffith family
Oak Grove, Louisiana

In the distance, along the ridgeline on his property, D.W. thought he saw something moving. He squinted his eyes and could just make out two men slowly making their way west. He eased off the roof into the waist-deep water and waded out to meet the young men. As it turned out, the men were oilfield workers who had stayed Wednesday night at his uncle Buster Welch's house. They were headed down the ridge toward Cameron, hoping for aid or rescue. Meanwhile, they had news to impart to the Griffith family.

"Your uncle Buster, his wife, and their three children all survived the storm and are safe. Coon Peyton, their neighbor, survived—but his wife, Bernice, drowned," reported one of the men.

There it was, another blow to the Griffiths. While Bernice Peyton was not a relative, she felt like family in many ways, because she babysat Cherie and Leslie every day at their home. In response to D.W.'s inquiry, the two men said there was no sign of his uncle Shine and aunt Lita Welch, who lived just east of D.W. and Geneva's home.

"My wife has a crushed ankle, and both she and my daughter have high fevers. I'm going to need help in getting them out of here." The men agreed to send a team with rescue equipment D.W.'s way, as soon as they came across help.

As luck—or more likely goodwill—would have it, a rescue team of sorts arrived within the hour. The two oilfield workers had indeed reported the family's plight to some people who could help them. Men arrived on foot from South Cameron High School nearby, where other survivors were gathering. These angels of mercy even brought a school chair to help support Geneva comfortably while they carried her.

Two of the men positioned themselves near the roof, and D.W. helped his wife into the chair they held for her. D.W. gathered Cherie in his arms and the rescuers helped the family off of the roof and into the waist-deep water. Leslie walked beside his father and grandmother, as they began the one-mile trek to the school. At long last the small band of survivors waded out of the woods that had offered them protection during the storm, the woods that had for years surrounded their home.

The going was slow as they gingerly picked their way across the top of the Front Ridge. Snakes were the immediate concern. The men kept a sharp eye out for any that might swim in their path or be floating atop debris. The murky water was cluttered with litter and tree branches from the storm's aftermath. All manner of household items massed against trees and fences, forming debris fields. What had once been homes and outbuildings now became obstacles above and below the water's surface. Geneva kept her foot floating near the surface, but the legs of the chair repeatedly became snagged in the submerged debris. Eventually, it was agreed that the chair had to be abandoned. Geneva had long ago lost her shoes in the storm and now had to hop on one bare foot through the water while the men supported her as best they could.

Along the way, the group passed homes in various stages of destruction. Some were completely gone, while others—like the home of Dr. Stephen Carter's parents—stood but were almost unrecognizable. The Carter house had an eerie resemblance to its former self. The first story had been completely gutted by the storm surge, while one room upstairs seemed intact with even the bedspread in perfect order. Leslie's eyes widened at the grotesque remains of the house. Geneva worried about the Carters, who were nowhere in sight, and about her friend Ducie. *Had Ducie stayed there with her in-laws last night?*

Although she was waist deep in water, Nannie had stopped her silent weeping for now. She was in a state of shock and exhaustion but placed one slender foot in front of the other as she quietly followed her son. He was the head of the family now.

D.W. continued to lead the way along the ridge. Within the hour, the band of refugees arrived safely at the high school just before dark. Water from the gulf was still deep along the coast highway, but the brick school sat a bit higher on a gentle slope, and parts of the structure had survived the storm. They followed other new arrivals into the room that suffered the least damage—the school gymnasium. The Griffiths gave heartfelt thanks to their rescue team as they parted ways.

Longtime friend Ruby Rutherford approached the family, sharing a warm, welcoming hug with Geneva.

"Don't worry. We have plenty of food and dry clothes," Ruby assured her.

"Where in the world did you find food and clothes?"

"We discovered canned goods that were still on the shelves in the cafeteria. As far as the clothes, the guys came across plenty of band uniforms on the top shelves in the band room. Luckily the uniforms were in their original plastic wrappers and were completely dry. Why don't y'all get changed, and then we'll get you something to eat."

In the privacy of the girls' bathroom off the gym, Nannie helped Geneva balance on her good leg while she unbuttoned her tattered blouse and skirt and dropped them to the wet floor. She shivered with fever, and also from the cold. When she stripped down to her underwear, Geneva found her wallet still stuffed inside her bra. All their other material possessions were gone. No home, no clothes, no cars or trucks. No barn, no livestock. Everything had been destroyed. The money in her wallet was the only money they had left in the world.

Somehow, none of that mattered. What did matter to Geneva was that her family had survived. Her children were safe. She looked again at her mother-in-law, sharing her sorrow at the loss of Papa Griffith. Nannie had her home in Port Arthur that the elderly woman could return to, but it would be an empty retreat. Without her husband of fifty years, Nannie's home would be filled only with memories.

Soon all the Griffith family had changed into the warm, dry clothing Mrs. Rutherford had provided. Back in the hallway outside the gymnasium, Geneva, Nannie, and Leslie looked at one another in their identical uniforms with the bright shiny buttons. Except for their bad hair and their bare feet, they looked just like the high-stepping marching Tarpons of South Cameron High. The ragtag ensemble was even complete with a majorette. Cherie was so small that the only uniform she could fit in was the band's white majorette uniform. They would have smiled at the sight had they not been so tired.

Geneva's feverish thoughts traveled back in time to her own high-school days, when she wore the uniform of the Port Arthur High School marching squad, the Red Hussars. Her eyesight blurred and her lids slowly closed of their own volition. A faint smile crossed her face as she leaned against the damp wall to steady herself and unconsciously ran her hands down the front and sides of the woolen jacket, smoothing the thick fabric into place.

Her thoughts bounced and spun once again, this time to her sweetheart, D.W. After high school, D.W. joined the Coast Guard. Geneva soon married her tall sailor with the dark wavy hair, and during the young couple's first year of marriage, they lived in the lighthouse at Port Aransas along the Texas coast.

The sound of their son's voice interrupted her wandering reminiscences.

"I'm going to find Dad," Leslie announced as the door closed behind his retreating barefoot steps.

Night fell upon Cameron Parish. Geneva and her family had been some of the last survivors to make it to the safety of the school. Many others had not been so fortunate and now faced the harsh elements outside in the long dark hours ahead. Many who had survived that day would not live to survive the night.

In the high-school gym, friends and neighbors shook hands and embraced while they mingled slowly around the large room. In a time-honored Southern custom, many people didn't just say hello—they hugged. Foremost on everyone's mind was learning who had survived and who had been lost. All the survivors were in a state of shock, but all were calm as they shared their terrifying experiences. The horror of that day had taken a large toll on the small community.

Several of the men worked hard with the school's wide utility brooms to get most of the water off the wooden floor and out of the doors. D.W. gathered the family together as Mrs. Rutherford opened cans of food for the refugees. The lunchroom's plates and bowls were put to good use. Geneva was weak with fever and had no appetite, but Ruby and D.W. both insisted she eat something.

"Please, Geneva. You have to keep up your strength in order to battle the fever until you can get medical treatment," pleaded D.W. He was trying so hard to care for his family. The worry lay heavy on his mind and furrowed his brow.

"Well, I might be able to eat a little canned fruit if you have any."

Ruby wasted no time in checking the labels of canned goods on the shelves of the pantry. She strained her eyes in the darkness and soon returned with a huge gallon can of peaches for her friend. Eventually, Geneva was able to eat a few spoonfuls before settling in for the night.

Some men removed the gym mats from their hooks on the walls

and placed them on the floor for the people to sleep more comfortably. By now, the gymnasium was dark. The deep chill on that summer evening seemed so unnatural. The Griffith family moved closer together to keep warm on their mat.

"Careful of your mother's foot, kids," reminded D.W. gently, as a hush gradually settled upon the large room.

"D.W., I want you to hold on to this," Geneva whispered to her husband, as she dug into the trouser pocket of the warm band uniform. Reaching across Cherie's tiny form between them, Geneva handed D.W. her sodden leather wallet.

He leaned up on one elbow and opened the small billfold. A tired smile crossed his face. There was just enough light to make out the currency inside. One crisp photograph in a protective sleeve flanked the currency pouch. A cheery picture of Geneva and Cherie in their Easter finery was the only family photograph to survive the hurricane.

"I guess this is the only money we have left in the world," he sighed softly, brushing back the dark, damp hair from his brow. He reached over to caress Geneva's cheek, and again felt her feverish skin.

"You are burning up, honey."

"I know, but it feels so good to lie down and rest. I think I'll just enjoy that sensation for a while." Her ankle throbbed with pain, but she tried to close it off from her mind.

There in the darkness, one of Geneva's neighbors, Elie Conner, felt that something was missing. Before they ended that awful day, Elie thought the survivors had to do one more thing. She made her way carefully through the rows of mats on the floor and sought out Wallace Primeaux, pastor of the Oak Grove Baptist Church. In the forlorn darkness of the huge, impersonal gymnasium, the reverend stood devoutly with his head bowed and led the survivors in a prayer of thanksgiving.

"Friends and neighbors, let us bow our heads and pray. Oh, Lord, we are gathered together in your presence this night in great sorrow. In the midst of this devastation, we humbly thank you for having spared our lives," the pastor began. His thoughts and prayers held a personal request imbedded in his words—a hope and prayer that his son, who captained the Cameron Ferry, might have survived the hurricane.

Geneva and Cherie Griffith, age five, in their Easter bonnets, 1957. To this day, Geneva carries the faded photograph in her wallet.

Snuggled against his father's side, Leslie felt the strong man's shoulders tremble slightly in silent sobs. Leslie, too, was reliving the moment when he last saw his grandfather sinking beneath the waves. The little boy reached out and patted Nannie's arm resting near his own.

Thursday, June 27
The Austin Davis home
Cameron Louisiana

Toward the end of the long, horrible day, Miss Nona Welch walked the quarter-mile toward the courthouse with a hundred other people who also rode out the storm in the Austin Davis house. All day long the huddled masses had watched out of the upstairs dormer windows as other houses in the neighborhood floated past the home and disappeared into the marsh beyond town. As the storm surge pushed on relentlessly, the refugees started making bets on whose house would float past next—their own or someone else's.

They attempted lighthearted comments, despite the fear and heavy worry on their minds. In reality, the weight of 150 persons in the upstairs bedrooms probably played a large part in anchoring the Civil War structure to the ground below—that and the open doors and windows on the first floor. Whatever the factors, the Davis house boldly withstood Hurricane Audrey.

While the structure had survived the hurricane, the storm surge had taken its toll on the contents of the house. Cases of food had been scattered from their downstairs pantry out into the fields surrounding the house. There was no fresh water to drink. Everyone was hungry and thirsty, especially the fifty little children.

When the gulf waters receded far enough, the people at the Davis house searched and found cans of food in the yard. The rushing waters had washed away all the labels, but at least they had food. They grouped the cans according to product numbers on the cans themselves, then used pocketknives to open one can in each group to find out what contents were inside the rest.

Using what tools they could find, the men had worked hard to retrofit the Davis pump and access fresh water for the many thirsty survivors. Compared to most everyone in town, the group had shared a sad but sumptuous repast.

As the group trudged on to the courthouse, in her logical, precise mind, Nona knew that it would do no good to worry herself sick about her family in Oak Grove, and that she would probably have to wait until tomorrow to find out how they fared. But love of her kinfolk overrode her usual practical self. Nothing was more important to her than her family. Clearing her mind, she tried to focus on her immediate situation. Besides, she was also anxious to see if her own home, directly behind the courthouse, had managed to hold its ground, despite Audrey's powerful wind and waves. She was resigned to the fact that she would most likely be spending the night at her desk in the Voter Registration Office.

The thick soles of her sturdy brown, lace-up shoes crunched over debris, glass, and broken branches strewn across the shell road before her. Stress and worry took their toll despite her brave efforts, however, and with each step she took through the rubble of her beloved Cameron, tears rolled unchecked down Wynona Welch's face.

Thursday, June 27
The Johnny Meaux farm
Oak Grove, Louisiana

Dusk settled across the Louisiana coast. Residents of Cameron and Vermilion parishes desperately sought refuge before nightfall. In Oak Grove, many survivors found a haven at the South Cameron High School.

Deep in the forest, Raymond Bartie was not so fortunate. He had hoped that the water would go down faster, but the area surrounding Oak Grove had gotten some of the worst of the storm surge from the hurricane. With water still surrounding the woods as far as he could see, Raymond realized he must wait until the ground was visible before he stood a chance of getting all five children safely to shelter.

"It's over now . . . it's over," Raymond told his children. "I know you're all cold and hungry, but we can't get down from here until the water is gone. We're gonna have to spend the night in this tree, so try to get some rest. In the morning we'll go find your momma."

Remnants of the wind off the gulf chilled the humid air. Fearful, cold, and hungry, some of the children began to cry for their mother— but they remained seated in the boughs against the trunk of the tree. As the day drew to a close, pencil-thin rays of light filtered through the trees to the dark, liquid surface of the forest floor below.

For the Bartie children, their father's unfailing voice was the glue that kept them firm in their resolve. His words of encouragement sustained their strength throughout the long, cold night. Eventually the children lowered their heads against the strong oak and occasionally slept.

For Raymond, however, visions of little Walter accompanied his every waking moment throughout the night—the toddler's laugh, the way he always ran into Raymond's arms when he came home, and finally the way Hurricane Audrey ripped his child from those same arms. The man still held out hope for his wife, but in his heart he knew his son was gone.

Night fell slowly in the forest.

Meanwhile, about two miles away in the grove, Maybell Bartie waited for Johnny Meaux to return for her and Mrs. Stewart. When the storm surge calmed, and the water began to recede, Mr. Meaux had tested the murky depths below the tree with a long stick until he found it low enough for him to wade through. First he carried his wife, Esther, through waist-deep water to a nearby house, then returned to the tree for the other ladies, one by one. From the attic of the house, the occupants threw him burlap sacks to cover his nakedness, which otherwise would soon become evident as the waters continued to lower bit by bit.

In the fading light of early evening, Maybell eased her wounded leg over the tree limb and onto Mr. Meaux's shoulders. Embarrassed by the closeness, but unable to walk, she was grateful for the lift. As the two made their way from beneath the tree and out into the open marsh, she heard a loud caw directly above. Her storm companion— the blackbird—flitted to a lower branch, then flapped its wings and left the tree, following Maybell in flight. The bird circled just above the treetops and then rested for a moment in a nearby cypress. In the eerie quietness at the edge of the marsh, the soft flapping of the bird's wings seemed oddly out of place to Maybell, much like the sound of Mr. Meaux wading through the water.

As they approached the battered house, the bird hovered overhead, the black feathers of its outspread wings shining with a soft, dark patina in the cold mist. So often during that long day, Maybell had stared at the large bird amid the branches of the tree. They were opposites in so many ways. Her life revolved around the fertile earth; the bird's life revolved around the blue sky above. In the tree, the bird had hunkered down facing into the storm, while she had kept her back to the wind. She found it odd that the crow was reluctant to leave her presence now that their ordeal was over.

Mindful of Maybell's leg wound, Johnny eased her onto the porch with one hand and kept a firm grip on the burlap sack with his other. They both were injured and cold but glad to be alive. From the porch, Esther reached out to help her husband up the steps and into the house.

The crow flew back and forth above, until a bewildered Maybell finally turned and entered the house. With a final loud caw, the blackbird took wing and flew off in the direction of the forest for the night.

Thursday, June 27
The Cameron Parish Courthouse
Cameron, Louisiana

At the courthouse, the community leaders coordinated efforts to maintain safe and comfortable conditions inside the building as much as humanly possible, given the circumstances. As darkness fell, two men, Deputy Sheriff Constance and a Mr. Trosclair, passed around wastebaskets to collect all matches and cigarette lighters. This proved to be a wise decision, carried out just in case someone forgot the danger from gas fumes and oil-polluted water, which filled the basement below.

Despite the unsanitary conditions from the overflowed toilets, the hundreds of people inside the courthouse had no choice but to brave the stench of the dark bathrooms in order to use the "facilities," such as they were.

In the darkness of the recently vacated jail cell, Dr. Clark examined the cuts on Tommy's feet and legs with a flashlight. What few prisoners were there at the beginning of the hurricane had now been released, as more space was much needed inside the courthouse. The hard cot served just fine as an examining table. When he had exited the warehouse late that afternoon, Tommy had stepped into a submerged box of broken glass. One particularly jagged cut on his leg needed cleansing and stitches. Dr. Clark disinfected the gash, stitched closed the opening, and instructed the man to seek further medical attention as soon as they were rescued.

"Mr. DeBarge, be sure to watch for signs of infection," reminded the doctor as he moved to the patient in the next cell.

Upstairs, the Broussards drew together in the dim light near Clara's bench. David and Richard had missed their afternoon nap and were tuckered out. Whitney gathered the toddlers close and lay down with them on the floor at Clara's feet. Mary Ann, Ethel, and Elaine stretched out near each other as they did most nights, finding comfort in their routine. Clara lay down on the bench, with little Helen cradled beside her.

All my babies are safe, reflected Whitney.

Outside, distant flashes of lightning occasionally brightened the dark sky. Almost a thousand people lay exhausted and in shock in the courthouse. They covered almost all the floor space in the building. The chairs in the jury box were all occupied as well. Dr. Clark and one of his nurses moved about the room with a flashlight. The narrow stream of light was a beacon of hope to the survivors.

"Hello, my Broussard babies. Whitney, it's so good to see you all made it here safely," Dr. Clark declared as Whitney stood up to shake his hand. "Are you all okay? No injuries?" The doctor's voice showed his concern for his friends but also revealed an underlying weariness.

"We're all fine, thank you. We were very blessed, Dr. Clark, very blessed. I'm just hoping to get word of my parents soon." Whitney looked down at his family, thinking how close he had come to losing them that day.

"Have you seen Sybil and the kids this evening? Have you heard any word of my family?" Dr. Clark asked his friend bravely. Whitney paused slightly before answering and looked his friend in the eyes. Even in the dim light, Whitney could see the pain in the young man's face.

"No I haven't, Cecil. Were you separated in the storm?"

The doctor nodded his head. "Yes, Sybil and the children remained at home, while I tried to make it to the hospital. The storm stranded me halfway between the two places." The young doctor paused briefly. "If you see any of them, or hear anything, will you let me know, please?"

Richard stood up and tugged at the doctor's trousers. "Do you have any suckers, Dr. Clark?" The three-year-old had a good memory, and a hungry stomach. Dr. Clark reached down and ruffled the toddler's hair.

"No, I'm sorry, Richard. The suckers are at the clinic. Maybe next time, okay?"

The two men shook hands, and Dr. Clark moved off toward the next family. These were his patients, his people, and his community. Everyone in the courthouse felt better just knowing he was there with them. Clara watched her former student tending the injured by flashlight, pushing aside his own personal torment. She thought of her dear friend Sybil and the Clark children and stared off into the darkness, her mind full of worry. Little Helen stirred in her mother's arms, and Clara held her baby close.

Beneath the tall ceiling of the now-cramped courtroom, the soft humming sound of Clara Broussard's lullaby comforted young and old alike. In the darkness, Whitney reached out for her hand.

The injuries varied—cuts, abrasions, bone fractures, snakebites, lacerations, and puncture wounds—as the storm survivors continued to find their way to the courthouse. Once the emergencies were treated,

Dr. Clark solicited the help of a sheriff's deputy to accompany him to the drugstore. From what he had heard, the store had been damaged but was structurally intact, and he soon found for himself that it was true. By flashlight, the men gathered armloads of medical supplies and antibiotics, filling a basket to the brim.

Shock, exhaustion, pain, and hunger settled upon those taking refuge in the courthouse—and grief was taking a heavy toll on the small community. Those who had not lost family members had lost friends and neighbors. There were children now without parents—parents now without children. The losses were huge.

The doctor made sure that each new arrival into the building was checked for injuries. He would always ask the people if there was any word of his family. Several said that they had passed his property and saw his house was gone except for a few bricks. There was no sign of his family.

Late that evening, Dr. Clark administered 500 doses of Nebutal sleeping pills to the adults in the building. Just before midnight, almost everyone was asleep, except the deputies on duty, the doctor, and the two nurses. The doctor would often look back on the sound of the communal snoring reverberating in the large building as one of the loudest noises he had ever heard.

"Why don't you try to get some sleep?" Clark suggested in hushed tones to the nurses.

With a flashlight in one hand and a medical bag in the other, he checked on the newborn babies and on Tommy DeBarge's leg sutures, then walked out into the dark hallway. The doctor had been awake since he delivered the twins almost thirty-four hours ago. All night long he tended the storm victims and thought of his missing family.

He couldn't sleep. Work became the only anesthetic to dull the emotional pain he suffered.

6:00 P.M., Thursday, June 27
Calcasieu Lake

By the storm's end in Cameron Parish, Alice and her husband had been blown to the edge of the Calcasieu Ship Channel, where, dazed and confused, they tried to determine their location on the lake. Brown was almost too tired to think, but he noticed something in the distance to the west. He squinted his eyes for a better look. He slowly turned around to the east, then back again to the west. At six o'clock, there was plenty of light left to make out the landmark.

"I don't believe it," he stated flatly, standing up on the roof for a better look. "Alice, see those oilrigs way over there?" he asked, pointing. "That's Hackberry! My God, Alice, we've been blown twenty miles from our home. We're halfway to Lake Charles." Astonished, the man slumped back down onto the roof close to his wife.

"I think you're right. Yes. That's Hackberry." She shook her head in amazement. "And look over there, and there," she said, pointing. Scattered throughout the lake were several groups of survivors. Their voices carried over the water surprisingly well in the sudden stillness.

"Look." Brown spoke softly, pointing to an object floating off to their left just within sight. A long-sleeved white shirt gave evidence to a body drifting upon the lake. There were others off in the distance. So many sights of that day would be burned in their collective memory. Brown knew that he would never forget these events, even if he tried.

"I'm glad to be alive, Tootie . . . just glad to be alive."

"Me, too, honey."

Two hours later, dusk settled over the lake. Temperatures dropped even further, sending a deep chill upon all the survivors stranded on the water. The Marshalls could hear people calling out for help to others nearby—or simply to anyone who could hear their cries. Cattle could be heard bellowing and splashing about in the dark gray stillness of early evening. Like the humans who struggled to keep their heads above water on anything that floated, the animals too were determined to find higher ground.

Nutrias—marsh creatures that looked like beavers without the wide tails—called out as they always did in the darkness. Their cries carried across the lake, as well as across the now-submerged marshes, a sound almost identical to that of a baby's plaintive wail.

A new danger soon reared its ugly head. First one snake, then another, began to slither onto the roof.

Through the night the Marshalls fought off snakes, cattle, and other critters trying to get on their raft. Adrenaline fueled Marshall, for he had no reserves of strength left. Alice survived as best she could, caught in a death grip of emotions. Even in the dark, she could make out the snakes as they moved menacingly across the light gray surface of the roof. Things happened so quickly, and they were both so tired. They sat side by side but facing opposite directions so that they could spot a threat from all sides. When danger approached, Marshall stood and wielded his hammer, with surprisingly good results. Midnight loomed, and the Marshalls continued to fend off the assault, but they were both suffering from exposure.

Alice felt the first snakebite. As a water moccasin's fangs sank deep into her foot, she let out a startled cry of pain and looked down to see the serpent slither across her feet.

"Brown, I've been bitten!" Alice scurried away from the snake. A scramble ensued to distance themselves from the moccasin before Brown was able to kill the poisonous snake. After a time, delirium set in and Alice fought in a daze, pushing another snake away with her feet. Soon the venom sapped her ability to continue the fight, and Alice collapsed.

"I'm so cold, honey, . . . so cold."

Alice lay down on the roof and did not get up again. In the darkness, Marshall fought on, hammering several head of cattle off the roof. He was constantly on the lookout for snakes and for hours tried desperately to keep them at bay—but in the darkness, it was impossible to spot all the deadly vipers that crawled aboard.

Lying prone on the roof, Alice was unconscious and did not feel the next snakebite—or the next.

CHAPTER 6

Friday—
"Gone . . . Gone . . .
Everything's Gone"

2:00 A.M., Friday, June 28, 1957
The Port of Lake Charles
Lake Charles, Louisiana

One of the first boats to arrive at the dock at the Port of Lake Charles was a Coast Guard cutter carrying Brown and Alice Marshall from Cameron. The Marshalls had been picked up along the edge of the Calcasieu Ship Channel halfway between Cameron and Lake Charles around two o'clock Friday morning.

The seventy-five-foot Coast Guard vessel was on a mission. The crew had been sweeping a fog light back and forth ahead of the boat as it moved slowly through the deep ship channel. The channel cut through Calcasieu Lake on its far west side and continued fifteen miles up the Calcasieu River to the port.

The cutter's powerful engine hummed smoothly at very low speed, a muffled shadow in the background noise on deck. Twenty sailors lined the rail peering out into the darkness, searching for signs of life.

"There!" a sailor yelled out, pointing.

The rescue ship had caught sight of the floating roof at the edge of the channel. When the light was quickly swiveled back and aimed at the roof, the strong beam highlighted the two survivors against the black water. The man knelt beside his wife and raised his arm in desperation, calling out toward the cutter. His wife lay prone on the roof, not moving.

"Stop engines!" The captain's order rang out across the dark, silent lake, and within seconds the crew sprang into action lowering a small boat into the water. Five crewmen manned the craft and, following the fog light's beam to the point of rescue, pulled alongside the roof. Two men eased out of the boat and stepped onto the shingled surface, carrying a stretcher.

"Sir, are you all right?"

"My wife . . . my wife needs help," Brown mumbled softly. His hand rested on her shoulder. "Snakebite . . . help her." He shivered in the bright light of the beam. Shock was setting in, and the once-strong man was weak from the biting cold and exposure.

The two sailors gently lifted Alice onto the stretcher and soon had both survivors aboard the well-lit deck of the Coast Guard cutter. The medical officer covered Alice with a warm blanket, tucking the edges beneath her limp form, but not before Brown noticed the horrifying condition of her skin. Another sailor produced a warm blanket and wrapped it about the man's shoulders, while another offered him water, then hot coffee. He drank deeply of both. In Brown's exhaustion and state of shock, his senses and awareness were quickly shutting down. He sat on the deck beside Alice's stretcher and, as if in a haze, observed the movements of the medical officer around his wife. Brown cupped both hands around the steaming mug of coffee and carefully raised it to his mouth. The warmth registered, even in his dazed state. The coffee coursed down his throat and slowly began to heat his system.

"Thank you," he whispered to the sailor who refilled the mug from a steamy thermos. He took another deep gulp, reached out, and searched for Alice's hand beneath the coarse wool of the blanket. The medic raised her head and tried to get some water past her lips.

Kneeling down beside the couple, the medical officer put his hand on Brown's shoulder.

"Sir, we are taking you to Lake Charles, where we can get medical attention for you and your wife. We've radioed ahead for an ambulance and we should be at the dock within the hour."

Brown couldn't respond. He nodded his head to the officer and then, still holding his wife's hand, lowered his eyes to Alice's face.

The hum of the ship's engine imparted a sense of security to Brown, and the subtle vibration of the propellers through the deck was additional reassurance, but it was not enough to stop the welling up of silent sobs that shook his chest. He squeezed Alice's hand but there was no response. He sidled closer, lifted her head upon his lap, and brushed the wisps of loose curls from her forehead.

Within a short time of being rescued, Alice Marshall died in the arms of her husband. She had slipped into an unconscious state sometime during the final hours of their ordeal, and Brown had never gotten the chance to say goodbye.

"Sir, I'm no longer getting a pulse," said the medical officer. "I'm terribly sorry."

Sitting on the deck of the ship, Brown slowly gathered her close against his broad chest and gently rocked her body back and forth.

Thirty minutes passed and the ship approached the dock at the Port of Lake Charles. Despite the early hour, the dock was alive with activity as local authorities and rescue personnel awaited the arrival of word from Cameron. The mariners threw ropes to men on the dock, and soon the ship was tied off and securely at anchor.

Alice's limp body was placed back on the stretcher, and the medical officer gently pulled the blanket over her head and tucked the edges beneath her still form. Brown stood with difficulty. He suffered from exhaustion, hypothermia, and exposure. He was stiff and sore, dazed and in shock, and every muscle ached after he had suffered twenty hours in the hurricane and its aftermath. Brown had used his last reserves of strength to protect Alice and himself on the roof. He was now at the end of his supply and had nothing else to draw upon. The cattleman seemed old and tired. He reached out to steady himself against the deck's rail and eventually had to be supported by sailors who stood nearby. Taking no chances, the men placed Brown on a stretcher.

With a rattle of chains, the gangplank lowered with a solid thud on the wide, wooden dock. Sailors in pressed uniforms lifted the stretchers in solemn dignity. Moving with care, the small group followed the captain down the metal plank onto the dock, where they were met by Red Cross personnel and several sheriff's deputies. One man stepped forward and indicated they should follow him. He shook the captain's hand and introduced himself.

"Sir, I'm Chief Identification Officer Roberts, with the Calcasieu Parish Sheriff's Office."

Roberts turned and walked, stopping when the group approached one of the warehouses along the dock. He signaled to the sailors to place the body in the warehouse marked Shed Number Five. After a brief conversation with the captain, Deputy Roberts approached the second stretcher and spoke with Mr. Marshall, who was being attended by Red Cross volunteers.

"Sir, I'm Deputy Roberts. I'm very sorry for your loss. An ambulance will take you to the hospital in just a moment. I need to get some information from you first so that we can make arrangements for your wife, if that's all right." It was dark and cold on the wharf, but Marshall was awake and somewhat coherent.

Five minutes later, the ambulance carrying Brown pulled out of the dock area and headed for St. Patrick's Hospital. When the vehicle rounded the corner and was out of sight, deputies transferred the body from Shed Number Five to another ambulance. Mr. Marshall had left very specific instructions regarding the care of his wife.

As the ambulance pulled away, Deputy Roberts reached for his clipboard and began a list of the confirmed dead from Hurricane Audrey for the anxiously waiting people of Louisiana and the nation. The name of sixty-one-year-old Alice Cagle Marshall was the first entry on the list—the first confirmed death of Hurricane Audrey.

In the days to come, this list would grow exponentially to include over 550 names of the dead and missing. Almost 200 of those names would be infants, toddlers, and young children.

Friday morning, June 28
The Cameron Parish Courthouse
Cameron, Louisiana

A few hours after midnight on Friday morning, the first rescue boat from Lake Charles arrived in Cameron. The *Offshore LaFourche* moored at the dock about a mile from the courthouse and was soon joined by two other boats.

People began to stir just as dawn's gray light shone through the upper-floor windows of the courthouse. Many people had gone to sleep the night before not knowing if missing loved ones had survived. They hoped that today would bring them some answers. At dawn, Sheriff Carter entered each room and announced to all the survivors that boats waited at the docks to evacuate everyone to Lake Charles. The rescue boats had also brought with them a limited supply of fresh water. Dr. Clark established teams to carry the stretcher cases to the dock and ensured that townspeople accompanied the orphaned children.

For the Broussards, evacuation was foremost on their minds. Like everyone in the community, they needed to seek food and comfortable shelter. Before they left the building, Whitney and Clara passed drinks of water around to all the children. So it was that a slow exodus began in the early hours on Friday morning in Cameron.

"Goodbye, Mary Ann. I hope we will see each other soon."

Young Hattie Skidmore waved to her friend as they parted ways on the steps of the courthouse. Hattie's family headed east and walked through the rubble of downtown Cameron to their home. Hattie was fifteen, old enough to understand how lucky she was to have survived the hurricane's wrath. Without the Broussard's Jon-boat crew rescuing her family from the rising waters, she was certain they all would have drowned. The boat ride to the courthouse had been terrifying, and it was a miracle that any of them survived.

The absence of any sounds in the neighborhood struck her as odd. As she and her family walked through the sodden remains of their neighborhood, her thoughts again returned to her little dog.

How could she have made it through this flood? Will our house even be standing?

The roof was the first thing she spotted. Amid the drifts of debris piled around the trees and remaining structures, her home stood in the mottled sunlight beneath the ancient oaks. The outside was battered and beaten. The inside was muddy and water had clearly risen almost to the ceiling. It was there, standing in the sodden remains of her living room, that Hattie heard the bark of a dog, breaking the eerie silence of the storm's aftermath. Pushing open her bedroom door, the teenager was met with a welcome sight. The room was in mild disarray, the furniture having floated about in the high water, but her little dog sat patiently atop a pile of neatly pressed clothes on her bed, waiting for her return. The dog's barks became excited cries of joy. Hattie scooped up her furry friend and nuzzled her against her shoulder.

How is this possible? Hattie thought in amazement. As she looked around her once-spotless room, all the silent clues became evident. Her dog didn't have to say a word. Her clothes still lay neatly on the mattress where she had placed them. Looking up, Hattie realized that the mattress had floated up to the ceiling, for telltale tufts of dog hair were stuck in the ceiling light fixture.

"Good dog. Good dog," she affirmed as her squirming pet tucked her head beneath her chin. Hattie pondered the little miracle and stroked her fluffy coat. She had so much for which to be thankful. She had read somewhere that dogs become part of the family unit, that they are not merely pets. Today Hattie Skidmore was thankful. Her whole family had survived Hurricane Audrey.

It was deathly quiet outside the courthouse. The first thing that Mary Ann noticed, however, was the smell. She had looked forward to a deep breath of fresh air after nearly twenty-four hours in the crowded building, but the receding waters had left mud and death in their wake. She covered her nose with her hand, trying to ward off the offensive musty smell.

Piles of debris, some ten and fifteen feet tall, littered the entire parking area. The business district lay in shambles.

It's so quiet, reflected Mary Ann, as the Broussards walked down the front steps of the courthouse. Lifting Richard onto his shoulders, Whitney veered left and led the way through the rubble, following the jagged path toward the small Catholic church on the east side of the courthouse. Clara carried the baby and brought up the rear, keeping all her little chicks in sight. As they neared the small white wooden structure, Ethel again marveled at how the church remained steadfast against the storm.

Leaning hard on the door, Whitney forced it open past a layer of mud and grime. The walls were muddy, the pews filthy, but the raised altar and its white linens were pristine. The man's prayer filled the small church, a prayer of thanks that the family members would often recall in later years.

As the Broussard family continued the disturbing walk to the docks, Mary Ann couldn't help but notice the bodies. Averting her eyes, the teen tried to concentrate on simply placing one foot in front of the other, staring straight ahead. In the crowd of survivors in front of them, two men transported Tommy DeBarge by stretcher toward the rescue boats. The roadway had taken a beating, but it still led the way to the dock, a path he had often ridden on his bicycle to leisurely observe the boat traffic along the ship channel. His brother was gone, and his own immediate future was uncertain, but at this moment the elderly gentleman lay quietly, carried by his townspeople—all headed in the same direction toward safety. He took comfort in that thought.

When the Broussards approached the Cameron docks, the first rescue boat, the *Offshore LaFourche,* was just pulling away, carrying 400 passengers and ten casualties. On board were Dr. Clark's hospital patients, including Mr. and Mrs. Willis and the couple's newborn twins. As the captain had waited for his ship to fill with survivors, he made note of the Cameron landscape. As far as Captain Price could see, the only buildings still standing were the courthouse and a few other structures. Major sections of the Gulf Menhaden Company, the fish-oil processing plant, and some steel warehouses seemed to have withstood the hurricane. Every other building along the familiar shoreline was gone.

The Broussard family boarded the second boat, the *Arcadia,* which carried 200 survivors. It was still very early in the morning, but the docks were full of refugees from the town and the surrounding communities. The smallest of the three boats, the *Lafitte,* began taking on survivors also, and within thirty minutes, all three boats in this first rescue squadron cast off the Cameron docks and began the three-hour voyage up the Calcasieu River to Lake Charles.

Meanwhile, the Cameron Ferry was back in operation, carrying Red Cross units and equipment from the Holly Beach side of the river channel. At seven o'clock, shortly after the rescue boats departed, the first medical team from Lake Charles mounted the steps and entered the courthouse. Dr. Clark welcomed the three doctors and eight nurses into the controlled chaos of a building that smelled of gasoline and that remained without working sewer lines due to Audrey's storm surge. In his bare feet and rolled-up pants, Clark shook the hand of his medical-school classmate, Dr. Eli Sorkow, who offered to relieve him so he could get some rest.

"I'm fine, Eli . . . I'm fine. I need to keep working, keep occupied," contended the young doctor, his red eyes haggard from lack of sleep.

He quickly brought the relief team up to date on conditions and treatment options with the available medical supplies. Individual rescue teams arrived continuously on foot, bringing survivors to the courthouse. Soon helicopters, both Coast Guard and privately owned, began rescuing and delivering more survivors. Often these rescue teams also recovered bodies of the dead. Sheriff Carter instructed that they be brought to the small icehouse nearby, which had miraculously withstood the storm.

In the midst of all the disaster aftermath, the new medical team pitched in immediately, but their experiences were both frustrating and touching. When approached by the new doctors throughout the day, most persons declined treatment until Dr. Clark could see them. They waited in turn—in pain—until their trusted doctor could attend to their injuries. By now, all the townspeople in the building knew of his plight. Without begrudging them, he had sacrificed everything to stay with them, suture their wounds, and save their lives. Dr. Sorkow witnessed the phenomenon over and over again during the course of the day, the victims visibly relaxing as they looked into Dr. Clark's eyes with admiration and respect.

The metal deck of the *Offshore LaFourche* radiated the sun's heat against Tommy's bare, injured foot. The sensation contrasted sharply with the biting cold of the day before. The humidity intensified the heat now. He closed his eyes against the glaring sun.

Exhaustion and hunger took second place to grief and physical injury in these survivors, but all these factors manifested themselves on the countenances of those on the rescue boats. The Broussards, like most of the others, experienced the human body's mind-saving mechanism—shock. The survivors' minds simply shut down most of the senses, for they had faced more than enough horror and death during the previous day. The journey upriver was eerily quiet, save for the steady drone of the engines. Mary Ann shielded her eyes against the glaring sunlight and let her mind go blank.

All the while, a continuous stream of privately owned motorboats, much like at Dunkirk in 1940, headed south toward Cameron from the Lake Charles area. The drivers of these "mercy boats," both large and small, plied the waters of the ship channel with one thought in mind—rescue their neighbors, the survivors of the hurricane.

At ten o'clock Friday morning the three boats docked at the wharves at the Port of Lake Charles. As the *Offshore LaFourche* nosed against the landing, the dock itself was crowded with anxiously waiting relatives and friends who had no way of knowing if their loved ones had survived. Emotion filled the waiting faces: hope, anticipation, anxiety, and sorrow—but mostly hope. If nothing else, they hoped that the passengers could tell them some news of their loved ones.

Sailors cast off ropes to those in the crowd, and a respectful hush prevailed on the docks. Not a sound came from the refugees on the boat. They stood there in the sweltering heat with nothing but the clothes on their backs and their children in their arms. Everyone on the docks eagerly searched the faces of the passengers. The survivors, however, looked shoreward in a daze, staring straight ahead, their faces emotionless. The only sounds were of the authorities lifting and carrying the stretchers of the dead to Shed Number Five, as the crowd parted like a sea of humanity. Next came the stretchers of the injured, those unable to walk, transported by the Civil Defense workers to waiting ambulances.

"Oh, look. There's Mrs. Willis, and the twins. She had them the day before Audrey," someone in the crowd pointed out.

Mr. Willis walked beside his wife's stretcher carrying one of his newborns, closely followed by a man holding the other infant. When all the stretchers had been offloaded, those waiting on the docks reached helpful hands out toward the hundreds of survivors. Once on the wharf, the refugees stood motionless until they were ushered toward busses that would transport them to shelters. They were a strong, hardy people, but they were still in shock, weak from hunger and exhaustion. Their hearts beat, but they were broken. Their eyes looked but did not see.

Some people in the crowd, desperate for news of their families, began to ask the dazed survivors if they had seen a particular person or entire families. Most of the survivors could not speak. Some mumbled as they followed the other refugees to the busses. Those who did respond spoke softly in brief phrases.

"Gone . . . gone . . . everything's gone."

As the second boat unloaded at the dock a half-hour later, many survivors gave the same soft reply. In the crowd waiting onshore, two couples—the Ausmuses and the Sonniers—spotted the Broussard family at the same time. They extricated themselves from the throng of people and within minutes connected with their friends. Whitney seemed to revive when Mr. Ausmus reached for his hand and shook it. Grateful for the offer of help, the Broussards spent the day recuperating at their friends' home. Whitney found a room for his family at the Seiner Motel that evening.

The next day a new chapter in their lives would begin, as their oldest son, college student Whit, tried desperately to find out the fate of his family and reconnect with his loved ones.

7:00 A.M., Friday, June 28
The Joe Cagle home
Lake Charles, Louisiana

Joe Cagle sat at the end of the long wooden trestle table in the kitchen, a hot cup of coffee in his hands. Mary Belle always prewarmed

Joe and Mary Belle Cagle fish a Louisiana bayou in a wooden pirogue, circa 1955.

his cup while the coffee dripped. He could take his time and sip slowly, because the steamy brew remained hot, just the way he liked it. The electricity was still out in Lake Charles, since just before noon the day before. The gas stove, battery-powered radio, and several large flashlights were the only operating appliances in their house. The benefits of having a gas stove were readily apparent, and thankfully, his large family could continue to enjoy hot meals during the outage. Only he and his wife were awake, and they were enjoying the early-morning quiet before the rest of the family stirred. He took another sip and watched his wife pour cream into her cup, and he smiled. Her chin-length, dark-brown hair curled softly, tucked behind her ear. He gave her a wink, and she smiled back.

"Is the coffee dripped?" whispered Theda, Joe's older sister, as she entered the kitchen from the long hallway, closing the door softly behind her. "Good morning, y'all. What a night, huh."

She patted Joe's shoulder as she went past, opened a cabinet, removed a delicate china cup, and poured herself some coffee. Of all the nieces in the family, Theda most resembled her aunt Alice. With her light-brown hair, petite frame, and warm genuine smile, everyone adored Theda. Her laugh was infectious, and children naturally gravitated toward her. Theda and Charlie waited so long for their own children and now delighted in raising their two little ones, who this morning slept in one of the bedrooms down the hall. How they ever slept over Charlie's snores was a mystery.

"How did you sleep, Theda? Did you have enough room in that bed?" asked Mary Belle. The sisters-in-law immediately set about cooking a huge breakfast to feed the large family, plus the twelve other relatives who spent the night. Thursday had been a very long, harrowing day, and everyone in the house was sleeping later than usual.

When the hurricane winds subsided late Thursday evening, Joe had made a quick trip to his automobile dealership two miles from his home to take stock of any possible storm damage to the large fleet of cars and the buildings on site. Between Tenth Street and Broad Street, he first swung by Bob Self's home on Legion Street, knowing that Bob would want to accompany him to check any possible water damage to the office files, vehicle records, and walk-in vault.

Several trees and power lines were down in the neighborhood, but the most noticeable damage was to Bob's home—the roof had been ripped away from much of the structure. The pale-blue Lustron-steel house had taken a beating, but the walls remained intact. Bob, his wife, Jo, and their two children made it through Audrey without a scratch.

The Cagle Chevrolet showroom floor, office areas, Service Center building, and numerous other outbuildings were none the worse for wear, save for a few broken windows. Even without power in Lake Charles, the dealership's doors could open for business soon.

Now that he was almost fully awake this Friday morning with a second cup of strong Seaport coffee, Joe lit one of his ever-present cigars, reached for the radio on the kitchen shelf, and turned the switch. He wanted news of the storm, but a knock on the glass window of the kitchen door diverted his attention. Joe's older brother, Brantley Cagle, came walking in and removed his hat. Brantley wasn't smiling. He was the bearer of bad news.

"Good morning, y'all. I'm glad to see the house survived the hurricane in good shape." He paused and took a deep breath. "Joe . . . Theda, I've got some bad news."

Brantley lived only three blocks away and often stopped by for coffee. Joe respected this man above all others. Brantley Cagle was a retired army colonel, admired by every soul who knew him, especially by his younger brothers and sisters.

"I would have called, but the phones are still out." His voice threatened to fail him, so he took a deep breath and adjusted his wire-rimmed glasses. He handed Joe the morning edition of the *Press* that he'd picked up in the driveway. A lump formed in Joe's throat.

"Are Lou and the kids okay? Did the hurricane damage the house?" Joe asked his brother.

"No, not much damage. We lucked out. We're all fine." Mary Belle poured him a cup of hot coffee. "I've just come from Regina's," Brantley continued as he sat down at the kitchen table. He looked his brother and sister in the eyes.

"Aunt Alice is dead."

"Dead? Aunt Alice? I don't understand." Joe shook his head slowly, incredulously. "She was staying with Regina. I spoke with her."

"It's true, Joe. It's true. Listen. She left Regina's Wednesday evening, worried about her husband and her figs. Regina begged her to stay in Lake Charles, but Alice wouldn't listen. Alice said she had more than enough time to get back before the hurricane was due to hit. Regina's been beside herself with worry ever since."

Brantley paused, took a sip of coffee, and tried to maintain his composure. "I identified Aunt Alice's body this morning at Hixson's Funeral Home."

Theda started to cry softly.

"As you know, there was no word out of Cameron all day yesterday or last night. At four o'clock this morning a man from Hixson's knocked at my door, telling me I should come down to the funeral home to verify the identification of a body. The phones were out, so the man had to come in person. Mr. Marshall had instructed Hixson's to contact me and not to contact Alice's daughter."

Brantley hung his head, unable to stop the flow of tears.

"Now I know why Marshall had the funeral home contact me. No child should ever see their mother like that," he choked out the words. "He wanted to spare Regina that pain."

Brantley told Theda and Joe how he had gone to the mortuary, where he was shown to a back room to identify the body. What he saw shocked him. Alice lay on a table in a dimly lit room. The power was still out all over town, and there was no refrigeration at the mortuary either. The man held up a lantern, and it provided more than enough light to view the body. The body was purple, a very dark grayish purple, from head to toe. She was almost unrecognizable.

"They told me of snakebites. Many snakebites. I didn't tell Regina about that. She doesn't *ever* need to hear those words. She heard enough on the news already."

"What do you mean?" Theda asked.

Until now, the three had been listening quietly as Brantley related the heartbreaking news without interruption. Joe sat there in stunned silence.

"When I left Hixson's, I went straight to Regina's. She and Walter were already awake when I got there." Brantley removed his wire-rimmed glasses and paused to wipe his eyes. "Regina was so worried about her mother and had gotten up early to listen to the radio for any news of Cameron. Around five o'clock they caught a radio broadcast with news from the docks. The report said that Aunt Alice was the first casualty brought up from Cameron. Their house had collapsed in a tidal wave."

"She heard that on the radio? Oh my God. Poor Regina," whispered Theda.

Brantley paused to regain his composure. He was a colonel, a man who often had to deliver bad news during the war, but this news hit so close to home.

"What about Marshall?" Joe inquired.

"According to the radio report, he's okay. He's at St. Patrick's Hospital. I'm sure his family here in town is with him by now. We can check on him later today if you'd like. I told Regina that Mother, Theda, and the rest of us would go with her to the funeral home this afternoon." Brantley stood up to leave. "You'll tell Mother, Joe?"

"Yes, they should all be awake soon. You go home now and get some rest."

Brantley nodded in response and left just as the children were beginning to stir. One child entered the kitchen, rubbing her eyes, and plopped down on the long wooden bench alongside the trestle table.

"Good morning, sleepy-head," said Mary Belle.

"'Morning, Momma." The ten-year-old girl laid her cheek down on the table and closed her eyes. "Could I have some coffee-milk, please?"

Another daughter, younger by about five years, came running into the room and went straight for Mary Belle. Down the hall, a baby began to cry. The family's typical, busy day had officially begun.

Joe closed the back door behind his brother and stared out the glass door-pane into the backyard. Tree branches, roof shingles, and assorted debris littered the yard where toys normally stood. Soon the ladies left to tend to the children, and the room fell quiet once again. The smell of freshly cooked bacon and buttered biscuits filled the kitchen but went unnoticed by the young man.

Joe's composure dissolved. He covered his eyes with his hand to stop the flow of tears. It didn't work. His sobs racked his shoulders, and he had to sit down on a tall stool nearby. At the far end of the long kitchen, his young daughter sat frozen, wide-eyed, with her cup of coffee-milk. She had never seen her daddy cry. Not ever. It was a sight she would never forget.

She put her plastic cup down on the polished wooden table and walked across the kitchen's tile floor. Her bare feet didn't make a sound. She stood next to her dad for a moment, waiting. His head was lowered, and his hand covered his eyes as he cried. Slowly, the girl reached out and touched his arm.

"Daddy? What's the matter?"

Startled a bit, he lowered his hand and looked down at his child. Quickly wiping away his tears, he smiled. It was a small, sad smile. He took in a slow, deep breath as he squared his shoulders and composed himself somewhat.

"It's Aunt Alice, honey." He sniffed and reached deep in his pocket for his handkerchief. "She died in the hurricane down in Cameron."

The ten-year-old thought about the hurricane, recalling yesterday's events in their own home. She remembered how the dark slate shingles of the nearby church had been ripped off the roof and sent sailing through the neighborhood like deadly scythes cutting a path through anything they encountered. She remembered her parents' startled screams to get all the children away from the windows when one of the shingles crashed through a den windowpane.

"Daddy, how did Aunt Alice die?"

"She drowned. A tidal wave hit her house near the beach," he replied with caution, framing his words carefully. "The house broke apart and fell on top of her."

"Oh." Her eyes got wider. The child thought quietly for a moment and visualized the horrific scene. "But Daddy, if she's dead, how could she *tell* you what happened? How do you *know* what happened?"

"Her husband lived to tell about it. It was on the radio, honey. The radio said Aunt Alice was the first person reported to have died in the hurricane."

Alice Cagle Marshall (left) with sister-in-law Ona Griggs Cagle in front of the east wing of the two-story Marshall home in Cameron, 1956.

The two-story Marshall home was completely swept away during Audrey. This 1957 photo shows the front yard where the house once stood.

Other family members began to enter the kitchen, spilling over into the adjoining den, and then the living room. In a short time, twenty people milled about the common area in various stages of emotional conversation. It became very noisy, very fast.

One of the interesting dynamics of a large family is multiple-group conversation. While two or three conversations might be going on in the same room, family members often hear and participate in both discussions at the same time. Sometimes they will finish each other's sentences or pause to interject an additional comment to a statement made in the other group. Generally, they don't miss a thing.

This morning, the Cagle family conversation focused on their aunt Alice and Hurricane Audrey. Some people sat in silence near the portable radio trying to catch the news. Storm information was growing by the minute. Others read the reports in the newspaper. Others cried when first hearing the news of Alice's death. Some spoke in hushed tones about snakebites. Soon all the adult family members were brought up to speed on the latest information.

On this first morning after the hurricane, the front page of the *Lake Charles American Press* early edition carried the headline HURRICANE DEATH TOLL MAY BE 200. One of the front-page articles reported the rescue of the Marshalls and subsequent death of Alice Marshall on the rescue boat. It was a grim headline, one that was to be upgraded daily for the next several weeks as the death toll mounted.

Friday morning, June 28
South Cameron High School
Oak Grove, Louisiana

At sunrise that Friday morning, the people were already awake at South Cameron High School. The men had found some freezers full of food that the hurricane had washed out into the marshy field behind the campus. On a grassy high point on the school grounds, they set about building a small bonfire to cook the meat, anticipating the arrival of other survivors. They were still without power and there was no communication with the outside world. But the water had receded even more during the night, and everyone hoped they would be rescued soon.

Geneva and Cherie Griffith had suffered through the night with high fevers. Even though they slept fitfully, they woke with their strength somewhat renewed. Geneva's broken ankle throbbed, causing her almost unbearable pain. She still had no idea that a snake's bite contributed to her suffering.

More survivors began showing up after dawn. Around ten o'clock that morning, help began to arrive in the form of an army helicopter that landed behind the school. The soldiers had stopped to let the people know that help would come soon. A fleet of army ducks—amphibious trucks—was on the way to take them north to safety.

Meanwhile, someone arrived at the school in a small, shallow motorboat searching for their family. The man moored his boat nearby in still-deep water between the school and the edge of the receding waterline. He offered to take the injured to Creole, where a rescue station and field hospital had been set up. D.W. carried Geneva to the boat. She and Cherie along with a few others were taken to Creole, only a few minutes away.

Water continued to drift back into the gulf, and soon parts of the coast highway emerged in front of the school. The remaining Griffith family and the other able-bodied members of the group started out on foot, heading to Creole.

Doctors and nurses were busy treating the injured at the field hospital comprised of tents and makeshift first-aid stations hastily set up along the north-south Creole highway. Cherie stared at the Red Cross insignia, as she and her mother were laid on a cot in the middle of the highway. Waves of heat reflected off the blacktop, adding to the already intense summer temperature. Homes and businesses that once lined the road to Lake Charles now lay in tattered disarray in the neighborhood. Many were completely gone. Others had been pushed from their foundations and had come to rest at tilted angles that protruded into the streets.

Geneva noticed groggily that she was directly in front of the Nunez home. The activity of the field operation added a surreal dimension. This did not look like her familiar community, but here she was lying in the road in front of a friend's home. Cases of medicine were stacked neatly by the highway, and a bar had been set up nearby. It appeared that the bar already had several customers. Truth seemed stranger than fiction.

Cherie sat on the cot with her mother in the hot midday sun. The pain in Geneva's ankle intensified, but soon a doctor knelt beside the cot to examine her injuries.

"Ma'am, your ankle is crushed. I'm gonna give you a shot of Demerol to ease the pain," stated the doctor.

"No, please don't give me anything that will knock me out. I need to stay awake for my daughter. If a drink of that whiskey will deaden the pain, I'll settle for that until I can reach the hospital in Lake Charles. Please, I need to stay awake for my daughter," Geneva begged.

The doctor ignored her plea and administered a shot of Demerol on the spot. He quickly moved on to the next victim. Soon, the pain eased noticeably. Geneva was able to stay awake, although it required considerable effort.

Army personnel approached the cot and immediately placed Geneva and Cherie aboard an army duck. The duck was a strange sight, much like an army tank without a lid. The two were seated up front in the passenger seat, and other injured people soon filled the rows of seats behind them. The medical evacuation scene was extraordinary, so out of place in the once quiet community. Diesel fumes from the army vehicles filled the air, coupling with the intense summer heat and humidity. Cherie snuggled up to her mother as the engine of the duck revved up for the transport to Lake Charles.

Little did Geneva know that the ducks had been built by a workforce consisting mainly of women just like her, and that each vehicle was rich in history. The ducks were designed and built immediately following the Japanese attack on Pearl Harbor. Their function was clear—they were amphibious military carriers created to transport supplies from ships to areas that did not have ports.

General Motors won the government contract to build the unique army vehicles, which consisted of a standard four-wheel, two-and-a-half-ton GM truck surrounded by a watertight shell with the added propeller. To Geneva and the other survivors stranded on the Creole highway, the noisy army vehicles were simply much-appreciated rescue trucks, not technical marvels built in 1942.

These ducks were used throughout World War II, beginning with operations on the beaches of Sicily and culminating in probably their finest hour—the D-Day invasion on the coast of Normandy, France. Until the rescue of the hurricane survivors this awful summer morning in June 1957, most people were more familiar with the Higgins—the famous beach-storming amphibious vehicle with the drop-down front ramp—which happened to be designed by Andrew J. Higgins, an engineer from Lake Charles. Few civilians were aware of this lesser-known "war transport turned rescue vehicle," which offloaded from the same carrier ships, moved easily through the coastal waters, then drove up onto the beaches, transporting their soldiers to more inland zones of the Normandy countryside.

In the days to come, these army ducks would save countless lives on the Louisiana coast, and their contribution would never be forgotten by the people of Cameron Parish.

As they moved due north at a deliberate pace along the Creole highway, Geneva had a clear view of the wounded landscape. The water from the storm surge had receded but was still deep compared to the usual water level in the marsh. Water was still up to the roadbed—the twenty-five-foot-wide ditches along both sides of the road were completely full of water. Only the two-lane surface of the highway was above water. The duck approached the first culvert in the road, and Geneva could see that the bridge ahead was gone, completely washed away in the hurricane. Without slowing down one bit, the vehicle veered into the left lane, crossed the road, and dove into the wide ditch filled with water. A gasp arose from the passengers on board.

I have gone through all this, and now I'm going to drown in a ditch! thought Geneva, too stunned to scream. She tightened her arm about Cherie's shoulders.

The specialized army ducks were used to deploy troops and cargo directly onto the beaches of Normandy in World War II but were later called upon to transport survivors of Hurricane Audrey to safety in Lake Charles. (Courtesy of the U.S. Army Transportation Museum)

To her surprise, the duck righted itself quickly and simply "paddled" across the water to the other side of the road, where it easily climbed back onto the highway. The passengers continued the journey in silence. They were apprehensive of what maneuvers the amphibious vehicle would have to make next, but mostly they were horrified by the view that assailed them along the Creole highway. The storm surge had moved inland for twenty-five miles. After a day of assault, the waters began to recede, but the once beautiful marsh—which stretched thirty miles deep and fifty miles across—was left a debris field of death and destruction.

Overhead, the drone of a low-flying airplane was lost beneath the powerful rumble of the duck's engine. Beginning Friday morning, several newspaper and radio reporters gathered information by use of aerial flyovers of the area. The state of Louisiana needed word of the destruction and massive losses suffered in Cameron and Vermilion parishes. Some of the reporters filmed the stricken towns along the coast, from Holly Beach all the way to Pecan Island fifty miles away.

Utter devastation existed in Cameron, where only 10 or 15 percent of the structures remained, and some of those were barely recognizable as buildings. In downtown Cameron, store merchandise was strewn all over the streets. In the past, the town of Cameron had grudgingly accepted the offensive odors emanating from the pogy plant, the Gulf Menhaden Company's fish-oil processing facilities. After Audrey, the offensive smells came from raw sewage, death, and decay.

East of town, starting a mile or two past the Cameron Elementary School, all the way to Pecan Island, the devastation was much worse—"indescribable," one reporter had said. Only one in twenty-five homes—4 percent—was still standing. Sometimes a slab or a concrete step was all that remained where a structure once stood. It was in this area that the Marshalls, the Griffiths, the Clarks, the Barties, and the Meauxs all lived.

Just to the east of their neighborhoods, the Mermentau Bridge between Oak Grove and Grand Chenier was swept away. To the north, the shores of Grand Lake and the Intracoastal Waterway were littered with carcasses of animals and piles of debris from homes that once stood along the coast of Cameron Parish. Large boats, some over a hundred feet in length, were blown and swept away from the Cameron docks, across town, and into the marsh beyond. Summer homes and camps along the numerous beaches had disappeared. Only the plumbing pipes protruding out of the ground remained as eerie markers of Holly Beach.

From the airplane, the reporters could see occasional hillocks and patches of dry ground where survivors stood huddled together, waving upward for help. And everywhere, everywhere, there was water. As the day drew on, other planes scouted information on the storm damage. One such plane carried a young Texas oilman from Midland—thirty-three-year-old George Herbert Walker Bush, who had substantial investments in the area economy.

Arriving on foot at the rescue station in Creole, D.W. Griffith and the rest of his family were quickly transported along the same highway Geneva's vehicle had taken. The destruction that cluttered the marsh as far as the eye could see visibly moved D.W. and his son. Trees, vehicles, parts of buildings, and furniture floated in the marsh. Boards and timbers, which used to be homes, were piled like bonfire heaps against tufts of land out in the marsh as well as along the highway. The carcasses of thousands of animals floated in the still water and were trapped amid the debris. Hundreds of head of cattle from the huge herds in Cameron Parish drifted swollen in the hot sun, while some still struggled, ensnared by the piles of timbers. Leslie heard the cattle bellow as he watched them twist their heads, trying to free their long horns from tangled masses of uprooted fencing and barbed wire. Like grim, tattered flags, items of clothing hung from trees and sagging telephone wires.

The human death toll was out there too. It was impossible to ignore the bodies floating out in the marsh, but it was too horrible to register. Nannie Griffith averted her eyes and stared at her hands lying limp in her lap.

As they approached the huge riverlike canal of the Intracoastal Waterway, the passengers witnessed yet another sight so shocking and out of place. When the long canal was widened fifteen years before, the removed dirt was deposited along the sides of the 125-foot-wide canal, forming a manmade levee. Here along the south side of the levee, the floating debris from Hurricane Audrey was piled at its highest, 25 feet high in many places. In some areas the debris field stretched out for a mile back toward the distant coastal towns from whence it came. For the rest of his life, Leslie Griffith was to remember the unimaginable amount of timbers from broken buildings, tangled like giant matchsticks, and the animals trapped within the huge mass, which stretched east to west for a hundred miles along the levees of the Intracoastal Waterway.

The caravan of army ducks continued on its way to the Gibbstown Bridge, where all the passengers were to be offloaded. Open army transport trucks waited on the other side of the bridge, ready to begin the next part of the survivors' journey. Geneva's vehicle waited in line far ahead of D.W.'s group and had stopped on the pontoon bridge itself. She was struck by yet another unusual sight, only one of many in the past two days. For miles and miles, boats and barges of all sizes were backed up along the wide Intracoastal Waterway, unable to move past the Gibbstown swing bridge. Today the bridge had been locked in place, keeping the evacuation route open for the rescue teams. Those boats were going to remain waiting there for a long, long time.

In the midst of this strange scene, a man from one of the waiting boats came ashore and onto the bridge. He approached the army duck and held out a simple box of cold drinks for the storm victims. Cherie and her mother both drank deeply from the cool soda bottles, much appreciated because of their fever and the hot band uniforms. Geneva slowly, gently, moved the cold glass against her daughter's burning forehead. Oh, the coolness against their feverish skin! The condensation dripped down Cherie's tiny brow, and she smiled up at her mother. Geneva was never to forget the kindness of this stranger.

With this group of refugees from the coastal communities now seated in the open army trucks, the ride proceeded smoothly from Gibbstown, through Sweetlake, and on to Boone's Corner. The people rode quietly, seated on the two long benches as well as on the bed of the truck. Many were still suffering from shock and exhaustion. Geneva looked into the faces of her friends. There was hardly a family among the group that had not suffered a loss in Hurricane Audrey. One young woman had lost her children when a wave swept them off the roof to which they were clinging. Her eyes were glazed over. They were open, but shut off to the world.

Just north of the bridge, a long row of mud-spattered, yellow school busses soon joined the armed services vehicles to transport the growing number of storm survivors to safety. It was in one of these Calcasieu Parish busses that D.W.'s group made the second leg of their evacuation. Amid the confusion of the convoy and the change in transport vehicles, D.W. somehow managed to find Geneva, and the family was together again if only briefly. Several Civil Defense ambulances were stopped along the highway as well, waiting to take the injured to local hospitals.

"Aren't you Geneva Ellerbee?" called out one of the ambulance drivers. Wyonne Noble had been a classmate of Geneva's in elementary school, and now she and her husband belonged to the Groves Civil Defense in Texas. They had driven the two hours to Lake Charles to help out in the relief effort. Something familiar struck her as she saw the injured woman sitting there, in spite of the band uniform and tangled mass of long brown hair.

"I want to stay with Momma!" cried Cherie as Wyonne placed Geneva in her ambulance with several other injured people, but they were unable to take the little girl.

Geneva's broken ankle had to be set at the hospital as soon as possible, so D.W. and the rest of the family boarded a school bus bound for the refugee center at McNeese State College. While en route to Memorial Hospital in Lake Charles, Wyonne called the Port Arthur Police Department on the ambulance radio.

"Sir, I need your assistance. Please call the Ellerbee residence and let the family know that their daughter Geneva and her family survived the hurricane. All family members are alive, except Papa Griffith," relayed the driver as she whipped through traffic along Highway 385 with sirens blaring and one hand on the wheel. This would be the first word received by Geneva's anxious parents.

Friday morning, June 28
The Johnny Meaux farm
Oak Grove, Louisiana

As soon as daylight broke through the trees, the Bartie family climbed down from the elevated safety of the large oak to the relatively soggy but safe footing of the forest floor. The water level stood much lower than it had the night before. The children were disoriented and hungry, but soon the Bartie family arrived without incident at South Cameron High School, where they joined several other families already heading for the emergency rescue area at Creole.

By now, it had been thirty hours since they had last eaten, so it was with great eagerness that they approached a field of corn along the road to Creole. Miraculously, some green corn had withstood the storm. They knew that the unripe corn might make them sick, but the hunger they suffered seemed much worse. From Creole, the army transports took the family to a school in Lake Charles, where they were given food and shelter for the night.

All the while Raymond unsuccessfully sought word of Maybell, who by Friday afternoon was also in Lake Charles. Timing is everything, and in the throng of survivors, the two groups never saw each other. Rescued in a small motorboat from the Boudreaux home at the edge of the marsh, Johnny and Esther Meaux—and then Maybell and Mrs. Stewart—all were dropped off close to Creole, where they made the short walk to the emergency command center. Because of their leg wounds, Johnny and Maybell were flown by helicopter directly to Memorial Hospital for immediate treatment.

Friday, June 28
The Cameron Parish Courthouse
Cameron, Louisiana

All that long Friday, Dr. Clark received and treated the storm vic- tims, and continued to ask if they had any news of his family. With his outwardly calm and professional demeanor, few fully realized the inner turmoil and agony suffered by the young doctor. They could only imagine what he must be experiencing.

Despite the grim reports concerning his demolished house, he still held out hope—hope that Sybil and the children had made it to safety somehow, somewhere. Each time a rescue team departed for yet another search of the area, he asked them to look for his wife and children. Each time the door would open, he found himself looking anxiously for Sybil's flowing red hair and smiling face, along with the rest of his family.

Even when there was a spare moment to sit and rest, Dr. Clark kept busy. He organized crews to clean and disinfect the courthouse. He didn't wait for volunteers—he assigned jobs to the able-bodied men. Outside the building, he selected sites for latrines to be dug by the

Civil Defense battalions now arriving. He surveyed the storage of bod-ies in the icehouse and directed their removal to the boats now lining the docks. Often side by side, Sheriff Carter, Alvin Dyson, and Dr. Clark worked seamlessly to organize and assist in the areas of their respective professional expertise. In Baton Rouge, Gov. Earl K. Long barked orders and got immediate results.

The day remained blistering hot, with temperatures in the high nineties. Returning to the courthouse through the rubble in the street, the exhausted doctor came across first one shoe, then another—both for the left foot. Gingerly he slipped the mismatched pair on his swollen, bloody feet, grateful for the protection.

Throughout the morning, messages and reports came in regarding different families and their fates, but still Dr. Clark heard nothing about his family. By midafternoon, he could no longer deny the obvious.

At three o'clock, Dr. Clark's cousin, Assistant District Attorney Jennings B. Jones, entered the courthouse and sought out his lifelong friend. Cecil was easy to find. The man pulled Clark aside to a some-what private corner of the large room where he had been treating patients, as the doctor removed the stethoscope from his ears.

"Cecil, have you heard anything yet about Sybil and the children?"

He shook his head and whispered, "No, nothing."

The young doctor's strong façade crumbled. Tears welled up and spilled down the rough stubble on his face. The cousins embraced, both crying softly. Jennings had known this man for thirty years and had never before seen his cousin break down. The moment of emo-tional release was short-lived, however, as duty called the doctor back to the tasks at hand.

Friday afternoon, June 28
Memorial Hospital
Lake Charles, Louisiana

Memorial was a scene of assembly-line medical treatment. The hospitals of southwest Louisiana were treating thousands of injured victims of Hurricane Audrey. At Memorial Hospital on Oak Park Boulevard, gurneys lined the hallways while the most critically injured were rushed to surgery. Geneva was wheeled into X-Ray, where a Dr. Schneider confirmed that she indeed had a broken ankle. The nurses cut the trouser leg up to the knee, moved the fabric aside, then washed her leg. Moving quickly, the doctor set her ankle, then began to layer the plaster over the fabric of the cast. In the haste of the moment, the bad cut just below Geneva's ankle was left untreated. More important-ly, none of the medical staff noticed the two puncture wounds from the venomous snakebite.

White-clad nurses carried Geneva's stretcher out into the hall, where many other injured waited on cots. Time dragged on as medical personnel rushed back and forth along the hallway. More victims were brought to the hospital, and the process repeated itself over and over again. Desperate to be reunited with her family, Geneva prayed hard for help. She was frustrated, and immobile. In her weakened state, the cast weighed so heavily on her.

It was the Marines who came to the rescue. Geneva propped her-self up on her elbows and spied two soldiers coming her way down the hall.

"Is there anything we can do to help?" they asked as they stopped at each cot.

"Over here, please!" she hollered, waving at the two soldiers.

Geneva explained that she had to get to her children right away. Her family was at the rallying point for refugees at McNeese State College, and she needed to get there as soon as possible.

"Yes, ma'am!" one soldier replied, and without another word, the Marines picked up her stretcher, walked out of the hospital, and placed her in a waiting army ambulance.

"Good luck, ma'am." They raised a hand in goodbye, gave instruc-tions to the driver, and closed the back doors of the vehicle. She was on her way.

"Must be my uniform," sighed Geneva with a grateful smile.

In the back of her mind Geneva realized that she hadn't bothered to check out of the hospital, but she was determined to find her family regardless of protocol. No sirens were needed, and the ambulance headed south down Third Avenue, turning right onto the narrow blacktop of Prien Lake Road. The vehicle slowly curved past the single ancient oak tree that grew in the center of the two lanes. The massive oak was a traffic hazard, but no one had the heart to cut down the beautiful tree, so the road simply flared out and continued around it. Five minutes down Prien and the driver turned left onto Ryan Street, a straight shot to the McNeese campus.

There was moderate structural damage in many areas of Lake Charles. Businesses remained closed, and the city was under a state of emergency. Trees had been uprooted, downing power lines throughout the city. Debris littered the residential streets, while road crews began the task of clearing the major arteries. Hurricane Audrey had left her temporary mark on the city, and the power was to remain out for days.

The scene at McNeese offered hope to all refugees. Literally thousands of survivors arrived at the college via armed services trucks and helicopters. Despite the sweltering heat, flight conditions were good in the clear sky, and helicopters landed one after another on the Parade Grounds near Kaufman Hall. The loud, pulsating sound of the helicopter blades punctuated each aircraft's landing on the grassy field. There they deposited their precious cargo, the people from Cameron Parish. The gymnasium and the McNeese Cowboy Arena had been opened and made ready. Personnel from all of the armed services joined with the Red Cross, the Salvation Army, the Civil Defense, and the local community to offer immediate aid.

Geneva's ambulance pulled alongside the east entrance to the arena. The army medical team carried her stretcher into the vast building. The "Cow Palace," as the college students fondly referred to the domed structure, was a large, dirt-floored rodeo arena. It was circled by row upon row of elevated bleachers, which could seat thousands. This day, 600 cots had been set up on the dirt floor. The arena became a haven for the homeless storm victims.

The men carried Geneva to a cot, set her down, and left. Within the vast confines of the building, many voices melded together to echo off the domed ceiling. The earthy smell of the arena floor reminded Geneva of the Griffiths' barn. Dust particles flickered above her in the rays of light coming through the skylights high overhead. Geneva sat up and looked around at a sea of cots in various stages of occupancy. The arena was bustling with activity. By that evening, the Cow Palace would affectionately be called Cot City by the *Lake Charles American Press*.

Geneva was not alone for long. She was soon joined by Dr. Stephen Carter's wife, Ducie, and her three children. The women rejoiced in seeing each other. Ducie asked about the family.

"Yes, the children and D.W. are safe. They are here somewhere," replied Geneva, looking around. "D.W.'s parents were with us at our house during the storm. We lost Papa Griffith."

Geneva recalled passing the Carter home—Ducie's in-laws—and seeing it demolished as she had waded to the high school the afternoon before. *Was that just yesterday?* mused Geneva.

"Ducie, how did you manage to survive? I saw your in-laws' home as we waded past on our way to the high school. Are they all right?"

"Yes, they are fine. We actually joined Stephen's parents at his grandfather's house in Creole. Both Stephen and his father thought we would all be safer spending the night there—and they were right." Ducie shifted the baby in her arms and continued. "As you know, his grandfather's house is a huge two-story home, much larger than ours, and it has weathered many storms over the years." Ducie glanced away briefly in thought, then looked again at Geneva.

"Stephen's brother, Brandon, who lives close to your house, lost his wife and two children. Brandon himself ended up being swept into his grandfather's yard in Creole. The water was so deep, and we were all in the attic. The men pulled him into the attic window to safety. . . ." Her voice trailed off, and the young mother took a moment to quell her tears.

Ducie looked down at her newborn, then at her twins, who were holding her skirt. Their rosy cheeks were smudged and the matching twin outfits were dirty, but the little ones still looked identical.

"His children were swept away. They're gone," Ducie spoke barely above a whisper. She and Geneva shared the same unspoken thoughts.

"What will you do now, Ducie? What are your plans?"

"Stephen and his grandfather have set up a temporary doctor's office in his home in Creole. They won't evacuate. They are staying to tend to the injured that have flocked there. Until things have settled down, I'll take the children to New Orleans and stay with Mother. I can't think past that point.

"Geneva, would you mind the children for a moment? I need to get them a change of clothes from the volunteer workers. They were nice enough to give me this suitcase, but I don't have any clothes to my name," she sighed with a smile. "After the children are cleaned up, we're catching a bus to New Orleans."

Ducie set down the suitcase and headed off in the direction of the volunteers. Geneva cradled the baby against her chest, and the twins played at her feet in the soft dirt. "Now don't wander off, you two. I've only got one good leg, and no crutches."

"Yes ma'am," they said in unison, not bothering to look up from the dirt swirls they were making with their fingers. Soon they began to cover Geneva's bare foot with the dirt.

"Resilient—that's the word for a three-year-old," she thought out loud.

One worker passed by carrying a stack of cotton diapers. Seeing Geneva with the baby, she stopped to ask, "Ma'am, do you need a diaper?" When she saw the cast on Geneva's leg, she said, "Oh, you poor dear. Here, take the whole stack."

Geneva placed them inside Ducie's empty suitcase, which contained two toy guitars. The twins had played their wind-up musical instruments all day long as they rode out the storm in the attic. Not even the roar of the hurricane winds could drown out the tune of the dueling guitars. After being subjected to the same song for ten hours, their parents retired the toys to the suitcase.

Within a few minutes, the young mother returned with a clean set of clothes for the children and said her goodbyes. Geneva was glad to hear that her doctor, Dr. Carter, was staying behind in Creole and that his grandfather had come out of "retirement" to tend to the injured as he had for the past fifty years in Cameron Parish. It was a sign of their character, of ideals and ethics handed down from father to son, and now to his grandson.

Other friends stopped by to greet Geneva, who was grounded on her cot. One friend took off to locate a pair of crutches for her. Another, Mr. Francis Ezernack, stopped and asked if there was anything he could do to help her.

"I'm trying to find my family, and I'm hoping they are here at McNeese."

"Describe them to me, and I will go look for them." When Geneva mentioned the little white majorette uniform Cherie was wearing, Mr. Ezernack interrupted.

"Oh, I saw her not long ago! Everyone was remarking about that beautiful little black-haired girl in that white band uniform."

He took off on a mission. Geneva watched as he moved about the huge arena, losing sight of him after a few minutes. Her strength was failing, and her skin burned with fever. The untreated snakebite and the angry gash on her ankle were undermining her recovery and sapping her strength.

"Momma! Momma!" the welcome voices of Leslie and Cherie called out as her family came into view, with Nannie not far behind.

D.W. knelt and embraced his wife. A long, relieved sigh escaped his lips as he opened his arms wide to include their children. The four clung to each other for a long moment. The young father could rest now. His family was safe.

Had she not been so dehydrated, Geneva would have wept in emotional relief. As it was, invisible tears of gratitude flowed deep in her very soul. Hurricane Audrey had taken the lives of so many children, yet hers had been spared.

She looked into the eyes of her children, then into her husband's.

"How is Cherie's fever? Leslie, did you get anything to eat? Nannie, how are you holding up?" Her voice was weak now, and her concerns tumbled out in a jumbled stream. D.W. felt her cheeks and worried anew.

After the pair of crutches arrived for Geneva, the grieving but reunited family prepared to leave Cot City for the home of a Lake

Charles cousin, Lucille Crosby. When reports of the devastation in Cameron Parish had spread through Lake Charles, Lucille had hoped against all odds that her relatives had made it safely out of Oak Grove. On this Friday afternoon, she had come to the arena and had gratefully found her cousin.

Nannie held the hands of her grandchildren, while D.W. helped Geneva maneuver on the crutches. Her movements were awkward, and the cast felt heavy as she bent her knee to lift the cast off the ground. *This band uniform is so hot, so hot.* As the small group began to exit the arena, her vision swirled. Her head begin to spin dizzily. Blackness encroached on her peripheral vision and gradually engulfed her sight. The whole arena was whirling around Geneva as she fainted and hit the soft dirt with a solid thud.

Unconscious now, and burning with fever, Geneva never felt her husband carefully roll her over on her back to lift her from the arena floor. Dust clung to her disheveled hair. A passerby sprang into action, kneeling down to support Geneva's heavy cast.

"Lucille, let's get her into your car quickly," instructed D.W. as he shifted Geneva into his arms and stood up.

"Mother, hold on to the kids' hands, and follow close behind Lucille. I don't want anyone getting separated from us in the crowd or in the parking lot outside."

Cherie trembled beside Nannie and clutched the folds of her skirt. Everything was happening too fast for the little one. Leslie had already thought to retrieve the two crutches and seemed aware of the need for urgency. For being only eleven years old, Leslie Griffith had aged a great deal over the past two days. He understood more about life, and certainly more about death.

"I've got Mom's crutches," he informed his dad, looking up to the man in charge.

"I'll be right behind you, son. And Cherie, don't worry. It will all be over soon. Stay close to Nannie, sweetheart."

The five Griffiths made their way through the cots and out of the large, wide doors of the McNeese Arena. D.W. stared into Geneva's dirty face as he carried her limp form out of the arena. Several friends waved in concern as the family passed by, finally exiting the building. Out in the bright afternoon sun, Lucille's husband, Lucky, waited at the curb with the car, waving his white hat in the air for them to see. He hurried to open the passenger-side door for D.W. Soon everyone was settled inside the Crosbys' spacious station wagon. An army serviceman stepped out into the drive and held up a hand to halt an NBC News vehicle heading their way, allowing the car to pull away from the curb.

A large army-green transport truck pulled into their empty space and offloaded more weary survivors into the arena. Another helicopter, this one a volunteer from an oil company, landed in the open parade grounds near the arena, deposited more tattered survivors, and then immediately took off again toward Cameron Parish.

All the survivors appeared dazed. Some wore borrowed items of clothing or blankets wrapped around their shoulders. Some were obviously families; some were lone children temporarily assigned to friends and neighbors, calling out for their parents. Civil Defense personnel met them all at the wide entrance doors, offering cool water and comfort while each person was registered, placed on a list, and assigned a bed. Their eyes searched for missing loved ones among the throng of people inside the arena. Shouts of joy occasionally rose from the group around the large message boards, as news of a loved one was posted.

Councilman Conway LeBleu moved about the arena, offering reassurance and comfort to his townspeople. He was their anchor, as was Sheriff O. B. Carter, who remained at the Cameron Parish Courthouse coordinating rescue efforts in town. The rescue cycle continued throughout the day, and by nightfall 600 refugees slept in Cot City.

In the backseat of the station wagon, Cherie leaned against Nannie's side, still clutching her grandmother's skirt. She remained quiet, tired from the long day in the hot sun and from being separated from her mother when she was at the hospital. While Cherie had no external injuries, her fever stemmed from the long hours of exposure in Audrey's chilling rain. After clinging to the tree limb for so long during the hurricane, Cherie clearly needed physical contact with her family.

"Here, baby, come sit on my lap." Nannie's arm surrounded her tiny shoulders and held her close, while Nannie's other hand patted Leslie's knee. The young boy looked over at his grandmother, thinking instantly about his Papa. He tried to smile reassuringly at Nannie, but his lips quivered in the attempt, so he gave it up and looked down at his mother's crutches on the floor. The raw, fresh vision of Papa slipping beneath the waves invaded his thoughts once again.

"Leslie, do you have any idea just how much your grandpa loved you?" Nannie asked softly for his ears only. He looked up again, slowly, and blinked away a tear that threatened to form on his pale lashes. Nannie waited until she held his attention. "Your Papa loved you with all his heart, from the tip of his boots to the top of his bald head."

Her sad smile warmed his tender psyche. Leslie nodded, barely moving his head, but this time his little-boy smile stuck.

"I loved him too, Nannie." A whirlwind of memories filled his thoughts, as he and his Nannie shared the private moment. He nodded his head again, still smiling, and turned to look out the car window. Leslie leaned his head against the glass and watched the storm-wrecked scenes flash past as the car drove north up busy Ryan Street. Despite his brave smile, he wept silently, tears dropping on the shoulder of his striped T-shirt.

As they drove along, he saw several downed trees lying mutely on front lawns. He thought of his dog. If Bootsie were with him, she would be standing on his lap and leaning out of the window, her ears and tongue flapping in the breeze. In a short while, however, Leslie's innate curiosity rose to the forefront, and he sat up sharply to get a better view of the devastation around Lake Charles itself.

In the front seat, D.W. cradled Geneva on his lap as Crosby drove with great haste across town to his home. D.W. smoothed back the hair that fell across her forehead. Geneva was burning up with fever.

"Here's a handkerchief, D.W." Lucille reached into her fashionable straw purse and handed him the soft cloth. He began to wipe her face as best he could. The dust from the arena clung to her damp skin.

"We need to get her fever down fast," D.W. murmured to himself, to everyone, as he continued to wipe her brow. He fanned her face with the handkerchief and then, setting it aside, began to loosen the buttons at the neck of the uniform with his free hand. Geneva's eyes fluttered open gradually, focusing on the face of her husband above.

"Hi, honey," she whispered weakly. "What happened?"

"You got kicked out of the band. The Tarpons want their uniform back."

Friday afternoon, June 28
Hixson Funeral Home
Lake Charles, Louisiana

Congested traffic near Lake Charles High School slowed Joe's progress along Enterprise Boulevard. The campus was bustling with army, Red Cross, and relief personnel transporting refugees to the school's gymnasium. As was the situation all over the city, there were several uprooted and fallen trees in the grassy median. Several blocks farther down Enterprise, at the intersection of Broad Street, a traffic cop signaled for Joe to proceed.

Hundreds of downed trees snapped power and telephone lines all over town. Some eight thousand telephones had been knocked out of service. Broad Street, normally one of the busiest, was littered with debris. Near Hixson Funeral Home, the traffic was rerouted around the thick tree trunk that was being sawed into smaller pieces for removal by the work crews. Joe took the one empty parking space along the curb.

Joe, his mother, and sister Theda were escorted to a small private room where they viewed Alice's body. A closed-casket service would be held that evening, rushed because of the lack of refrigeration in all the town's mortuaries, and because of the mounting number of bodies being brought up from Cameron.

Even though Brantley had told his family of his experience in identifying Alice's body, it didn't register in the proper magnitude. They felt compelled to go and say a private goodbye to the aunt they so loved. Now, however, standing there beside the casket, they were all shocked at the sight of the blackened, bruised body.

"Poor Alice . . . how horrible, horrible," Theda cried softly as they drove home.

The news coming out of Cameron and Vermilion parishes was worse than anyone could have imagined. By the hour, the death toll rose. Survivor accounts filled the late edition of the *Press*. Joe had gone into the office that day but found it hard to concentrate. A skeleton crew had manned the showroom floor to answer questions regarding vehicle damage. Since the power and phones weren't working, the rest of the staff was sent home. Meanwhile, Joe formed a plan for the next morning.

Friday afternoon, June 28
The Griffith family
Lake Charles, Louisiana

Nannie Griffith asked that they please make one stop along the way to the Crosby home. They drove to the Beam residence, home of Nannie's sister, Carrie Beam, and her husband, Charles, where Nannie was greeted with open arms. The two sisters clung to each other on the front porch—one in relief, one in anguish—both crying softly as they went inside the house.

D.W. and his uncle spoke in hushed tones about the loss of his father.

"I have to find my father's body." D.W. took a deep breath and swallowed hard before continuing. "I want to begin searching first thing tomorrow."

The two men huddled together on the front steps, making plans for the next day. His uncle placed a hand on D.W.'s shoulder as they parted ways.

Nannie would remain at the Beam residence while the rest of the group continued on. Within thirty minutes, Lucky turned the station wagon into the driveway of the Crosby home. The going had been slow through several parts of town, with traffic rerouted by Gulf States Utilities crews around fallen power lines.

D.W. carried Geneva inside, ignoring her protests to use the crutches. "I've seen you perform magnificently on crutches, Geneva," he teased.

Once they arrived at their comfortable home, Lucille and Lucky took over the care of their guests. Lucky fired up the barbeque grill in the backyard while Leslie played with their dog. With the electricity still out all around town, there was a need to use the frozen items in the rapidly thawing home freezers. After ten minutes, the charcoal briquettes burned a hot red-orange. Soon they would eat like kings.

Inside the house, Lucille prepared a basin of water for Geneva's sponge bath. D.W. carried his wife to a vanity stool next to the bathroom sink, where he helped get her out of the hot dirty uniform and into a soft, pale-blue robe that Lucille handed him. The nurse at the hospital had already cut the trouser leg when the cast had been applied, so the task went smoothly. Lucille shooed him out to join the rest of the guys in the backyard.

"We saved extra drinking water in the bathtub just before the storm hit, so we do have some clean water available. Until we get the 'all clear' from the water company, we'll continue to drink only this water, not what comes out of the pipes," declared Lucille. "We don't have electricity, but we do have plenty of charcoal and water!"

Lucille worked effortlessly without rushing one bit, pampering the Griffith girls as if they were at a day spa. In the dim bathroom, she first lit candles, which reflected subtly off the mirror, adding more light to the room. Next, she set out fluffy towels and matching washcloths, sweet-smelling shampoos and lotions. All the while, Lucille spoke in soft, soothing tones about nothing really. The calming effect was evident almost immediately. Cherie opened a small glass jar of luscious-smelling hand cream that Lucille passed to her. The little girl bent to sniff the jar and got a bit of the pink cream on her nose. She smiled and even giggled, looking over at her mother. Geneva returned her daughter's smile and felt the tension between her shoulders begin to relax. The soft rug on the bathroom tile floor felt wonderful against her bare foot.

"Okay, you two, first I'm going to wash your hair, then leave you alone for your bath," said Lucille, smiling as she knelt down between them. She tried to gauge the amount of strength Geneva had left.

"Come here, my little majorette, and let me get you out of those clothes. I think I can manage your zipper," Geneva said, and Cherie carefully stepped over the large white cast to get within her mother's reach. Sitting on the low stool, she helped her daughter out of the costume. Lucille went to work on the pair. The mother and daughter's tangled tresses were lavished with shampoo and conditioner.

"This feels so good. Better than a back massage," purred Geneva, as all remnants of the salty gulf water rinsed down the sink's drain. After the ordeals of the past two days, simple pleasures now felt like luxuries.

While Geneva and Cherie continued with their baths, the men were placing meat on the grill. The hickory scent from the smoke filled the yard and came in through the open windows of the house. Lucille set the table, and everything was ready by the time the men carried in the platters of barbequed beef and spicy Cajun sausage, a specialty of Abe's Grocery.

Cherie emerged from the bathroom, resplendent in one of Mr. Crosby's white undershirts that draped to her ankles. She had a towel wrapped about her head, in a tall turban, and she felt like a princess again—albeit a homeless princess.

The two families took their places at the table. Saying grace over the meal took on special meaning that evening, as they openly gave thanks for their bounty and inwardly mourned their loss.

Dusk settled over Lake Charles, and the death toll in Cameron mounted by the hour. As more survivors were found and brought to Lake Charles, so too were more corpses.

"Start your search at the docks," Mr. Beam had whispered to D.W. that afternoon on his front porch. The old man wiped his eyes quickly. When Nannie and her sister, Carrie, had gone inside the Beam home and were out of earshot, D.W.'s uncle had continued to answer his question. It would have seemed indelicate had Nannie overheard.

"Today's newspaper said the bodies were being brought up from Cameron to the Port of Lake Charles docks. A Coast Guard boat brought the body of Alice Marshall there before dawn. From what I understand, a temporary morgue has been set up at the docks because now the bodies are coming in so fast," Beam continued as he placed his hand on his nephew's shoulder.

"But first, you need to get some food and rest, I would imagine. Get your family settled in, and get a good night's sleep. Besides, it's going to take a while for the bodies to be recovered. You've got a tough job ahead of you, son." This sudden news of his brother-in-law's death was hard on the man, but Mr. Beam could only imagine what D.W. himself had been through. "The evening edition of the *American Press* will no doubt have more information that can help you in your search. In the morning, I'll come by real early and pick you up at the Crosbys'. Okay?"

D.W. nodded his head silently, too afraid to speak for fear of breaking down.

Friday afternoon, June 28
The Mermentau River

The pointed bow of the narrow, wooden pirogue easily cut through the water of the Mermentau River, which ran between Oak Grove and Grand Chenier and emptied into the Gulf of Mexico. On this day, however—the day after Hurricane Audrey devastated the coast—the river looked different. Today the murky, salty remnants of the storm surge emptied from the once-freshwater marsh back into the gulf from whence it came, the water level inching lower by the hour.

When conditions around his house had improved, Randolph Fawvor wanted to survey the damage to his neighborhood. His truck was inoperable now, but the small trusty pirogue needed nothing but its paddle to navigate the Mermentau. With each dip and pull of the oar, water dripped off the paddle like melodic pearls in the humid stillness of the air. Slowly, almost in awe of the devastation, Fawvor cruised the muddy water, cautiously avoiding the floating debris in the river, until he came across a sight that made him stop midstroke and pull up to the bank for a closer look.

There was no mistaking it now. The body of a small child hung tangled in the strands of a barbed-wire fence. Finding a manageable spot along the swollen riverbank, the man beached his small craft and stepped out of the boat onto the sodden grass.

Fawvor carefully, gently disentangled the child's body from the wires, then lifted him into his arms. All the while, silent tears coursed down his face unchecked, for Fawvor knew this little boy to be one of the Bartie children. Returning to the pirogue, the man placed the small body on the floor of the boat, smoothed out the tattered cotton T-shirt, and paddled off down the Mermentau in the direction of the cemetery.

Mr. Fawvor had navigated only a short distance when cries for help came from the marsh. Ahead on the riverbank, two people stood waving their arms in exhaustion and desperation. There was not enough room for more people in the small, narrow boat, so Mr. Fawvor lifted the child's body carefully and placed it gently on the riverbank. Once the survivors were transported to safety out of the marsh, Fawvor returned to the spot on the riverbank and retrieved the body.

Several times during the course of his journey to the cemetery, Mr. Fawvor repeated the process, rescuing victims from the marshy banks. Each time that he was forced to stop, he tenderly placed the child's body on the riverbank, returning as soon as the mission was completed.

In the waning hours of the afternoon, Fawvor—with his tiny cargo on board—pulled up near the shattered pilings where the Mermentau Bridge had stood the day before. With the toddler's body cradled against his chest, he began a solitary walk to the small church about a mile away. He thought about the rest of the Bartie family and wondered if any of them had survived the hurricane. At the cemetery, Mr. Fawvor used his hands to dig the small grave in the soft, damp earth. Looking about for something to use as a headstone, he came across a short plank that suited his purpose. He diligently carved the marker with his pocketknife, so that if the Bartie family had survived, they could find the grave of their little boy.

The late-afternoon sun cast long shadows among the headstones in the quiet church cemetery as little Walter Bartie was laid to rest.

"Into your hands, dear Lord, we place this little angel."

The simple funeral was unattended by mourners other than Randolph Fawvor, but it was a reverent and solemn occasion nonetheless.

7:00 P.M., Friday, June 28
The Cameron Parish Courthouse
Cameron, Louisiana

Upstairs on the second floor of the courthouse, State Rep. Alvin Dyson paced the radio room. Night would be falling soon on his dev-astated town, and the death toll continued to mount. Seated at the worn wooden desk, the short-wave radio operator had been busy for several hours sending and receiving messages for the state official.

Dyson had regained much of his strength since battling the nine-foot storm surge—and an angry cow—inside his home during the storm. Trapped in the living room with nothing but a floating chair between himself and the animal invader, the man tread water and sang hymns for eight hours. Even when his home washed off its foun-dation and floated past the courthouse, he kept on singing—and kept pushing back on the cow with the chair as they both occasionally bumped up against the ceiling. At storm's end, Dyson could barely walk, but eventually made it to the courthouse before dark. His ener-gy had been restored overnight, but his voice had been depleted.

"This is K5CTS. Would you repeat that last message, sir? Over," Mr. Dyson asked the distant operator in a hoarse voice as he halted mid-step in his pacing.

"Yes, sir. Repeating last message: *Sybil, John, and Joe Clark are safe in Lake Charles.* Over."

Representative Dyson tore out of the radio room and ran down the stairs in his eagerness to locate the doctor. As he expected, Dyson found Dr. Clark examining a recently rescued family, who luckily seemed to have only minor injuries. The nurse carefully cleansed the woman's abrasion as Clark moved toward the next cot to check the husband. Dyson took hold of the doctor's arm and pulled him aside with gentle determination.

"Dr. Clark, your wife and two oldest boys are safe in Lake Charles. We just received the news through a radio transmission."

For a moment Alvin Dyson's words were met with stunned silence. Cecil had all but given up hope for Sybil and his family, but even in his suddenly elated state, the doctor still had the presence of mind to catch the discrepancy in Dyson's simple statement.

"Alvin, it must be a mistake," he responded with guarded optimism. "The two boys were with my mother. They must mean my *mother* and the two boys. Is there any way you could check that for me?"

The doctor slowly sat down, while Mr. Dyson ran back upstairs to the radio room. Joy, sadness, confusion, hope, and disbelief—a myriad of emotions combined in an effort to override the despair under which he had been functioning for two days. He stared unseeing at the two borrowed, mismatched left shoes covering his wounded feet. It took several minutes, but Dyson returned with a solid confirmation of the message.

The beginnings of a deep auburn sunset graced the calm waters of Calcasieu Lake, as thirty minutes later the young doctor flew over Cameron Parish in the last helicopter to leave town that evening for Lake Charles.

Friday, June 28
The Clark family
Lake Charles, Louisiana

When the doctor stepped off the tarmac at Chennault Air Base in Lake Charles, his friend Jo Briel whisked him away from the activity at the airport and drove straight to the Briel home, where Sybil lay recuperating. Dr. George Briel and his wife, longtime friends of the Clarks, had gently tucked Sybil away from the world in the privacy of their home.

Sybil and her neighbor, Plum Nunez, had survived thirty hours in the water of Calcasieu Lake before being rescued around noon that day, Friday, June 28. All through the long night, the two women heard sounds of other survivors on the lake—heard their cries for help, and their screams of anguish.

Once they were finally safe aboard a rescue boat, a nurse administered sedatives and offered food and water, but Sybil refused to eat. Grief-stricken, she lay still and silent on the deck. Her tattered corduroy shirt and pedal pushers lay damp against her bruised skin, and her long red hair lay tangled against her shoulders. Several hours later, Sybil was transferred from the Lake Charles docks to the Chennault Air Force Base Hospital.

"Please call Dr. George Briel. I want to go to their home," Sybil informed the hospital nurse who helped her into the crisp white sheets of a hospital bed. The nurse dialed the doctor's home, hoping for a good connection. Fortunately, the Briel home—like the military hospital—was located in an area of town that had not lost phone service from downed power lines.

Just before Mrs. Clark's friends arrived, the nurse was able to impart a bit of good news—her husband was alive and well at the Cameron Parish Courthouse. A short time later, Sybil learned that their two oldest children had survived the storm by clinging to a tree with their grandparents for eight hours.

In the familiar surroundings of the Briel home, Sybil received much-needed tender care for her injuries. The doctor first treated the bad laceration around her neck inflicted by the antenna wire, then tended her hands, which were imbedded with long, jagged splinters of wood. Her palms, almost devoid of skin from the long hours battling debris in the lake, required special attention. Her wedding ring was so bent out of shape that the doctor had to remove it with a small medical saw. All the while, Sybil spoke very little—and the doctor understood her invisible wounds.

By the time the helicopter landed at the base, Dr. Clark was already considered a hero in Cameron Parish. Word had also spread through the survivors and refugees who found safety in Lake Charles and Sulphur, and who related their stories to the news media. For the moment, however, Cecil and Sybil shared a private reunion at their friends' home, as he opened the bedroom door and tenderly embraced his wife.

An hour later, the Briels' telephone began to ring nonstop. Reporters had located the young doctor. His community needed help, and for two long hours he graciously answered the reporters' detailed questions about the conditions in Cameron Parish, before finally crawling into bed at two o'clock Saturday morning. For the first time in more than three days, Dr. Clark closed his eyes and slept.

Being a nurse, Mrs. Clark understood certain things without question. The duty to care for the injured and the sick was one of those things. So it was with complete understanding that she kissed her husband goodbye three hours later when he left for the airport. At dawn Saturday morning, the army helicopter carrying Dr. Clark flew over the Intracoastal Waterway heading due south for Cameron, Louisiana.

The really great men are always simple and good.

CHAPTER 7

Life After Audrey

"It is a matter of fate whether the infants will be buried beside their parents. These families are scattered in death, as the hurricane scattered them in dying." —Calcasieu Parish Coroner, Dr. Harry Snatic

Saturday morning, June 29, 1957
The Joe Cagle home
Lake Charles, Louisiana

Stars glimmered high above in the dark, predawn sky as Joe flicked on the porch light, closing the front door silently behind him. He removed the gold paper band from the Anthony & Cleopatra cigar and struck a match. Drawing quickly with short, shallow puffs, he soon had the cigar tip glowing a deep amber-orange. At 5:00 A.M., a truck pulled up in front of the Cagle home.

A friend since their childhood, James Corbett readily complied with Joe's request to make an early-morning run down to Cameron. Joe was still worried about the Fawvors, his friends in Cameron, and thought it might be wiser to go down to the coast in a truck instead of his sedan. That's where James entered into the plan. Since their late teen years, James Corbett always drove a truck.

For the past several years, Corbett and his family enjoyed the rural life on the Cagle farm south of town at the far end of Ihles Road. In addition to holding down his regular job in town, James had agreed to move to the farm and keep an eye on things for his friend. James and his wife, Pug, a local pharmacist, had plenty of room in the crisp, white, two-story farmhouse on the property. Although somewhat drier now, the farm came close to completely flooding during the hurricane. The storm surge from Audrey had pushed twenty-five miles inland, advanced over the Intracoastal Waterway, and finally stopped at the southern boundaries of the Cagle farm itself.

On this Saturday morning, light traffic moved smoothly out of Lake Charles, south down Highway 385 toward Creole. Military vehicles seemed to be the only traffic at this early hour. James lit another cigarette and the two friends smoked in silence, listening to the radio. A somber broadcast reported the latest on the conditions in Cameron Parish. The next segment grimly listed the dead and missing.

Dr. Harry Snatic, the Calcasieu Parish coroner, described the unidentified bodies one by one—their approximate age, height, coloring, clothing, and jewelry—any detail that might help identify each corpse. All area radio stations broadcast this report daily for the next month, long after some of the nameless bodies were buried. It was gruesome chapter in Louisiana history. It was also a grim, necessary task.

The highway became a little bumpy, so James slowed the truck to half-speed. They had turned at Hackett's Corner a few miles back, and the marsh—or Cameron Prairie, as it was formally called—lay just ahead. Following a caravan of army transport trucks, James slowed as they approached then crossed the Gibbstown Bridge over the Intracoastal Waterway. The area surrounding the pontoon bridge was a beehive of army and Civil Defense activity.

"We're halfway there now, James."

Joe rested his elbow on the rolled-down window, enjoying the cooler early-morning temperature. The wet, muddy smell of the marsh began to fill the air. This air smelled different than usual, however—intense, as if it had been concentrated and ill seasoned. He realized that the freshwater marsh smelled salty now. Joe and James often fished and hunted ducks in this marsh, and they knew what normal smelled like. Normal didn't smell like this. The marsh was ailing.

James squinted and leaned forward for a better view. There was something odd about the road. The usually smooth highway must have taken quite a beating in the storm, and the residual mud didn't help. The army trucks were farther ahead now; James was alert and on edge.

"From what I understand, the water actually came over the road all the way up to here," indicated James. In the dim light, they couldn't see much on either side of the road at this point. "Twenty-five miles inland that flood came—to the back edge of the farm. I suppose this mud on the road was left by the receding waters."

Joe rotated the cigar, got a firm bite, and placed both palms on the dashboard. Light was just beginning to break through the humid haze over the marsh.

"Whoa!" said James, pressing on the brake as the truck slipped and hit another bad patch of road.

They slowed to a crawl. James was certain now—something was definitely wrong with the road. Joe felt it too, as though they were driving over a slippery, corrugated-tin roof.

"Look at that! I swear this road is moving," blurted James. He gripped the steering wheel with both hands, correcting a slight skid.

"Oh, damn . . . oh, damn. Joe, do you see what I see?" James gasped and stopped the truck in the middle of the road. The road indeed was moving, quivering in the dawn light. They could see it clearly now.

"Snakes!" they both gasped at once.

And snakes there were . . . lots of snakes. Black water moccasins of all sizes slithered in the muddy residue from the receding storm surge. The snakes covered the highway. For miles on both sides of the road, salt water had invaded the vast marsh during the hurricane. The storm's floodwaters still covered the many small islands and tufts of marsh grass normally occupied by the mammals, birds, and reptiles. This left little dry land for the numerous creatures of the marsh to vie for, including the snakes. With nowhere else to go, the snakes congregated on the highway. Snakes hated salt water. Joe hated snakes—especially now, after what they had done to Aunt Alice.

"Get us out of here, James. Get us out of here right now." Joe rolled up the truck window and started to squirm nervously in his seat. James was well aware of Joe's fear of snakes. He'd teased him about it for decades. But this situation was serious, and James knew to keep quiet. He moved out in first gear, carefully maintaining traction. After a few hundred yards, the snakes were less evident. In several minutes, the truck cruised down the road toward the outskirts of the small town of Creole, out of harm's way.

Military personnel saw their approach, walked to the center of the highway, and halted the truck.

"Sir, state your business. Are you residents? How did you get past the roadblock at the Intracoastal?" It was a short conversation.

"Only official rescue personnel are allowed into the area at this time, Mr. Corbett, Mr. Cagle. The Seabees are in the process of repairing these access roads. I understand your concern, but you will have to return to Lake Charles until the small bridges have been repaired and we have been given the all-clear."

Instructed to pull over to the side of the road, James turned around, waited for another military caravan to pass, then pulled in behind them. In less than one minute, the well-intentioned pair was sent back to the safety zone north of the Intracoastal Waterway.

"Okay, James. Stick close to that truck. We have to go back through the snakes, remember." Joe removed the cigar from his lips and used it to point the way, punctuating his sentences with the glowing end.

"Don't worry, Chief. The heavy army transports will squash most of them."

A born prankster, James was serious for a change. This was the one time he had no intention of teasing his friend. Joe wasn't so sure about that. He raised his eyebrow and gave James the "evil eye." Fortunately, Joe trusted this man with his life. He calmed down after a few moments, and his thoughts returned to the scene at hand.

As the two friends drove back north, the bright sunrise afforded them a different view from the one they had seen thirty minutes before. Both men now witnessed the condition of the countryside. Debris littered the marsh everywhere. Bloated cattle, pieces of buildings, farm equipment, cars—it was a scene like no other. The barbed-wire fence rows hung in tatters, draped with a myriad of former household items, such as torn remnants of clothing and fabric, power lines, and bent pieces of tin roofing. Although the water level was still well above normal depths in the marsh, with each hour over the past two days the water slowly receded. As a result, more bodies became visible.

In the distance, marsh buggies and helicopters now searched the marsh, recovering human corpses. Hundreds of bodies floated, scattered over the vast expanse of the once-beautiful wetland. This horrific sight burned in Joe's brain as something he would never forget. In the years to come, he would rarely, if ever, speak of that day. The marsh of southwest Louisiana had become something other than just a sportsman's paradise—it was now hallowed ground.

"These poor people . . . do you think the Fawvor family survived, James?"

His friend thought for a moment, choosing his words carefully. "Well, Alice's husband survived."

Joe slowly nodded his head in agreement.

The two friends continued the short drive back to Lake Charles in silence. Each man quietly processed the experiences of the past few days in his own way. For both men, however, none of this loss of life made any sense. The one-hour drive to safe inland areas was an evacuation route that the community had taken en masse several times in previous hurricane seasons. They had experience. They knew the drill. They were packed and ready to go. But no amount of preparation—and no amount of prayer—could restore the twelve lost hours that Audrey stole from this community.

The following day, Alice Cagle Marshall was quietly buried in the Merryville, Louisiana, cemetery located next to the football stadium, Cagle Field, named for a former star football player and war hero in the family. Numerous relatives and friends surrounded Regina as her mother was laid to rest, and in the crowd, a number of Alice's former students paid their respects to their teacher.

The afternoon was hot and humid in the cemetery. Far to the north, the stormy remnants of Hurricane Audrey still packed fifty-five-mile-per-hour winds—and caused yet another death—as the storm crossed Lake Erie, and the United States border into Canada.

Saturday morning, June 29
The Griffith family
Lake Charles, Louisiana

Just before seven o'clock Saturday morning, Mr. Beam pulled along-side the curb in front of the Crosby home. There was no need to honk the horn, for D.W. was waiting on the porch, eager to begin the search for his father's body.

"Good morning, D.W.," he said, passing him a well-worn metal thermos before shifting into first gear. "Have you had any coffee yet? Catch up on your sleep? You look well rested. How's Geneva's leg?"

So began the long hard day for D.W. He would look back on these times and often think how much more difficult it would have been without the support and help of family. Family was everything. To his surprise, D.W. found that he actually had slept well last night. The barbeque feast left them all fully satisfied. After dinner, he and Geneva briefly discussed plans for the next few days ahead of them, before exhaustion overtook them all. This morning Geneva would wake to find him gone, but she knew the task he faced today. The Crosby cousins provided a welcome place of safety and comfort for the Griffith family even while the city was without electrical power or telephone service. Resting assured that his family would be in good hands, he could now concentrate his efforts on finding his father.

D.W. stood in a slow-moving, long line on the Lake Charles wharf. There was no shade on the docks, and the sun's burning heat radiated down from a cloudless sky. His arms were already starting to redden a bit, adding to his deep tan, but a borrowed hat shaded his brown eyes from the worst of the bright sun. There was not even a hint of a breeze coming across the waters of the wide Calcasieu River ship channel. On a normal day, these people would have passed the time visiting or chatting about the weather, or possibly about the latest baseball game. But this was not a normal day, and no one in the long line wanted to chat about the weather. They had come to view the bodies of Audrey's victims. Weather was the enemy.

As more people arrived on the docks, deputy sheriffs were in place to answer their questions and show them toward the viewing line. All of the newcomers had the same look, the same pain evident in their faces. One by one they made their way to the end of the line, each footstep resounding on the wooden pier. Often, they paused to shake hands with someone and ask if anyone had word of their child or spouse. No one wanted to face what waited inside Shed Number Four and Shed Number Five, but in some cases, such as D.W.'s, the outcome was already known. He was searching for the body of a loved one, not a survivor.

News media from around the country were evident in most areas of the port that day. All the reporters described in detail the scene before their eyes. Occasionally the correspondents conducted an interview. Almost to a man, the press behaved with respect and empathy toward the hundreds of storm survivors and kinfolk from the area who now crowded the docks. As the day progressed, more and more bodies were recovered from the Cameron area and brought to the sheds.

Inside the wooden warehouses of Shed Number Four and Shed Number Five, the authorities and volunteer workers spoke in hushed tones. Women volunteers assembled makeshift desks from available planking and boxes within the warehouse, and typed up the lists describing each body as it was brought into the warehouse. The details included race, sex, approximate age, height, weight, hair color, clothing and/or jewelry, and any identifying marks, such as tattoos or birthmarks. For hours on end they typed without rest, sometimes slumping their heads down but for a moment on folded arms atop their typewriters.

A quicker embalming process used in emergency situations—spraying the corpse with formaldehyde—was performed on each body. The bodies were then placed on the floor of the shed in neat, formal rows, interspersed with large, dripping blocks of ice about three feet square. Many of the dead were without clothes, so the workers covered each one and made it presentable for viewing.

Sadly, family members were not placed together at the temporary morgue. During the hurricane, the rushing storm waters separated many family members when their homes were demolished. Bodies were found in every conceivable place—floating in the marsh, snagged in barbed-wire fences, draped in trees, pinned under collapsed roofs, entangled in rubble, and trapped in debris fields, all of which stretched for miles throughout Cameron and Vermilion parishes. It was impossible for authorities to tell who belonged with whom.

Despite all the sanitary efforts, the smell of death inside the sheds was almost unbearable, even for family members making brief inspections. Most of the workers wore surgical masks soaked in bitter-smelling ammonia just so they could breathe during the endless hours, while the viewers covered their noses with handkerchiefs sprayed with the same acrid solution.

By the second day, pine boxes were hastily constructed to serve as temporary coffins. After embalming, each body was placed in a box and covered with a heavy sheet of green wrapping paper. The box lids were set beside the neat rows of coffins, until positive identification was made. Never before had the Port of Lake Charles stored such cargo in its warehouses.

Sunday, June 30
The Griffith family
Lake Charles, Louisiana

Without phone service, there was no way D.W. could know that his wife's parents, and her sister, had driven in from Port Arthur and were now searching for Geneva. Three lifelong friends also made the drive from Texas to search for her. Late Friday evening, Geneva's parents had checked the registration boards at the McNeese Arena, found D.W.'s name, and walked through each row of Cot City. When they failed to find the family at McNeese, they checked at the refugee centers at Lake Charles High School and First Ward School. There was no sign of Geneva or her family.

The next morning they had searched at each hospital and found their first clue. They viewed their daughter's X-ray at Memorial Hospital, but there were no discharge papers to lead them forward in their search. Each location was crowded with people searching for their relatives, just as Geneva's parents were doing. The Ellerbees had one advantage, however. At least they knew their daughter and her family had survived.

With much of the area telephone service still out, the Ellerbee family hit a dead end. Finally, on Sunday afternoon, Geneva's mother made contact with Carrie Beam, Nannie Griffith's sister.

"Yes, dear, I know where they are!" Aunt Carrie replied, beaming.

Aunt Dora and Uncle Buster Welch, who lived next door to Geneva in Oak Grove, came to the door to greet Geneva's mother as well. Mrs. Ellerbee was relieved to find that they too had survived the storm.

"We ended up clinging to one of our oak trees for eight hours, and it saved our lives. Our neighbors, the Warren Jones family, along with his eighty-nine-year-old mother, survived the storm in our huge fig tree. Besides being the oldest fig tree in the country, I now believe it's the strongest as well!" offered Dora with a half-hearted, sad smile. "We had no idea that your daughter and her family were in a tree on their property until we saw them that night, immediately after the storm. I know you'll be glad to hold them in your arms again, dear."

At the Crosby home, the windows were open wide throughout the house in hopes of catching even the slightest of summer breezes. Leslie closed the front door behind him as he went out onto the porch to look at the funnies section of the *American Press*. Geneva sat quietly on the living-room sofa with a copy of the day's newspaper on her lap, while Cherie emptied a box of crayons on the floor nearby, and chose magenta to draw a flower on her mom's cast.

"Keep your foot still, Momma."

That won't be hard to do, thought Geneva. *I don't have the strength to move my big toe.* She had just taken some aspirin, but it hadn't yet brought down her fever. Her ankle throbbed with pain. Once again she read the list of the confirmed dead on the front page, which included the names of the Veteran's Affairs officer and his family. Their little boy had been identified first because of his cast.

So many friends and neighbors . . . so many children, she agonized silently.

Geneva closed her eyes and simply tried to breathe without crying. She tried not to cry around the children. She was experiencing so many unfamiliar and unpleasant feelings. If she had not been burdened by fever, she might have been better equipped to begin healing. As it was, Geneva was finding it hard to heal mentally as well as physically.

Cherie soon finished her flower and climbed up on the sofa next to her mother. She laid her head in Geneva's lap and closed her eyes. As she often did now, she gently took hold of her mother's skirt in her tiny fingers. Geneva stroked her daughter's soft dark curls and watched Leslie through the screen window. *Thank heavens Leslie is in good health. Cherie is still weak with this fever. It's lasted over three days now.*

D.W. had been unsuccessful again today but planned to resume the search for his father within the hour. By noon that day, three days after Hurricane Audrey struck the coast, many of Sheriff Ham Reid's deputies had been awake for sixty-five hours, working round the clock to facilitate the identification of bodies at the sheds. As the makeshift morgues at the docks began to fill, bodies were transferred to several funeral homes in the area. On Broad Street, Hixson Funeral Home soon required much more space, and rented the house next door to accommodate the number of bodies, which grew each day.

The Combre and the Gilmore funeral homes also spilled over into outbuildings and garages near their own facilities, where the sorrow-filled chants of Negro spirituals echoed through the neighborhoods. Their religious dirge was an achingly beautiful sound, for these hymns were sung by devout souls burdened with broken hearts. With electricity and therefore refrigeration still lacking, the offensive smell of death hung like a pall in the neighborhoods.

D.W. had returned to the Crosby house around midday for a brief respite and now sat at the kitchen table, holding his mother's hand. Nannie looked down at her cup of coffee.

"I want to go home, son. I need your father's things around me—to make me feel closer to him, you understand."

Through the porch windows, Geneva saw the car coming down the street slowly, and her heart rose in her throat. *Could it be them?* Leslie heard the car and looked up. He rose curiously to his feet, then bolted down the steps. At the sidewalk, he turned back to shout, "Mom! Mom! Look!" He pointed to the oncoming car.

The Ellerbees spied Leslie waving ahead and within moments parked in front of the Crosby home. Geneva's family poured out of the car and raced up the walk. Geneva's sister spun Leslie around in a joyous hug. Soon the living room was full of people all talking at once. Lucille immediately started a fresh pot of chicory coffee with a quick strike of a match to the gas stove.

Going straight to her daughter, Geneva's mother sat down beside her and saw the cast for the first time. She had so many questions, but right now she just needed to hold her daughter close.

"Oh, Geneva, Geneva," she whispered against her hair. Geneva had no words—she just clung to her mother.

Her father removed his hat, approached D.W. and Nannie, and spoke tenderly to them about their loss. Then, he moved to the other side of the room to find Geneva. His wife was now hugging Leslie and Cherie, kissing their foreheads. Geneva's father bent down on both knees to embrace his daughter, who remained immobile on the sofa with her heavy cast.

"Come here, baby," he said softly and gathered her in his arms. Without her even knowing it, those were the words Geneva needed to hear. She was once again the child, surrounded by her parents. She was so ill and in such pain from her injuries that most things didn't register very well. But this—this was basic. This was a primal need.

"Oh, Daddy," she sobbed against his shirt, and he held his child for the longest time, rocking her gently from side to side.

"Don't worry, sweetheart. Everything's going to be okay," he whispered. "Do you hear me? Everything is going to be okay." He patted her back and felt the fever through the thin cotton blouse. He rocked her for a while till her breathing became more regular.

"Daddy, take me home," she spoke near his ear.

For the next hour, the families shared their ordeals, and tried to make plans as best they could, based on the limited options available. Geneva and Cherie still had fever and needed care, so it was decided that she and the children would return with her parents to their home in Port Arthur. There was nothing to pack—no clothes or personal items—except for Geneva's wallet. Nannie, too, would return to her home in Port Arthur, while D.W. stayed in Lake Charles to locate the body of his father. Stealing away for a quiet conversation, Geneva's father spoke with D.W. on the front porch.

"You've always been a good son-in-law, D.W., but I have never been more proud of you than I am at this moment. I want to thank you for saving my Geneva, and those precious babies." He reached for D.W.'s hand and shook it fondly.

The hour passed quickly, and soon D.W. carried Geneva to her parents' car. With her arms around his neck, the two said their private, temporary goodbye as he walked down the sidewalk. He then set her down in the front seat, ever mindful of her cast. Leslie walked beside his dad, carrying the crutches once again. Everyone piled into the rather crowded car with another round of heartfelt thanks to the Crosby family. A final wave goodbye, and the car pulled away from the curb and headed for Texas.

In the days to come, Geneva would continue to battle the infection from the two untreated wounds hidden beneath her cast.

The next day, D.W. found the body of his father.

Monday morning, July 1
The Port of Lake Charles
Lake Charles, Louisiana

D.W. started out early as usual for the sheds. He wanted to beat the heat, which rose to blistering temperatures on the Lake Charles docks. At least this morning a steady breeze blew in from the south, from the beaches of Cameron. The water in the ship channel rippled in response. D.W. noticed something about the crowd. He was seeing many of the same faces in line each morning, and again each evening, all looking for their loved ones. It might be that these are the people who would never find their missing families. By now, four days after Hurricane Audrey struck, the bodies would be unrecognizable unless they had been kept on ice for the last few days, and that was highly unlikely.

A young athlete from McNeese was there again. D.W. saw him exit Shed Number Five and walk out into the clean air.

His face is hard to read today. I wonder if he found the rest of his family, or his girl, D.W. reflected. The young man stopped to bend over, bracing his hands on his knees. He hung his head and took several deep breaths. Chief Identification Officer Roberts followed him out of the morgue carrying a clipboard and waited quietly for the student to collect himself. After a time, the young man righted himself and stood tall once again. The deputy began asking questions and filling in the form. For the McNeese athlete, Hurricane Audrey proved to be the critical, overwhelming opponent.

It was a private moment, and D.W. felt compelled to look away. The line shortened and moved ahead at a reasonable pace. The morning edition of the *Press* reported that the bodies were processed rapidly now. Their full descriptions were documented here at the sheds; then the deceased were removed quickly to either the area funeral homes or the icehouse. Today the remaining unidentified dead would be buried in the first of several mass graves in Lake Charles.

Several officers and Civil Defense volunteers stood at the rough wooden door of the large, cavernous warehouse.

"I'm looking for my father, Mr. Dudley Griffith. Have more bodies been brought in since yesterday afternoon?"

D.W. supplied the physical description of his father, including the clothes he wore, his watch, and his wedding ring. Chief Identification Officer Roberts carefully checked the column listing the bodies of male victims brought in since yesterday evening. His finger moved slowly down the page, then stopped at a particular entry. The weary officer looked at D.W. and read the documentation respectfully.

"The body of this gentleman was brought here, then transported to the Lake Charles Ice Plant. If you think this description might fit your father, that would be the place to start looking today," Officer Roberts informed D.W.

The traffic up Ryan Street bottlenecked in front of St. Charles

Academy and came to a complete stop at the second large building, the Immaculate Conception School, even though students were gone for summer vacation. Traffic cops in sharp beige twill finally motioned for D.W.'s lane to proceed. At the corner of the block, just past the tall palm trees in front of the three-story, red-brick ICS, Borden's Ice Cream was closed—no power, no ice cream.

In happier times, the Griffith family enjoyed many a frosty treat at Borden's soda fountain. D.W.'s thoughts wandered to those days. Each time they had come here and pushed open the heavy glass door to enter Borden's, the cold air-conditioning made them all shiver. The college kids employed as soda jerks provided excellent service at warp speed. But the Griffiths took the time to wait for the nice lady with the blue eye shadow who called all the children "darling." Geneva loved her milkshakes, and the lady always managed to slip an extra red cherry on top of Leslie's hot fudge sundae. She would wink as if it were their own secret, and he would smile.

Those simpler, good times seemed so long ago now. His family was in Texas, and he was on the way to the makeshift morgue. The traffic picked up speed a bit near the courthouse and past the Calcasieu Marine National Bank. A few traffic lights were being restrung above the main artery, but so far few signals were operable.

The tall sign atop the Paramount Theater seemed to have weathered the storm well, but several large windows at Muller's Department Store had obviously been replaced with new glass already. Muller's trademark, custom canvas awnings had been ripped from above several of its windows. Lake Charles' elegant department store remained closed but seemed none the worse for wear.

In the next block, a maintenance crew worked to remove the freezer tape that crisscrossed the glass display windows of Jake's Produce & Grocery Store. Jake's was known for having some of the freshest produce in town, and for maintaining a time-honored tradition of taking grocery orders over the phone, then delivering the groceries to their customer's doorstep. Cleanup efforts took place up and down Ryan Street as owners waited for the electrical power to be restored.

As Ryan Street narrowed to its less-traveled, north portion, it began to slope down toward the river and the ice plant. The green army ambulances and assorted emergency vehicles jockeyed for parking spaces along the front of the temporary morgue. D.W. was forced to turn the corner and park along the edge of River Road, where several locals were fishing. An elderly man dipped the long pole of his net and scooped up a large brown crab from his baited line. The white shell road crunched beneath D.W.'s feet as he passed the men, rounded the corner, and walked up the wooden steps of the building. Behind him, life along the river continued at its own time-honored pace.

Thick, insulated walls retained the frigid cold inside the freezer vaults of the ice plant. The air was chilled, yet the smell of death permeated the hallways and the vaults. In room after room, large blocks of ice stacked in rows provided the necessary temperature for a morgue set aside for the victims of Hurricane Audrey. It was there in one of the vaults that D.W. found and identified the body of his father.

Recovery teams found the body in the oak grove just north of where he drowned. He was lying on the ground amid the trunks of the hackberry trees at the base of the next tree line. Papa's body had been taken to the small icehouse in Cameron. From there it was transported up the river to the docks in Lake Charles, with a hundred other bodies.

Dudley Griffith had completed his life's journey. The family held his funeral in Port Arthur at the Trinity Baptist Church, which filled to overflowing despite its large size.

Nanny is strong today, thought Leslie. In her sorrow, she offered comfort to those around her with poise and dignity. He had noticed the change in his grandmother once Papa's body was found. His dad called it "closure." Nanny seemed at peace knowing that Papa's body would be buried in nearby Greenlawn Cemetery. Before the service began, D.W. explained the large crowd to his son.

"All his life, your grandfather believed in honoring the dead, Leslie. He always tried to take off work to attend funerals of his friends and relatives. He was always there in their time of need to pay his respects. Today, this community is paying him back."

Eleven-year-old Leslie stood beside his grandmother in the front row, as the powerful pipe organ led the standing-room-only crowd in

"Amazing Grace." The robed choir was magnificent, their voices fill-ing the room with deep, rich harmony. Goose bumps rose on the young boy's arms, and his spirits also rose. The recitation of his Papa's life's work and the heartfelt tributes that were shared combined that day to honor his grandfather in the manner he deserved, leaving an indelible impression on the boy. He was so touched by the ceremony, Leslie Griffith joined Trinity Baptist Church the following Sunday, and was baptized shortly thereafter. Every time the boy walked into the church, he felt close to his grandfather, and he smiled.

Geneva remained at her parents' home, too sick to attend the funeral. She slipped in and out of feverish sleep all that day, remem-bering how she said her goodbye to Papa down in the water as she struggled to survive the huge waves. The sound of the hurricane winds screamed vividly in her dream. Geneva turned her head back and forth on the damp pillow, trying to escape the sound. Her leg throbbed with pain, and she relived the moment on the roof when her ankle was crushed against the trunk of the tree. *I prayed to God, but why didn't He answer my prayers?*

Friday, June 28
St. Louis University
St. Louis, Missouri

The morning after Audrey, college freshman Whitney Broussard, Jr., followed his usual routine before going to his first class of the day. As was his habit, he purchased a newspaper from a sidewalk vendor, rolled it up and tucked it under his arm along with his books, and pro-ceeded to a nearby restaurant for breakfast. As the waitress poured him a cup of coffee, Whit unfurled the St. Louis newspaper.

CAMERON, LOUISIANA COMPLETELY DESTROYED BY HURRICANE AUDREY, read the headlines. The article reported "hundreds killed." The news propelled Whit into stunned silence, since "only hundreds" lived in Cameron. To further hammer home the dev-astating news, a picture of one of his friends accompanied the article on the front page. With limbs swollen from injuries, Lillian Theriot lay on a stretcher, exhausted from her fight to survive the hurricane.

Desperate to find word if his family had survived, Whit repeatedly tried calling his home in Cameron, but the operator continuously replied, "All circuits are down. Please try again later."

Whit did not hear from his parents until Saturday evening, when they reached Bourg, Louisiana, about four hours east of Lake Charles. Relatives had driven over in two cars to bring the family to Bourg, which had working electrical and telephone service. The wait had been agony for the young man, who naturally feared the worst—that he had lost his entire family. When he received the phone call from his parents, the sound of his mother's voice came through the receiver like a miracle.

"Yes, son, everyone is fine. We are being cared for very well. There is no need to worry any longer. Just keep up with your schoolwork."

Relief was not instantaneous, however, and Whit insisted on speaking to each of his siblings one by one, to make sure they were all okay. Only then could he breathe a partial sigh of relief; but still he knew it would be impossible to concentrate on classes so far away from his family. Visions of Cameron's devastation raced through his mind, working overtime along with reality—his family had lost everything, and they were homeless. They were planning to stay with relatives in Bourg for the summer while finalizing plans for the next school year. Foremost in his parents' plan was finding a temporary home until they could return to Cameron.

After saying goodbye to his father, the young man hung up the phone. His decision was made before the receiver was even back in the phone's cradle. He immediately withdrew from St. Louis University and purchased a train ticket to New Orleans. Whit Broussard was going home. There were plenty of colleges in the south, and he wanted to be near his family.

After two days on the train, he arrived in New Orleans and eventually the town of Bourg, where he embraced his family once again. Whit insisted on joining his father, who had returned to Lake Charles to help the Red Cross revive and rebuild Cameron. His uncle Nick, a physician, administered the necessary immunizations, which would protect him from any possible pestilence and disease that often resulted from natural disasters. The next morning, Whit left for Lake Charles, feeling once again a deep connection with this land, and these people. For several months, he and his father worked with the Red Cross, based out of a building on north Ryan Street across from the Weber Building. Whit spent long days typing reports, forms, and correspondence all related to his hometown. Record keeping and transferring information between other relief agencies was important in the rescue and reconstruction efforts. Father and son often worked side by side. Whitney, Sr., worked tirelessly with local and federal agencies to slowly rebuild the infrastructure of Cameron Parish, including the school system.

During this time, as soon as the roads were passable, Whitney and his son returned to Cameron to check out the damage to their home. The smell of death filled the air. Cleanup crews set rotting cattle corpses ablaze in large bonfires topped with old tires. The black smoke rose in dark columns against the crisp blue summer sky along the coast. Debris had been bulldozed from the main street in Cameron, resulting in twenty-foot-tall piles of broken warehouses and businesses alongside the road. Rats and snakes roamed the piles of debris at will. The threat of pestilence hung over the parish, spurred by the lack of fresh water and sewage facilities.

The Coast Guard and the armed services labored round the clock with local agencies and volunteers to rescue the stranded survivors, retrieve the dead, and transport both up the ship channel to the docks at Lake Charles. Sheriff O. B. Carter rallied the troops, the elected officials, and the civilians as the clear leader of Cameron Parish during these trying times. He was everywhere at once, and he was the entire community's source of inspiration.

Within two or three days after Audrey, the Red Cross provided food to 1,000 people in Cameron Parish, serving meals three times a day in field kitchens and also mess centers staffed by the army from Fort Polk, Louisiana. The Air Force flew in cooks from Maxwell Field in Alabama. This lifesaving service continued nonstop for the next three months. Cajun favorites such as gumbo and jambalaya were often on the menu for the appreciative residents and work crews.

Whitney drove carefully through the town, now totally unrecogniz-able save for the courthouse. The going was slow, and the coast high-way was in bad shape, but he reached the edge of town without mishap. On one side of Marshall Street, the motel was nearly demol-ished. On the other side, the elementary school was a gutted shell, shattered and broken from the force of the hurricane. Damage to the two buildings was a double blow to his career, and source of income. Dan Street, like all the roads in the parish, suffered greatly in the storm. Whitney stopped the car in the former parking lot of the motel, and the father and son began the short walk to their house. For decades they had taken this same road, passed the same homes, waved at the same families in this neighborhood. Their walk today was in stark contrast to all those other walks home.

No longer filled with lush gardens and brightly colored flowerbeds, Dan Street had taken a beating. Several empty lots gaped where love-ly houses once stood, with now only cement steps marking the spots. Drifts of boards, tree branches, and household items littered the road and yards. Mindful of snakes, the two men watched where they stepped. A tangle of small school desks massed around the trunk of a mulberry tree toward the end of the block. Familiar schoolbooks, well worn from years of use, lay ruined in piles of mud and debris.

Toward the end of the block, Whitney strained to see around the corner, hoping to catch sight of the home he shared with Clara and their children. After all the devastation he had seen coming through town, Broussard was prepared for the worst. Now, standing with his son in their front yard, the man lowered his head and cried softly into his hands.

There it stood, his southern cottage, amid the tall pines and oaks of the neighborhood. The house was intact structurally, with only minor damage in evidence. Whitney quickly wiped his eyes on his shirtsleeve and surveyed the damage. The screens on the porch would have to be replaced, as would many shingles on the roof. Beyond the house he could see that the garage, too, had stood its ground. Anchored in place for safety's sake, the swing set waited patiently like a nanny in the green grass for the children to return.

Whitney Broussard was one of the fortunate ones. All of his family survived Hurricane Audrey, as did his home. Before he took another step, the devout Christian offered another silent prayer of thanks.

July 1957
The Griffith family
Port Arthur, Texas

Geneva could not get past the terrible memories of the storm and all that her family had suffered that day. Her fear was deep and genuine. She felt safe only here in the home of her youth. Here in Port Arthur, she could also escape the sound of the breakers crashing on the shore of Cameron's beaches.

Geneva's sister wiped a cool, damp washcloth across her brow, trying to bring down the fever. She lifted Geneva's hand and wiped up and down the slender arm, then covered her once again with the pale pink sheet.

This is not good, her sister thought to herself. *This is not right.*

Naturally worried about his daughter, Mr. Ellerbee had arranged for his doctor to make a house call the very day Geneva arrived. The doctor checked out both Cherie and Geneva and gave each of them some medicine for their fevers.

A few days later, one of Geneva's aunts came over to help and observed her niece's deteriorating condition. Aunt Ordra was visibly upset. She held her niece's hand and spoke firmly, insisting that she see a doctor immediately. That afternoon, Geneva and her mother drove to the doctor's office. Geneva's progress was slow on the crutches, but once she was inside the reception area, the nurse took one look at her and quickly seated her in a wheelchair. In a short time, two nurses lifted her onto an examining table.

"I want this cast removed," Geneva insisted to the doctor who had seen her earlier during the week. The nurse took her vital signs while Geneva continued to point at her leg.

"Something is terribly wrong. I know there was a deep cut on my ankle before this cast was applied."

"Has your fever subsided at all since I saw you last?" He read the chart. Her numbers were high.

"No, it hasn't, and I think the fever is coming from the untreated cut. Please, doctor, take off this cast!"

"Nurse, if you will please bring me a saw." The doctor's request was met right away, and the nurse stood by to assist in the removal of the cast. "Okay, young lady, let's see what we've got here."

Slowly, carefully, the doctor sliced through the layers of plaster and gauze with the short stainless-steel saw, keeping the leg as immobile as possible. He paused and pushed his glasses back firmly against the bridge of his nose. The nurse set aside pieces of the heavy cast in a surgical tray as his work progressed. He moved his head closer to the cast to better observe his precision cuts.

The tension of the moment was compounded by the grating sound of the saw and the chalky dust floating in the still air of the small examining room. From the chair nearby, Geneva's mother reached over to hold her daughter's hand. Even before the doctor removed the last layer of gauze next to her skin, he could smell the putrid infection. Within moments the cast was completely removed. The experienced doctor was horrified by what he saw.

Geneva's ankle and leg were black. She had gangrene.

"Oh, my God," Geneva's mother gasped. Her hand drew to her mouth, instinctively covering her words from her daughter's ears. But it was too late. Geneva had already pulled herself up onto her elbows for a better view. More than anyone else in the room, Geneva wanted to know what was going on with her own leg. Her eyes were fever-fuzzy, but she could see the black flesh.

"I told you," Geneva stated flatly.

"Lie still, Geneva."

The nurse supported the back of Geneva's neck and laid her back gently against the table, patting her arm. "Try not to move while the doctor examines your leg, okay?" She offered Mrs. Ellerbee a weak smile, but it did nothing to allay the mother's fears.

The doctor literally ran out of the office and came back with his associate. The second doctor, the younger partner in the clinic, joined the first in a thorough examination of the blackened tissues, while the nurse tried to divert her patient's attention, wiping the moisture from Geneva's brow. The young colleague bent down and closely checked a spot on her ankle.

Moving to stand near Geneva's shoulders, he looked down into her eyes. He knew she was in pain, suffering from the rapidly spreading infection. The gangrene had already moved from the untreated wound on her ankle up to midcalf.

"Geneva, let me ask you some questions." When her eyes focused on his, he continued. "Yes, the untreated wound on your ankle has become infected. But there is something else. Is there a possibility that you were also bitten by a snake? We have found two puncture wounds, like fang marks on your ankle."

"A snakebite?"

Like flashes of lightning, the scenes replayed in her head, quick and vividly sharp in her memory. *The snakes! The large cottonmouth. The snake in the tree. The orange beads, and the wind. Water was everywhere, and snakes were in the water. Papa was in the water.*

"Yes. Snakes were in the water, the trees, everywhere. My ankle already hurt so much that I wouldn't have felt the bite . . . yes, it could have happened." Her voice failed her. She closed her eyes. Mrs. Ellerbee saw the tear fall and gently squeezed Geneva's hand.

The physician immediately started Geneva on a series of anti-venom shots for the snakebite, as well as a separate treatment for the gangrene. Over the next several days, she continued the shots until her fever finally subsided. Her leg, too, began a slow healing process. In time Geneva's blackened tissues healed, and she suffered no after-effects from the gangrenous leg. She hobbled around on the crutches but never mastered the technique. Her maneuvers remained clumsy at best, but she was finally healing, and getting stronger by the day.

Mr. Ellerbee often sat with Geneva early in the mornings when others were not yet awake. Geneva always woke up early. Lately, he brought her coffee in bed on a small wooden tray, and they spoke softly so as not to wake Cherie. One day he placed the tray across her lap and felt her head.

"Daddy, I'm not going back to Cameron Parish. I will not raise my family there. Not along the coast, no sir." She sipped the steaming dark coffee slowly. If she hadn't been sporting a heavy new cast, she would have tapped her foot defiantly.

Geneva could no longer put it off—she had some important decisions to make about her future. While Cameron Parish was rebuilding, they would have to live elsewhere. D.W. was with his family as often as he could be, but he was also juggling his offshore work schedule and trying to find them a place to stay in Lake Charles. Soon, he planned to take a leave of absence from the oil company, so he could begin to rebuild their home.

Geneva's father let the moment pass without comment as she unfolded the newspaper and scanned the headlines.

On a warm July evening, Mr. Ellerbee sat in the shade of the veranda enjoying a beautiful Texas sunset with his daughter. The green metal chairs of the patio furniture had weathered the years well and offered an inviting place to enjoy the end of a long summer day. The heady smell of the freshly cut grass hung in the humid air.

"I truly believe the sunset is one of God's most beautiful creations," he commented. The deep golden rays beamed down between the few lingering clouds, gilding their edges in glorious tones of gold and silver.

"I agree," Geneva sighed, keeping her eyes closed and enjoying the moment. She tried to soak up the last of the warm rays before the sun dipped from view. Her father took another sip of ice tea and studied her face.

He had realized for some time that his daughter was still suffering from the emotional trauma of Hurricane Audrey. He knew he could never fully comprehend what she and her family had gone through that awful day, even though she recounted their ordeal on several occasions. She was obviously struggling with a lot of unresolved issues, but he never pressed her to discuss them. Leslie and Cherie seemed to have bounced back a bit easier—a bit quicker.

But Mr. Ellerbee was sure of one thing—he knew his daughter, and he knew she had amazing inner strength. Her faith was powerful as well. Geneva would be forced to draw upon this inner strength in the months to come. Her leg was improving quite well now, but the emotional scars would take much longer to heal.

They say time heals all things, he thought to himself and took another sip of tea.

Behind her closed eyes, Geneva's thoughts were falling into place. Once her fever had gone away, she had been able to think more clearly, and she thought often about the events that had happened. She could see that her body was going to heal, and that meant she had some important decisions to make. But the dilemma had brought her to a standstill. For the past several weeks, she had been in a quandary about what to do with her life at this moment in time. She knew for a fact that she did not want to return to Cameron Parish—not now, not ever.

She broke the silence with a huge revelation.

"Daddy, I don't want to move back to Oak Grove. I want to stay right here in Port Arthur." She spoke evenly, decisively. Her soft green eyes remained downcast, brimming with emotion and despair. "I don't want to live along the coast ever again."

Geneva's father slowly leaned forward and set his glass down on the round patio table. He took his daughter's hand in his old one, and kissed her knuckles, all the while pondering her declaration and framing his response carefully.

"Geneva, look at me, honey." He waited until her green eyes met his. "You have to go back. You must go back."

She looked away without blinking, but the tear rolled down her cheek anyway.

"Baby, look at me," he continued softly, and waited until he had her attention once again. "D.W.'s job is in Cameron Parish. That's where he works, and that's where he wants to live."

"I can't go back. I can't," she interrupted, shaking her head. Her long ponytail bobbed about in parallel confusion. It was more a plea than a statement, and Mr. Ellerbee's heart broke for his child.

"Listen, baby. I don't have all the answers, but I do know one thing for certain. You love your husband, and he is a good man. You love your children. You have been blessed with a wonderful family, and you have to keep your family together. You must move back to Cameron Parish."

The two Texans remained quiet for a while, settling back in their chairs. One was worried, stubborn, and scared; one was blessed with old age and experience. Geneva closed her eyes again, trying not to face the obvious. Mr. Ellerbee knew that his daughter was chewing over his words, and he let her mull over her conflicting thoughts quietly. She had a big decision to make, and it was going to take some time. He swirled the melting ice around in his tall glass and took a long, cool sip. The condensation dripped against his hand. He waited.

When finally she opened her eyes, Geneva studied the amazing sunset with renewed interest.

"Daddy, can you explain why God did not answer my prayers when I had begged Him for help and claimed His promise to show me what to do?"

There it was, sort of a missing link in the healing process. He set down his glass and contemplated her downcast eyes.

"Baby, don't you know that He did indeed answer your prayer, but not in the way you expected? God gave the knowledge to the strongest one, and that was not you—it was D.W."

Puzzled, Geneva looked up into his wise face, a face she trusted. She had never thought of it that way. She raised one eyebrow and gave him a thoughtful, unhurried nod of her head.

Later, when she was alone with D.W., she asked her husband about his solid, deliberate decisions, pressing him for answers.

"How did you *know* what to do? And why did you bring inside *those* three things from the barn—the ropes, the ax, and the saw? How did you know to untie the children from the tree limbs?"

D.W. thought about it and shook his head. "I don't know, Geneva. It just seemed the right thing to do."

They were both quiet for a moment, deep in thought. He kissed her forehead and gathered her close. It was at that moment that Geneva realized that every decision her husband had made during the killer storm had been the right one. She realized that death lay waiting right behind each move they made, ready to claim them had they made the wrong choice. As it was, it was a miracle they had survived at all—and God had indeed answered her prayers through D.W.

That sudden realization was a defining moment in her life.

Fall 1957

In the remaining summer months following Audrey, Whitney Broussard divided his time between Bourg and Lake Charles and often drove to Cameron to help rebuild his community. While the Broussard home underwent repair and refurnishing work, life continued at an adjusted pace for the large family. Their friends, the Ferdinand Sonniers, found them a comfortable rental house in Lake Charles and set about cleaning it in advance of their arrival. As the fall school term approached, Whitney and Clara settled in to their temporary housing until their own home in Cameron would again be ready for occupancy.

In September, Elaine and Ethel registered and began classes at the Immaculate Conception School. Naturally shy, Elaine faced the new town, the new school, and the new classmates with trepidation. She became quiet and withdrawn. Her older sisters tried to ease her anxiety and held her small hand as they walked into the front lobby of the school on that first day. Mary Ann, who boarded at the high school across the schoolyard, looked forward to seeing her classmates again. Kissing her mother goodbye, she rushed outside the lobby and entered St. Charles Academy, the original and older school in the educational compound, built in 1882.

Sister Ligouri, the short but imposing teacher with gentle eyes, greeted Clara and her daughters. Most students attending ICS entered in kindergarten or first grade and had basically the same classmates until they graduated. A new student entering the fifth-grade class, as Elaine was doing, was an unusual occurrence at the school. The rosters remained the same for many years, and the waiting list was legendary. This term, however, saw exceptions to the rule, as refugees from Cameron became integral parts of the student body.

"Hello again, Mrs. Broussard. Welcome. Girls, are you ready for your first day of school?" Their crisp uniforms of white blouses with navy skirts looked identical to those of all the other girls who walked the halls, but Elaine still felt different. In the past two months since Audrey, her life had been turned upside down. And today, she thought, promised to be no different. The tiny, elderly nun reached out for Elaine's hand.

"Why don't you come with me, Miss Broussard, and I'll show you to your classroom." With a glance to her mother, and a wave goodbye, Elaine crossed the marble floor of the busy lobby with her guide and walked up the stairs to the second level. In the hallway, students rushed past carrying armloads of fresh school supplies and book sacks, slowing only as they approached Sister Imelda's office. All the while, Sister Ligouri spoke softly for Elaine's ears only, and held her hand. The girl's tension eased, but only just a fraction. Entering the class-room together, the kindly nun introduced Elaine to the teacher, Sister Fatima.

"Welcome, Elaine. I have a desk reserved for you. We are seated alphabetically in this classroom, and your desk is here, next to Miss Cagle." The little girls exchanged smiles as the loud school bell rang out in the halls. By the end of recess that first day, the two began a friendship that lasted for years.

There was no kinder woman than Sister Fatima, and the teacher made a special point of making the school year of 1957-58 wonderful for little Elaine.

No school bells rang out in Cameron that September. As his chil-dren left for ICS that morning, Mr. Broussard experienced an empty ache. Hurricane Audrey had destroyed his school. But even though he was no longer a principal, he had secured a teaching position in near-by Westlake, fifteen minutes from Lake Charles. No matter where he taught school, there was that comforting thought that Broussard fully appreciated—he was still one of the fortunate ones, for they had sur-vived Hurricane Audrey.

Even in illness, the man's gratitude and faith remained strong. Halfway into the school year, he contracted spinal meningitis and spent several months in St. Patrick's Hospital recuperating from the debilitating illness. When he was well again, he returned to teaching, and also spent much of his spare time supervising the repair and refurbishment of the family home in Cameron.

At the time of Audrey, Clara was in the early stages of pregnancy, and was unaware that she was again with child. The following March, Clara gave birth to their newest daughter, Patricia, bringing the number of children to eight.

June rolled around and the Broussard family returned to Cameron when school let out for the summer. Elaine had grown to love her new school, her new teacher, and her new friends, but she was also happy to return to her childhood home. Construction began in earnest to rebuild the Broussard Motel.

One year after Audrey, in the late summer of 1958, a new school constructed in hurricane-proof design and materials neared completion on its original site across from the motel. The new Cameron Elementary School stood on a thick slab built atop seven-foot-tall concrete and steel piers. The new structure would perform a secondary but necessary function in the community as a hurricane shelter in future years.

Cameron Parish rebuilt its infrastructure—public utilities, schools, government offices, roads and highways—at varying milestones during the year. For many families in Cameron and Vermilion parishes, the healing process would take much longer.

September 1957
Office of Cagle Chevrolet
Lake Charles, Louisiana

"So, what's our total to date?" Joe asked Bob Self.

"As of last week, the number stood at 246. It seems to be leveling off. No more recovered vehicles arrived last week, so we can probably call this our final number—246."

After Audrey, operations at Cagle Chevrolet progressed at a different pace. For the past three months, several employees revised their job descriptions. They joined the wrecker crew. Their job entailed recovering damaged vehicles from Cameron Parish.

For the people who rode out the hurricane in Cameron, Oak Grove, Grand Chenier, and Creole, not one vehicle survived the storm surge. The usual movements of daily life, or what remained of it, came to a standstill. Even those residents whose homes survived the hurricane did without transportation. Everyone walked about town or rode bicycles.

Cagle sent his recovery team to retrieve these ruined vehicles, towed them back to the dealership, and worked with the owners' insurance companies to get them compensated for their loss. Every day for three months, the crew pulled crushed cars and trucks from beneath piles of debris, from trees, and from the marsh. Some places could only be reached by boat or marsh buggy. One by one the vehicles were towed to Lake Charles.

The employees of Cagle Chevrolet also joined the numerous civic efforts being performed for the devastated area by many local businesses—including Joe's good friend and competitor, the Ford dealer. Food and supplies were trucked to Cameron Parish. It was a true community effort.

As far as replacing their customers' vehicles, time was of the essence, but insurance checks were slow in coming. The people of Cameron Parish needed cars now, not later. Cagle enabled many customers to get new cars long before their checks came in the mail.

The physical layout of the car dealership also changed. In addition to the new and used car lots, a separate location was set aside for the crushed and muddy vehicles from Audrey. The Cagle wrecker crew stacked 246 trucks and cars on the back lot of the Broad Street property.

A major problem arose, however. The snakes embedded in the muddy vehicles soon slithered their way out and onto the property. For months the snakes hid, then reappeared, then hid again. Several close encounters ensued, but finally the snakes met their end.

Being the prankster that he always was, James Corbett lapsed into his former self. He took one of the dead snakes, placed it on the front seat of Joe's car, closed the door, and walked away. At the end of the workday, Joe opened the car door to begin the drive home. His shriek could be heard for miles.

"James Corbett!"

But James was a fast runner and was already well out of earshot. For most, life in Lake Charles was getting back to normal, and laughter proved to be a great healer.

The next morning at breakfast, Joe went to the cupboard and selected one particular jar of preserves—fig preserves. Seated at the long trestle table, he twisted off the outer ring of the Ball jar and lifted up the inner lid with a snap, releasing the wonderful aroma. The jar was filled with thick jam and tender chunks of figs. It was also filled with fond memories of his aunt Alice. A gradual half-smile warmed his face.

Christmas 1957
The Griffith family
Oak Grove, Louisiana

Once Geneva's cast had been removed in mid-August, the Griffith family moved to temporary quarters in Lake Charles, where housing had become scarce. D.W. rented a makeshift home with a small kitchenette—a former neighborhood grocery store at the intersection of Common Street and School Street, across from a fire station. They would stay there for about six months while Cameron Parish continued its massive cleanup effort. Now that she was able to get around without a cast, Geneva made the daily commute to her job at the Cameron Parish Courthouse.

In September, the 1957-58 school term also brought changes for Leslie. From their apartment, the sixth grader walked several blocks to LaGrange High School to attend classes. The high school, like others in the area, made adjustments to fit several elementary and junior high classes within its building.

D.W., in the meantime, worked on rebuilding their home in

Cameron. First, he and his uncle Will Welch gathered as much of the original structure's timber as they could, including the roof that had saved their lives, from the debris that Hurricane Audrey left on his property. Within a week after the storm, the Red Cross provided tents to the hundreds of homeless residents throughout the parish. D.W. set up his dark canvas tent in his front yard, close to where Geneva's rose garden once grew. From the remains of their former home—along with a stack of freshly hewn lumber—a smaller cottage began to take shape on the exact spot where the destroyed house used to stand. This one-room structure would house the family for the next year, until the final, permanent home was constructed nearby.

A few days before Christmas, Geneva and her small family were able to return to Cameron Parish. She wasn't exactly dragged there kicking and screaming, but she was not happy about it at all. Geneva's job was to paint the cottage, while D.W. began construction on the "big house."

"This paint is probably going to peel off the walls in no time at all," she half-laughed, half-cried with Aunt Nona, pointing her dripping paintbrush toward the cottage wall. "There's more water than oil in this paint, from all my tears."

It was nearly a fact. Geneva had cried, practically nonstop, over having to return to Cameron Parish. She could hear the constant roar of the gulf just two miles away in front of her home. The sound of the waves crashing on the beach would prompt the tears to fall and the disturbing memories to come flooding back. She was thankful to God for their lives but fearful of the place itself. She had to be strong for her children, however, so the emotional tug of war raged inwardly for months on end.

True to his word, D.W. situated the "big house" on the high point along the front ridge—the spot he first saw emerge above the receding storm waters. A major change existed in the design of his new home, however. The house was constructed on stilts, sturdy piers about ten feet tall, closely approximating where Audrey's deadly storm surge had risen. First, a wide deck was laid atop the tall piers, becoming the floor of the future house. Stacks of lumber lay beneath the well-made, robust deck, and the site was soon cleared of all debris from the hurricane.

The large green barn was gone, along with all the livestock. D.W.'s herd of cattle perished along with thousands of other head of cattle during the hurricane. In the aftermath, the surviving herds were scattered around the marsh and the lowlands of the parish. The roundup had been a massive effort organized by Hadley Fontenot, John Paul Crain, and Sono Savoie.

Christmas came and went in Oak Grove. It was bitter cold that winter, and for the first time in seven years, it snowed. As the months passed, Geneva welcomed the spring's warmth with open arms. The children played in their yard as they had all their short lives.

One spring day when the sun blazed in a clear sky, Leslie ventured out to find the tree that had saved his life. With the sound of his father's hammering in the background, he walked away from the cottage toward a big stand of trees adjacent to the open area where the barn once stood. The green grass was already an ankle-deep carpet after the short winter season. Beneath the tree limbs, the forest's lawn cushioned his steps in the quiet woods.

As boys are required to do, he bent to pick up a stick from the ground and waved it at the air, at nothing, at everything. It was a spear. It was medieval knight's lance. It was a sword and he whacked a tree trunk within an inch of its life.

On their thirty acres, the grove consisted of scores of oak trees, many of the ancient oaks having huge trunks five feet in diameter.

"Which one was it?" he wondered out loud. Unconsciously he stole a glance at the skies above, then continued his quest for the tree. Within a minute or two his search was over. As his eyes fell upon one particular oak, there was no mistaking that he had found the right one. He paused about twenty feet from the sturdy, trusted tree and took in the full view. It wasn't huge like many of the ancient oaks nearby. *It seemed much bigger during the storm, that's for sure. I think that one . . . yes, there's my tree limb. It's so high. So high up.* For a moment he thought he could hear the wind shrieking, and he looked down at the grass, shaking the scary thoughts away.

Twelve-year-old Leslie had grown a lot since last summer. He looked up again and slowly walked toward the oak. As fate would have it, the tree was not terribly far from the "big house" that was under construction. With his long stick, he reached up and traced the wide angry mark that ran down along the trunk. The scar was devoid of bark. The roof bumping against the trunk had left a stark, vivid reminder of the wrath of the hurricane. When he had seen the scar, he knew without a doubt this was the tree.

He remembered now. He had seen the mark before when the water receded that day, but his mind had been so assaulted and he had forgotten. He reached out and stroked his hand along the rough, grayish-brown bark. *Hello, mister oak tree. You saved my life.* He stroked the bark again. *I guess we both made it, huh.* Leslie didn't know whether to thank God or thank the oak, so he thanked them both. The boy leaned his tousled blonde head against the tree trunk and closed his eyes, but he didn't cry. After all, he was twelve now.

With each nail that D.W. hammered, the frame house began to take shape. The lines were clean and sharp, topped by the gentle slope of a shingled roof. Geneva's life took on a new shape as well. Her father had been right, as fathers usually are. She loved D.W. It was a plain and simple fact that overcame everything else after the storm. She had returned to Oak Grove, and the family was together.

On this early spring evening, Geneva drove home from the courthouse as she had so many times in the years past. The drive along the coast highway still displayed the damage from Hurricane Audrey. Many homes were gone, many families lost forever. Still, the majority of survivors struggled to rebuild, starting from scratch. The mighty oaks stood tall and defiant along the cheniers, reminders that life does go on in spite of deadly blows to a close-knit community.

Geneva turned off the road and pulled into their new shell driveway. The sound of the crushing shells beneath the tires was an unofficial signal that her workday was done. She was home. She rolled up the car window, ever mindful of the sudden rain showers that could crop up along the coast in the night. The setting sun glowed, shining off the gulf waters.

D.W. balanced high on the rungs of a ladder, silhouetted darkly against the deep-red sunset sky. He had shed his shirt in the warmth of the day, and his lean, muscular form was a handsome sight in jeans. Once again, she was struck by the sight of this man—her husband. His thick, dark hair blew gently in the evening breeze, and his skin glistened in the light of the sunset as the taut muscles strained to position a rafter in place. *Oh, my, how I love this man. Daddy was so right.*

Geneva often thought of her beloved father. He had lived long enough to witness the start of construction on their new house, but died from a heart attack several months later. In time, the house became a home. The family moved in to the "big house" just before the holidays the following year. Leslie and Cherie thrived in their new, yet old, surroundings. Santa arrived as well. Almost a thousand people assembled on the grounds of the courthouse to listen to a marching band's Christmas music while the children visited with Santa Claus.

As it turned out, not everything had been lost in the storm. Besides Geneva's wallet, there was one piece of household furniture that was found several months after Audrey. Along Highway 27 near the Gibbstown Bridge, a man had come across a worn and battered desk in a ditch, half-covered by debris. The drawers had been nailed shut, but upon opening them, the man learned the owner's identity. Leslie's leather tooling catalogs bore his name. Along with other items inside, the young boy's tools remained intact. Even though the piece of furniture was quite damaged, the man sought out D.W. and returned the desk to its rightful owner.

To this day Leslie Griffith still has those treasured tools of his youthful hobby.

Life After Audrey

That June in 1957, life along the coast of southwest Louisiana became divided into two distinct timeframes—before Audrey, or after Audrey. It was a common phrase, a reference point understood by all the community. When the history of Cameron Parish was discussed, events fell into one or the other of those two timeframes.

For many families, Audrey was a serious and permanent line of demarcation. For some, it was the end of a normal life, the end of a happy existence. The loss of a child was indescribable. And, as expected, each surviving parent healed at their own pace.

Even while many of the people of Cameron Parish were in a state of shock after Audrey, certain familiar sounds would sometimes cause a moment of awareness, connecting them with the remnants of their former lives. For a time after the storm, the evening cries of the nutrias out in the darkness of the swamp would have some mothers standing at the edge of the marsh in inconsolable grief. They were adamant that the sound they were hearing was their baby crying out for help, crying out for their mother. In most cases, grim reality eventually regained hold of their reason—but some parents never recovered from this grief.

Everywhere the rescue and cleanup crews looked, signs of death dotted the landscape. Even those souls who had been buried for decades were caused to resurface by the incredible strength of Hurricane Audrey. Almost 150 burial vaults had been washed away from the small cemeteries throughout the parish. These crypts were scattered over many miles of swamp. Each time one was discovered, it was retrieved and brought to town. Cataloged and stacked along the roadways, the heavy cement vaults were eventually returned to the proper cemeteries for "reburial."

The Clark Family

Over the course of the next year, Dr. Clark helped to rebuild the medical infrastructure of Cameron Parish, and later the medical center, from donations that came from around the state and the country. Donations came from every walk of life. Inmates from Louisiana's Angola Prison took up a collection several days after Audrey—passing a tin can from cell to cell—and sent every penny they could. "For Dr. Clark," they said.

Only after the sick could be cared for in their hometown once again did Dr. Clark finally start to rebuild his own home, which was now noticeably smaller than the house he and Sybil had previously built for five children.

During Audrey, Dr. Clark performed as a hero to his community. After Audrey, the nation recognized his great courage in several ways. At its annual meeting in Philadelphia, the American Medical Association presented Clark with a gold medal, naming Dr. Cecil Clark as the nation's "Most Outstanding Family Physician for 1957," and "General Practitioner of the Year" by the AMA House of Delegates. The thirty-three-year-old was the youngest physician to have ever received the award.

The Cameron physician was also given the 1957 Distinguished Service Award by the Lake Charles Jaycees, the Junior Chamber of Commerce.

Dr. Cecil W. Clark, Jr. (far left), with Dr. Stephen Carter, Dr. S. O. Carter, and Dr. George Dix at the 1961 groundbreaking ceremony for the South Cameron Memorial Hospital, which was constructed to replace the medical facilities lost in Hurricane Audrey. (Courtesy of J. Wise, the Cameron Parish Pilot)

As the years passed, the young couple's family grew in size once again. In later years, Dr. Clark established a medical practice in Lake Charles, where he lived and worked with Sybil until his death in 1994, at the age of sixty-nine. He passed away on a mild February morning in his Cameron Hospital. Mourners at his funeral filled Our Lady Star of the Sea Catholic Church to overflowing.

Throughout their intertwined medical careers, Sybil had always tried to stay quietly in the background, supporting her husband's efforts and raising their family. Despite her own career, Sybil felt lost for a long time after his death, and eventually she moved back to Cameron Parish to be near her relatives and her community roots. Her sons returned to Cameron as well.

Sybil remains very active and continues nursing the infirm by volunteering in a Lake Charles rest home every other weekend. She still avoids the limelight, even though she is an integral part of a Louisiana legacy. To this very day, the hundreds of survivors from the courthouse still recall Dr. Clark and his devotion to their needs above his own.

The Broussard Family

In the fall of 1957, young Whitney Broussard, Jr., made good his resolution to stay close to home and family. He registered at Louisiana State University and graduated several years later with a degree in chemistry, which was soon followed by a second degree in pharmaceutical science.

Education continued to play an important role in the Broussard family values. Whitney and Clara's oldest daughter, Mary Ann, graduated from St. Charles Academy, attended college, and became a registered nurse. For a long time after Audrey, Mary Ann suffered through frightening dreams of the perilous boat trip. She would wake up feeling the ache in her fingers from clutching the stranger's shirtsleeve as he helped pull the Jon-boat to the courthouse. She never knew his name, but she never forgot how he helped save her life the day of the hurricane.

Thirteen-year-old Ethel grew up, graduated from college, and became a teacher like her father and mother. Oftentimes she remembered that day of Audrey, recalling the exact moment when she realized that it was more than just a bad storm. When she was safely inside the strong confines of the courthouse, someone had conveyed the terrible news that her friend and classmate, Roger Dale Savoie, had died. At that moment, the true gravity of their situation hit the young teenager—Hurricane Audrey was a killer storm.

In later years, Ethel continued to follow her parents' sage advice, especially when choosing her lifelong profession. She still teaches school in Lake Charles, and sometimes discusses Audrey with her students when covering a hurricane unit or reading about a recent hurricane in the news.

Ten-year-old Elaine grew up and attended college at University of Southwest Louisiana in Lafayette, graduating in 1969. That same year, her parents sold their home along the gulf coast and permanently moved inland to Lake Charles. Following in the footsteps of her mother, father, and older sister, Elaine taught school for many years.

Before Audrey, Elaine had always been a bit fearful of the water. Now she is deathly afraid, and to this day has never learned to swim. When the family first returned to Cameron, the children always kept a watchful eye out for their two horses, Timmy and Pops. Elaine remembers how for years she wanted to lay claim to each horse she saw that remotely resembled their missing quarter horses.

In the early 1970s, the younger Broussard children graduated from St. Louis High School in Lake Charles, after the century-old St. Charles Academy on Ryan Street was demolished. Today, an expanded playground for Immaculate Conception, Elaine's former school, temporarily fills the area within the compound. A third generation of Cagle children currently attends classes there, as did the Broussard children the year after Audrey.

Clara Broussard still lives in Lake Charles surrounded by family and friends. She and her children often set the dining-room table as they have for decades, with the very same china, silver, and crystal that miraculously survived Hurricane Audrey. Clara's china cabinet never toppled during the storm. It floated, more than half-submerged in the

Clara and Whitney Broussard on their sixtieth wedding anniversary, being congratulated by their friend Monsignor DeBlanc (center).

murky gulf waters that filled the dining room. To this day, the Broussard family meals begin with saying grace and end with the laughter of grandchildren—and the china and crystal are none the worse for wear after three generations of Broussard babies.

In 2004, almost fifty years after Hurricane Audrey, Clara's beloved Whitney passed away. The tall, gentle Cajun with hazel-green eyes loved his precious Clara until the day he died.

The Bartie and Meaux Families

Almost five days would pass before word of Maybell Bartie reached her family. A minister, Reverend Perry, sought out Raymond and the children while they were still temporarily housed at the school in Lake Charles, and imparted the good news. The large family shared a joyous reunion at Memorial Hospital.

After Maybell was released from the hospital, the family lived for a year in Westlake while Mr. Meaux rebuilt the two farmhouses and the barn. The spring following Audrey brought the families together for planting the crop of field peas and corn. In the summer of 1958, the Meaux farm was back in operation. The two families lived and worked in Oak Grove until almost a decade later, when the Barties moved to Lake Charles. In the big city, the children—now grown—found jobs and began their own lives. In 1981, Raymond passed away. Maybell, beautifully delicate and ageless, has been blessed with excellent health and still lives in Lake Charles near several of her children.

The Bartie family never forgot the compassion of Randolph Fawvor, and some time after Audrey, they were able to thank the man for his kindness in burying their little Walter.

D.W.'s uncle Johnny Meaux served with distinction as the Cameron Parish state representative in Baton Rouge for almost thirty years, but he and his wife lived on the farm most of their lives. At the age of ninety-one, Mr. Meaux passed away and was buried at the Sacred Heart Catholic Church cemetery in Creole, a few miles from their farm. Three years later his wife was laid to rest by his side.

The Marshall and Cagle Families

In the months after Hurricane Audrey, Brown Marshall regained his strength while staying at the home of his son in Lake Charles. The physical recuperation happened quickly compared to the mental trauma that lingered from the ordeal. The loss of Alice weighed heavily on his mind. For a time, her loss broke his spirit; but as Cameron Parish rebuilt, so did its townspeople.

When Brown returned to his land at Daigle's Corner near Cameron, his home, barn, and cattle pens were all gone—lost to the

storm surge, tidal wave, and hurricane winds of Audrey. His business—
the stockyard and slaughterhouse—had been scattered to the wind.
Marshall's herd of longhorn cattle faced starvation in the now salty
marsh in the days and weeks after the hurricane. Miraculously, the
Cattle Rescue Project recovered a number of cattle from his herd.

The long row of stalwart oaks along the front edge of his property
held their ground during Audrey, and many managed to survive the
storm relatively unscathed. When first he came to take stock of the
damage, the mighty oaks seemed somehow to be waiting for the man to
return and rebuild his life on the land he so loved. And rebuild he did.

Marshall worked alongside the contractors, overseeing construction
of a new house. While on a smaller scale compared to the former two-
story Victorian structure, the 1958 home fit his present lifestyle. He
opted for a single-story home without stairs, which he revealed to be
"planning ahead for his advancing years."

Choosing semiretirement, Marshall decided not to reestablish his
meatpacking business, opting instead to rebuild his herd of cattle.
Without Alice by his side, Brown turned to what he knew best, what
gave him comfort—the land and the longhorns. Like the grand chenier so abundant with massive oaks, his roots were deep in Cameron
Parish.

Marshall remained a cattleman until his death almost thirty years
after Audrey, in 1984. Just as Alice had been laid to rest near her parents and family in Merryville, Brown was buried in Lake Charles near
his relatives. Connected only by memories now, there exists a haunting distance, a gulf between the two loves.

Alice's grandchildren remember their short time with their grandmother with great fondness. Elizabeth Phillips recalls sharing life's
simple pleasures from a simpler time—trips to the big farmhouse, gathering eggs from the hen house with Alice, and gathering fruit and
pecans from the Marshalls' orchard. On rare occasions, the grandchildren had entered the meatpacking business and watched the butchers
at work.

Long before they grew to adulthood, Regina Phillips' three daughters became accomplished cooks in their own right, much like their

mother and grandmother. In an attempt to organize the heirloom recipes passed down from generation to generation, Regina and her daughters compiled a cookbook. *Fit For a King,* first published in 1970, is currently in its fourth edition and includes some of Alice's original dishes, the most notable being her recipe for fig preserves.

Elizabeth Phillips grew up and married a young man from Cameron Parish who, at the age of five, survived part of Hurricane Audrey inside a school bus. Elizabeth became a teacher like her grandmother and today lives in Grand Chenier, a short drive away from the Marshall home—and Alice's ancient fig trees.

Alice's nephew Joe operated Cagle Chevrolet until his retirement in 1985. During his forty years in the automobile business, the Louisiana Automobile Dealers Association elected him president of the association, as well as a director, for ten terms. In 1972, Cagle was named *Time* magazine's Automobile Dealer of the Year.

With his wife and nine children, Joe lived in Lake Charles until his death from leukemia in 1988. Several years before his death, he purchased eighteen acres of property on the coast highway in Cameron Parish. Massive, ancient oaks that survived Hurricane Audrey shade deep freshwater ponds stocked with fish. Ducks and geese enjoy a winter home on the ponds and wetlands of the property, while deer freely roam the dense forest—the grand chenier. Horses gallop and graze in the natural grasslands. The rhythmic sound of the breakers on the wide, sandy beach nearby adds a sublime ingredient to the scene.

Truly a sportsman's paradise once again, the land is now owned by one of Joe and Mary Belle's children—the ten-year-old daughter who spoke with him about the death of Aunt Alice during Hurricane Audrey that morning in the Cagle kitchen so long ago.

The Lawsuit

In the wake of the deaths and devastation of Hurricane Audrey, resentment toward the Weather Bureau simmered until it reached a low boil. Many residents of Cameron Parish blamed inadequate warnings

This photograph of Joe Cagle was taken at an LSU fraternity function circa 1940.

issued by the Weather Bureau, now named the National Weather Service, for the large number of fatalities. They also blamed the television and radio weather broadcasters, for failing to call for an evacuation on Wednesday.

The belief that the Weather Bureau should have protected the citizens became an emotional and ideological detonator. This anger resulted in something highly unusual for the time. Over one hundred families filed lawsuits against the National Weather Bureau.

In one such case, *Whitney Bartie v. United States of America*, Cameron attorney Jennings B. Jones and Baton Rouge attorney Alva Brumfield filed a suit on behalf of the plaintiffs. During the week of April 25, 1964, several years after Hurricane Audrey, the federal trial began in the United States District Court in Lake Charles, Louisiana. U.S. District Court Judge Edwin F. Hunter presided over the emotionally charged proceedings. The case was the first of its kind in the history of the United States federal court.

The fundamental question at issue in the trial was both simple and extremely complicated—did the Weather Bureau use reasonable care in evaluating the evidence upon which its forecasts were based?

In *Bartie v. U.S.*, the survivor sued the Weather Bureau for negligence, blaming the deaths of his family on their insufficient warnings. Cameron resident Whitney Bartie, an operator in a shrimp processing plant, lost his wife and five children in the hurricane. The families and attorneys of the remaining wrongful death actions followed the trial with intense interest. It had been decided by these plaintiffs that the Bartie lawsuit would be the test case for their own pending lawsuits against the federal government.

While the Weather Bureau conceded from the beginning of the trial that the hurricane had struck the coast hours before the storm bulletins had predicted, they pointed out that the unexpected increase in forward movement of the storm, along with the increase in hurricane-force winds, "unfortunately occurred in the night hours" well after the 10:00 P.M. advisory.

Both the Weather Bureau and the plaintiff's witnesses—including Sheriff O. B. Carter and Dr. Cecil Clark—pointed to the television and radio reports, neither of which specifically called for evacuation. The witnesses supplied testimony that the television broadcasts lulled the people along the coast with phrases such as "you can rest well tonight" and "get a good night's sleep, because the storm will not reach the shores before late tomorrow afternoon."

The U.S. attorneys described the Bureau's chain of command and the responsibilities of each Bureau level. They stated that the Weather Bureau Station in New Orleans was a forecast center only—responsible for issuing hurricane warnings for the Gulf of Mexico. These forecasts and hurricane warnings were passed to the Lake Charles Weather Bureau, which was responsible for *distribution* of these statements. The Lake Charles bureau did not forecast; they spread the word of the forecast.

The U.S. attorneys further explained that for Hurricane Audrey, the Lake Charles bureau distributed the warnings via public dissemination channels to ten parishes, including Cameron and Calcasieu. In summation, the attorneys pointed out that was where the National Weather Bureau's responsibility ended—that the Bureau "did not own, operate, or control any radio or television stations."

Judge Hunter ruled in favor of the Weather Bureau, citing numerous legalities based on the Federal Tort Claims Act, 28 *U.S.C.A.* § 2680. In his written opinion, the judge further cited the expert's testimony that the warnings issued "were as accurate as could be expected at that time." He cited several Weather Bureau bulletins and advisories. Two in particular—released on Wednesday evening, June 26—advised of high tides.

In the plaintiff's claim that no evacuation was called, the judge cited the chartered duties of the Weather Bureau. In his ruling, he explained that the current law stated that no such duty was imposed on the Weather Bureau by statute or regulation.

While the law was specific on that point, and he was required to base his decision on the *very specific, required duties* of the Bureau, the judge's written opinion called for a change. Judge Hunter urged that changes needed to be made in the way official advisories were worded in areas that urgently needed to evacuate, as well as in the responsibilities of local television and radio reporting of hurricane advisories.

The people of Cameron had lost the case, and subsequently, J. B. Jones filed an appeal. The ruling of the United States District Court was upheld on appeal, and at that point the numerous other wrongful death cases were withdrawn.

The Griffith Family

Several years after Hurricane Audrey, Nannie Griffith gave her grandson a special gift—a photograph. As it was with all those who lost their homes in Audrey, most Griffith family photographs were lost in the hurricane. Among the few remaining photos from his youth, Nannie's gift was a cherished picture of Leslie with his beloved grandfather and his cocker spaniel, Bootsie.

Leslie still has the photograph. The young storm survivor grew up, attended South Cameron High School and LSU, married, and still lives on the land that has been in the family since 1850. Groves of trees, marshland, and wildlife abound around the family homestead.

Five-year-old Cherie grew up, attended the same high school as her older brother, but never became a majorette in real life. After graduating from LSU, she remained in Baton Rouge and worked for Gov. Edwin Edwards. She married and raised her family in Baton Rouge, never returning to live along the coast of Cameron Parish.

In one way, Cherie has been blessed in that she has no direct memories of her terrible ordeal suffered during Hurricane Audrey—only secondhand recollections from what others have told her. Her trauma as a five-year-old was eventually forgotten . . . it faded and blended into the memory of a simply happy childhood. Fortunately, youth often has an advantage in that way.

After Audrey, D.W.'s aunt Nona Welch remodeled her small two-story house near the courthouse and lived there until she retired. After stepping down as registrar of voters, the auburn-haired lady moved closer to her family in Oak Grove. Miss Nona suffered an aneurism in her later years and was buried in the Rutherford cemetery in Grand Chenier.

For Geneva, it was hard to pinpoint the exact time that she grew to love the coast again. It was actually her bond with Cameron Parish as a whole that conquered her fear of living near the water, of hearing the constant roar of the gulf near her home. The people made the difference.

After Hurricane Audrey, Geneva returned to her job at the courthouse, where she eventually went to work for the new district attorney, J. B. Jones. During the forty-plus years she worked at the courthouse, she continued to write as a newspaper reporter for the *Cameron Pilot*, and later the *Lake Charles American Press*. She somehow managed to juggle these three jobs all at once. She became routinely involved with reporting most of the community events and the parish's successes in rebuilding. This love for the community began to ease her painful memories of the storm. In order for their lives to go on, they had to look to the future. This healing process was a community effort in the purest sense of the term.

After Audrey, D.W. sank his roots deeper into Cameron Parish. He took a year off from work to rebuild his home and their lives. He returned to being a ship's captain for Pure Oil Company soon thereafter. In later years, he worked for the Louisiana State Port Authority, until his death in a car crash in 1972.

He was a hero to his family in many ways, not just for saving their lives during Hurricane Audrey, but for the dedicated service he gave to his community, maritime shipping, and the oil industry.

Nautical life continues along the coast of Louisiana much as it has for centuries. Ships both large and small ply the waters off the coast, the shipping channel along Cameron's docks in the Calcasieu River, and along the Intracoastal Waterway. Ship captains play an important role in naval history and seagoing enterprises, and D.W. was no exception. Upon his death, the state of Louisiana wanted to pay tribute to this favorite son, and as a result, one of their vessels holds a special place in the hearts of Cameron Parish folks. Every now and then along the water's edge, it is possible to catch a glimpse of the massive tugboat named in his honor—the *D. W. Griffith*—aiding and assisting ships, ferries, and barges of all sizes as it travels east and west all along the Louisiana Intracoastal Waterway. It is a fitting tribute to the smiling sailor who so loved the sea.

After decades of residing in the "big house" on piers, Geneva sold the home to her son, Leslie. He in turn built her a new home of her own within shouting distance. Leslie's family soon outgrew the "big house" on piers, and he added on to its size by closing in the ground level of the structure, making it a two-story residence.

For over twenty years, his parents' old, original front patio—the long cement porch with the brick façade—had stood its ground, a gray reminder of his childhood home that was destroyed by Hurricane Audrey. When Leslie built the new house for his mother, he busted up the cement and constructed her new house on tall piers, precisely on D.W. and Geneva's original home site.

The oak tree that saved their lives is still there. A decade or so after the storm, a grapevine grew up the trunk and covered the limbs. The vine was heavy with fruit and made a tolerable bottle of homemade wine, according to Leslie's taste buds. Lightning struck the oak several times and finally killed the grapevine, but the tree itself is still alive and well.

When the vine died back, the scar from the roof showed itself once again. Unlike the other oaks in the grove, that particular tree never grew much after Audrey. It seems almost the same size as during the storm, sort of frozen in time. The scar never healed either.

Geneva's lifeline, the toothache tree, led a short life as far as trees go. It wasn't too many years before the tree died, and eventually a wild pecan tree took root and now grows in the spot. Most of the family would agree that pecans are better to have than toothaches.

After Audrey, the LSU Extension Agency provided oak seedlings to plant throughout Cameron Parish. Leslie and Cherie helped their parents plant a dozen or so on their property. Today those seedlings are huge, over four feet in diameter.

"They are way bigger than the tree we were in," reports Leslie in amazement.

Geneva's story continues to this day. Upon D.W.'s death in 1972, Geneva devoted herself to her family, to Cameron Parish, and to the press. At age eighty-three, she retired from the *Lake Charles American Press*'s Cameron desk. In 2004, she moved from Oak Grove to be closer to her daughter, Cherie. Busy beyond belief, she wrote a weekly column for the *Cameron Pilot*, called "Retirement Notes." To this day, Geneva can endure the heat but cannot stand the cold—the cold that is so reminiscent of Audrey's wrath. She never remarried. Geneva remains Geneva Griffith.

Shortly after Hurricane Audrey, the National Weather Bureau retired the name Audrey, never to be used for a hurricane again.

CHAPTER 8

Epilog

Each year has seasons. Each life has chapters. For the families that survived Hurricane Audrey and returned to live in Cameron Parish, a half-century would pass before they were again so sorely tested by nature's wrath.

As of July 2005, Hurricane Audrey remained the deadliest storm in recorded history ever to hit the Louisiana coast, but to those outside of Louisiana—to most of the nation—Audrey was a forgotten storm. This is in spite of the fact that the death toll was much higher than in Florida's Hurricane Andrew (23), or in Biloxi's Hurricane Camille (256), both extremely destructive storms that continue to receive media mentions each hurricane season, as they should. Each year, however, the local Louisiana and Texas television stations and newspapers mark the June 27 anniversary of Audrey with thoughtful and respectful coverage, and have never forgotten the impact on its residents.

The hurricane season of 2005 set many unprecedented records, and for the first time in recorded history, three Category 5 hurricanes (Katrina, Rita, and Wilma) formed during this period.

It was the worst of times for Louisiana.

Hurricane Rita
September 2005

Leslie Griffith always knew this day would come. Glancing at the dark clouds approaching over the Gulf of Mexico, he shook his head in silent resignation and turned to place the last toolbox alongside the suitcases in the back of his heavy-duty truck. The weather had been incredibly hot that day, which made the packing job even harder, but as night began to fall in Oak Grove, the wind picked up considerably. Leslie removed his baseball cap and wiped his brow once again in the fading light.

The tall Cajun baby-boomer smoothed back the hair at his graying temples, then replaced the cap snugly. He paused in the gravel driveway between his home—the house D.W. built after Audrey—and his mother's home, the one Leslie himself built for her twenty-five years later. A meandering brick walkway formed a permanent path from his house over to Geneva's front steps. Though the home was built eight feet above ground on tall, dark, wooden piers, its stairs were mostly unnecessary, now that Leslie had installed a small elevator for her convenience at the back door.

On this day the communities of Cameron Parish braced for a Category 5 hurricane—Hurricane Rita—heading their way. For decades now, the residents fully appreciated the value of early warning, and prepared to leave their homes in haste.

Evacuation. The word had new meaning for many other residents along the entire U.S. gulf coast following Hurricane Katrina's deadly blow to Louisiana, Mississippi, and Alabama just weeks before this evacuation day. In that storm, New Orleans had endured catastrophic loss of life, and many questioned if the Crescent City would ever rebuild to its former size and historic grandeur.

For Leslie, the choice had been clear cut and simple. For the past two days, he and his wife, Peggy, worked long and hard to move their cattle and horses inland, miles away from the coast. They packed family heirlooms and photographs, tools and valuable equipment—everything necessary to rebuild their lives, if necessary. From his boyhood desk that survived Hurricane Audrey, Leslie removed each of the drawers and carried them upstairs . . . just in case there would be flooding during Rita.

On this Thursday evening, he closed the tailgate of his truck and paused for a long look at the two homes on the Griffith property. This

lush, green land of his youth was in his blood. He clung to it tena-
ciously, just as the hanging Spanish moss clung to the nearby oak
trees. A sudden gust of cool wind whipped the leaves, returning his
thoughts to the task at hand. Leslie looked around the property one
last time and told the place goodbye. It was a ritual of sorts, one he
performed with each evacuation. After all, there was no guarantee he
would have anything left when he returned.

With a reassuring nod to his wife, Leslie followed her sedan out of
the driveway. The couple drove out of Oak Grove and headed to safety—first to Lake Charles, then on to Cherie's home in Baton Rouge,
where Geneva waited anxiously for his arrival.

A strange sense of apprehension had plagued Geneva most of the
summer, brought on by the unusual number of hurricanes and tropical
storms. The constant worry left her tense. With haunting memories of
Audrey resurfacing more frequently, she desperately wanted her two
children close beside her during this approaching storm.

In Grand Chenier, ten minutes from the Griffith property,
Elizabeth Phillips Richard, Alice Cagle's granddaughter, gathered several more boxes of cherished items from her home, and then she and
her family blended into the line of traffic with the other evacuees. The
sheriff and his deputies made a final sweep of the parish before they,
too, sought refuge farther inland. Soon, Cameron Parish was one huge
ghost town.

Three million coastal residents of Texas and Louisiana evacuated in
advance of this massive hurricane. There was 100 percent evacuation
in Cameron Parish and 95 percent in Lake Charles. Those without
relatives inland desperately tried to find accommodations in hotels,
already filled to capacity with last month's homeless and displaced victims of Hurricane Katrina.

As the few remaining hours ticked away, Rita's wind speed dropped
a few miles per hour to Category 4 intensity as the eye wall fractured,
then re-formed. Just like Audrey, Hurricane Rita's wind speeds now
measured at the top of the Category 4 scale, around 145 miles per
hour. Landfall predictions ranged somewhere between Galveston and
Cameron.

Shortly after midnight on Saturday, September 24, 2005, Hurricane Rita unleashed her fury on Cameron Parish. In the empty darkness of the courthouse, the clock above the elevator stopped at 2:50 A.M. as a churning fifteen-foot storm surge rose to the ceiling. Ghosts of the past were the only witnesses to the shrieking sounds of the hurricane winds and the terrifying destruction to come. Almost half a century after Hurricane Audrey, her ugly cousin Rita slammed into the southwest Louisiana coast.

At daybreak Sunday morning, Louisiana and the world waited to hear news of Cameron Parish. Houston and Galveston had been spared a direct hit. The eye of the hurricane passed directly over Sabine Pass on the Texas-Louisiana line, placing Cameron and Lake Charles on the most damaging, "dirty side" of the hurricane.

Several facts were already known by Saturday evening. Media coverage showed that Lake Charles, forty miles inland from the coast, had taken a major hit from the hurricane-force winds and suffered substantial damage from downed trees and flooding. The greater metropolitan area was completely without power, but most residents had complied with the mandatory evacuation order, and there was no reported loss of life.

Strong winds, darkness, and a deluge of tropical rain prevented efforts to get word on Cameron's fate. In the aftermath of Hurricane Rita, there was no way to access Cameron Parish except by boat or by plane. The first aerial reconnaissance and live media feed took place at morning's first light.

The Griffith family, like much of the nation, had been glued to the television for days. Now, they sat together in Cherie's home and watched the first news footage of Cameron and Holly Beach on CNN.

Along the beach to the west of the ship channel, Holly Beach was gone. Of the 200 beach homes in the small vacation community, all that remained were occasional plumbing pipes sticking up through the sand like architectural skeletons. There were no large piles of lumber from broken homes. Holly Beach had been erased from the map. Two lone palm trees flanked a weathered walkway, which led to an empty spot where a lovely beach home once stood. Only the heaviest remnants of human life remained—the bumper and taillights of a vehicle protruded half-submerged from the sand.

Then, like an impervious medieval castle, the Cameron Parish Courthouse flashed across the television screen. Their Louisiana fortress stood tall and proud amid the flooded streets. Cameron was a demolished town, but the defiant, time-honored symbol of the community's spirit remained intact. All the walls were standing. The roof, too, had held.

Relieved cries filled Cherie's living room in spite of the tears. The initial footage of Cameron Parish was brief, without an aerial shot of their homes in Oak Grove, but they had seen enough to know that the damage around Cameron was extensive. Leslie's one thought was to return to his property as soon as flooding receded, and as soon as the National Guard reopened the roads.

Several days after Hurricane Rita, Pres. George W. Bush flew over Cameron and Calcasieu parishes in Marine One for a firsthand view of the devastation, much as his father had done almost fifty years before as a private citizen. Most of Cameron's roads were still under water.

A week after Rita's landfall, Leslie returned to Cameron Parish. South of the Intracoastal Waterway, the entire parish was closed to all residents and visitors alike, but Leslie was a parish official, and the National Guard allowed him entry at the roadblock. From atop the Gibbstown Bridge, Leslie could see debris randomly scattered for miles throughout the marsh, but nothing compared to Audrey's depth of wreckage that had jammed up against the waterway. Over the past fifty years, the once-prominent banks of the canal had eroded, allowing the new rubble to be pushed unhampered farther north, across the waterway into Calcasieu Parish.

Proceeding cautiously on the two-lane road, he made slow but steady progress around piles of out-of-place objects that had come to rest on the highway—large storage tanks, pieces of buildings, and parts of small bridges that used to cross the ditches on each side of the road. He was thankful that the emergency crews had temporarily bulldozed the debris to the sides of the road as much as possible.

He continued the drive south, all the while searching for signs of familiar landmarks. Several miles north of Creole, large sections of metal football-stadium bleachers hung suspended fifteen feet high in the trees along the highway, together with clothing and assorted debris—another ominous indication of the power and depth of Hurricane Rita's storm surge. A few minutes later, Leslie cautiously entered the town. Creole had been demolished.

Turning left onto Highway 82 along the coast, Leslie soon passed the battered remains of his alma mater, South Cameron High School, which had offered such welcome refuge to his family after Audrey. Back then, only the gymnasium, band room, and cafeteria had survived the storm. Today, the red-brick building was filled with fond memories of his school years but little else. Many of the walls were standing, but it appeared to be a total loss.

Leslie kept on course without stopping. He knew that there was only one mile left between the school and his home. Memories of Audrey flashed through his mind—memories of his family's dangerous walk through the deep water to reach the school before dark, along with memories of his grandfather. Today, the road seemed somehow narrower than before, most likely because of the downed trees and shattered structures that the dozers had pushed aside. Building after building, house after house—all structures along the final mile were either completely gone or half-missing. In contrast to the structural damages, a noticeable reminder of the town's namesake—the oak grove—still lined the road, as the trees had for a century.

Leslie slowed his truck considerably as he neared the Griffith property. *Only a hundred yards left to go.* The trees prevented him from having a clear view until he pulled into the driveway and brought the truck to a complete halt.

Leslie was a realist. He had known to expect this degree of damage, but knowing it and seeing it were two different things entirely. Only one house remained on the property. Geneva's raised cottage was gone. He had built it to withstand a massive storm surge, using even stronger piers than were on his own home. The dark piers, some metal stairs, and the shell of the heavy elevator were all that remained—no roof, no walls, no heavy bathtub, and no floor. To his shock, the home seemed erased, as if by a tornado.

Before Rita, Oak Grove had been a thriving, rural community of thirty-five families and over one hundred structures—including their homes, farms, barns, outbuildings, and a few small businesses. After Rita, only four structures remained, each with varying degrees of damage. One home was Leslie's, and another belonged to their former neighbors, the Carters.

Leslie's two-story home had survived, albeit battered and broken. The upstairs portion, the portion his father built in 1958 after Audrey, seemed structurally intact upon the sound platform, which rested high on the old piers. D.W. would have been proud—the tall, thick creosoted timbers had proven their worth. When Leslie enclosed the bottom floor several decades later, he opted for a completely brick exterior on both the upper and lower levels. The fifteen-foot storm surge had completely gutted the ground-floor addition, but several of the brick walls held in place. Only a thorough inspection by structural engineers would tell if the house was sound enough to be repaired.

Well . . . my house looks like the house Dad built after Audrey . . . a house on pilings, thought Leslie with a sad but grateful sigh.

All furniture on the ground floor was gone—including his cherished desk. The powerful, fast-moving storm surge had swept everything away. Upstairs, the contents of the home fared only a bit better. The hurricane winds and the water had ruined most of the remaining household items beyond repair.

Taking inventory, Leslie walked the property, mindful of where he stepped. Debris littered the yard. As the initial shock began to wear off, he noticed the offensive smell that permeated the area. Everything seemed to be covered with a layer of sticky, gray mud. Still wet in most places, the thick "gumbo mud" stuck to his boots. It smelled of seaweed and swamp water, of marsh mud and sandy beach. In the marshes along the coast, it was a normal, muted, hydrogen sulfide, eggy smell, tempered by salty breezes—part of the normal life cycle of all tidal marshes—but on dry land it was concentrated, and out of place, left behind by the retreating storm surge.

On a bitterly cold winter day in February 2006, five months after Hurricane Rita, electrical power is connected to a white FEMA trailer parked beside the remnants of the Griffith home. For the family, it is a bittersweet situation, compared to the Red Cross tent that provided them with temporary quarters following Audrey, nearly fifty years before.

Bricks lay scattered about the backyard. Halfway submerged in the mud, a white highway sign posted the speed limit. Fresh deposits of white sand and seashells, some rather large, gave evidence that only days ago this land had been part of the Gulf of Mexico. In the back of his mind, he could hear the sound of Audrey's shrieking wind, and he shook off the sensation. He slowly turned and looked about for his tree.

Earlier that summer, a sudden storm with strong gusty winds had caused the uppermost portion of the tree to crack and splinter apart from the trunk, leaving the oak tree about half as tall as it had been during Audrey. The lifesaving tree limb that he laid upon had broken off, but Cherie's was still there, as was the branch his parents and

Remnants of Geneva's home after Hurricane Rita in September 2005. Only the piers, some metal stairs, and the elevator shell remain.

grandmother had stood on for eight hours during the hurricane. It had been a strange, awkward moment when Leslie later cleaned up and removed the downed limbs from the property.

Today, after Hurricane Rita, he took a few steps amid the stand of trees and located the one tree trunk that had the easily identifiable scar. It was a brief moment, but a necessary one. He'd had almost fifty years to deal with the scars from Audrey and put them behind him, but today the memories were unavoidable.

He thought of his father, and he knew without hesitation that he would rebuild his home and his life in Oak Grove.

Across the Mermentau River, just east of Oak Grove, Grand Chenier is located a bit farther back from the coast, by a mile or two, but damage there was extensive nonetheless. Elizabeth Phillips Richard, Alice's granddaughter, lost her home and the local school where she taught students for the past twenty-five years. Jobs in Cameron Parish would be nonexistent for a long, long time.

Leslie Griffith, 2005, in front of the scarred and broken oak tree that the Griffith family clung to for eight hours during Hurricane Audrey.

Although D.W.'s aunt Nona Welch had passed away two decades before Hurricane Rita, her home on Henry Street once again withstood a hurricane in the neighborhood next to the courthouse. Several blocks to the east, the lovely, centuries-old timber of the historic Austin Davis home—where Nona rode out Hurricane Audrey—stood tilted and wounded. The southern mansion had finally succumbed to the more powerful forces of Rita, and bulldozers cleared the property four months later in January 2006.

Between Cameron and Creole, the community at Daigle's Corner had suffered greatly from a severe storm surge. The neighborhood nearest the intersection with Highway 82 (Marshall Street)—where Brown and Alice Marshall once lived—had been completely swept away. Not only were the homes gone, but so were the trees, leaving everything in shades of dead grass, gray and beige. It was like viewing an old black-and-white movie, it was so devoid of life.

Several months before Rita, the Marshall property had been sold for development. The home site and the surrounding timberland had been bulldozed clean to the ground. There was no trace of the smaller home that Mr. Marshall built following Alice's death from Hurricane Audrey. Alice's fig trees, the long row of oaks, and the fruit orchard had been removed as well. In many ways, the preemptive loss was easier to take than having a storm demolish Tootie Marshall's home for a second time.

The most important factor in comparing the two storms was the loss of life. Audrey's death toll of over five hundred had devastated three generations in Cameron and Vermilion parishes. In the aftermath of Rita, several accidents and heart attacks were later attributed to the storm, but loss of life during the hurricane itself was zero. There was also a new demarcation phrase in the local dialect—"before Rita" or "after Rita."

Two weeks after Rita, Geneva Griffith composed her regular "Lagniappe Two" column with care from her home in Baton Rouge. In addition to the two houses in Oak Grove, she also lost her vacation home on Rutherford Beach, which she purchased in 1994. Last but not least, Geneva lost a mobile home to Rita as well—four homes in all. Distraught with grief over this hurricane, and the second loss of her beloved Cameron Parish, the eighty-three-year-old veteran reporter wrote from the heart. Tears—and memories of Audrey, of D.W., and of their home—came flooding back with each stroke of her pen. She wrote, in part:

> My son, Leslie, has just returned from Cameron with the bad news. We, along with most everyone else, have lost everything, but no loss of life, thank goodness for that. I don't want to see it, so I guess I will never go back. . . .
>
> I remember that my father-in-law drowned in my arms during Hurricane Audrey, but there was no way I could save him. I had waved to my family up in the tree and told them goodbye, because I knew I was going to die also. But I guess God was not ready for me to go, so my husband finally got me up into the tree, also.
>
> D.W. loved it on Oak Grove, where his family had lived over a hundred years. However, even though I had grown to love the people there and had gotten involved in everything, I do not want the bad memories. . . . I want to remember Cameron as it was and not now that it has been swept clean. I want to remember all the good times we had back then.
>
> "I have to stop thinking about it, or I will cry. . . .

One month later, Geneva retired from writing her column in the newspaper when it became too painful to write about the devastation in her beloved Cameron Parish. Each life has chapters, and Geneva realized that she had no other emotional option but to turn the page.

Twice the Griffiths had lost a great deal to a massive hurricane—as did most of their neighbors throughout Cameron Parish. For months after 2005's Rita, an overwhelming sense of déjà vu permeated the daily existence of those who suffered through 1957's Hurricane Audrey.

A month after Rita, the parish officially allowed residents to return to view their property and salvage what they could. In a poignant visit, former president George H. W. Bush—now in his eighties—also returned to Cameron, his former Louisiana base of operations for

Zapata Offshore. After his helicopter landed, the president climbed the steps of the courthouse and entered the building. Upstairs in the same courtroom where the Broussard family endured Audrey, the now-private citizen took a seat in the jury box to attend a meeting with local authorities concerning the state of emergency in Cameron Parish. When he spoke, Mr. Bush recalled 1957's Hurricane Audrey, and also 1965's Hurricane Betsy. The former president had been connected to Cameron in a business sense, but more importantly he had never forgotten the lives lost in Audrey.

Twice Cameron Parish had been ground zero. Twice people by the thousands had become homeless and jobless—but in these fiercely independent, resilient communities, Hurricane Rita had met her match. The people of southwest Louisiana were made of stronger stuff. Just as their deported Acadian ancestors regrouped and rebuilt after a political storm three centuries before them, many of these displaced Cajuns of southwest Louisiana began to regroup with quiet dignity.

Like his father before him, sixty-year-old Leslie Griffith loved this land with every fiber of his being. A month after Rita, he was busy cleaning up the property, hoping to rebuild as soon as possible. His wife, on the other hand, had strong feelings to the contrary, much as another Mrs. Griffith had fifty years before her. Eventually Peggy relented, as did Geneva so long ago.

Leslie's thoughts on the matter have always been formed and tempered by the land itself. As the sun filters through the tall pines and gnarly oaks, the gulf breeze soothes the senses and combines with the blue air subtly scented with resin. Standing in the oak grove between his house and the tree that saved his life during Audrey, Leslie is crystal clear on one point.

"When I returned on that Wednesday after Hurricane Rita, and the house that we built after Audrey was still there, I knew that I had no choice. I could not abandon my home or my land. The house—at least the top portion—was still there. I will move my kitchen and living room back upstairs as the house was 'post-Audrey.' If Rita did not take it, then I figure that no storm will take it. It will take a while for it to be livable again, but we will survive—or die trying. It's the prettiest place on earth as far as I am concerned. I could not live anywhere else."

In downtown Cameron, cleanup crews continue to work from dawn till dusk each day. High above the entrance to the Cameron Parish Courthouse stretches a long, wide banner that states simply . . . CAMERON WILL RISE AGAIN.

That is their promise. That is their future.

Acknowledgments

This book would not have been possible without the gracious consent, cooperation, and input of those I now fondly call "the Ladies of the Storm"—Geneva Griffith, Sybil Clark, Clara Broussard, Clara's daughters—Elaine, Ethel, and Mary Ann—and Maybell Bartie.

We began the process in September 2004, and their patience during the following year of interviews and correspondence resulted in a documentation of our collective family histories surrounding the events of Hurricane Audrey. As expected, each family recalled elements of the hurricane in their own unique, reflective rendering depending on where they were situated geographically during the storm. While not always physically related, the families of Cameron Parish who experienced Audrey share a common bond emotionally.

Leslie Griffith's thoughtful insight into Hurricane Audrey played a key role in helping me relate the effects of the storm through a child's eyes. I tip my hat to Geneva's son, who himself is a backbone of present-day Cameron Parish. He is determined to rebuild the family home a second time, after suffering yet another major blow to his property during Hurricane Rita in 2005.

A special recognition goes out to my dear aunt, Theda Cagle Heath, for her crisply detailed and accurate recollections of our family's history and firsthand accounts of our aunt Alice, before and after Audrey. Regina's daughters—Elizabeth, Kathleen, and Frances—supplied the cherished photographs and warm memories of their grandmother Alice.

I started the book on Audrey after many years of contemplation on the subject. I knew years ago that I wanted to document that part of our family history for my own children, but I rarely considered a project of this magnitude—a full-blown book. Undertaking such an intimidating endeavor called for a jolt of inspiration, and mine came from a most unexpected source—observing the hard work and finely honed talent of two tiny teenagers, my friends Farah Fath from "Days of Our Lives" and Kirsten Storms from "General Hospital."

Three people encouraged me to take up writing years ago, even though I pooh-poohed the notion at the time—my mother, Mary Belle Cagle, her twin sister, Betty Bernsen, and my great-aunt, Sister Rita Estelle Broussard of St. Mary's of Notre Dame. When she was 100 years old, Sister Estelle told me to stop doing whatever it was that I was doing for a living and take up writing. She then sat down, put her opinion in a letter, and mailed it to me posthaste, just to reinforce her advice. Nuns know stuff.

For historical data, I drew upon consistently reliable information from the Carnegie Library, the *Lake Charles American Press* archives, the *Beaumont Enterprise*, the *Cameron Parish Pilot*, the Lake Charles Weather Bureau, federal court documents, and Frazer Library at my alma mater—McNeese State University. At the Carnegie Library in Lake Charles, the genealogy librarians provided greatly appreciated assistance. Noteworthy gems of information were also found online at various weather-related Web sites.

In southwest Louisiana there are several journalists and writers who have devoted their lives to decades of reporting the life and times of their communities. These professionals—Geneva Griffith, Don Kingery, Jerry Wise, Nola Ross, and Don Menard—have contributed a great deal toward preserving the local history surrounding Hurricane Audrey.

In one area in particular—documenting the existence of the tidal wave—I am most grateful. While the eyewitness accounts were well known, it was through Don Kingery's efforts in 2003 that three staff members of the Lake Charles weather service revised the tidal-wave estimates. These men based their new calculations on several factors—the wind velocity, tide, storm surge, windblown waves, reach of the continental shelf, and more.

These weather experts even measured the high-water mark left halfway to the top of the Cameron courthouse. They took into account the recorded drops in water level over time and the distance between the coastline and the courthouse. The study was a comprehensive evaluation. The result validated the eyewitness accounts. The weather experts estimated a tidal wave of fifty feet. This was *in addition* to the already existing storm surge (averaging ten feet deep) and windblown waves (ten to fifteen feet).

The journalist now had the data he needed. After the weather service staff read the information, and concurred in every detail, the *Lake Charles American Press* published the full-page feature article by Kingery in June 2003. It was the newspaper's forty-sixth-anniversary coverage of Hurricane Audrey.

These combined sources validated stories handed down through the generations who were involved in Hurricane Audrey. I had heard of brothers Tommy and Sidney DeBarge and of their ordeal through "Audrey conversations" over the years, but I was finally able to satisfy my own curiosity regarding the end of their story by locating Sidney's obituary and funeral arrangements. It was comforting to learn that Tommy was able to say a final goodbye with a proper service.

My sister Beth, a natural-born Nancy Drew, and her husband, Billy Loftin, who must surely have been a Hardy Boy in some former life, both used their considerable skills to research information and track down two of the families in the book.

All along, I felt that historical photographs would be an important component in relating this historical narrative. My daughter Dianne Fruge set aside her own busy schedule and spent days helping me gather these rare pictures from the survivors' families.

At Pelican Publishing Company, Editor in Chief Nina Kooij championed my book through the entire, long road to publication. Production Manager Terry Callaway provided the technical skills and expertise required in restoring and reproducing the fragile historical photographs for the book. I owe them both my heartfelt thanks.

My first unofficial "editor" and invaluable critique guru was homegrown. My daughter Sarah Gergen often stayed up late at night after her children were in bed and read the draft manuscripts into the wee hours. The next morning I would get a feedback phone call from Lincoln, Nebraska, as she rushed off to teach her science classes.

And finally, no amount of encouragement or acquired knowledge could have made this book possible without the constant support and involvement of my incredibly patient husband, Dave. Dave is my rock. Without Dave there would have been no book.

Saffir-Simpson Scale

The Saffir-Simpson Hurricane Intensity Categories

Wind Speed and Storm Surge	Typical Effects

Category 1 Hurricane—Weak

| 74-95 mph | Minimal damage: Damage is primarily to shrubbery, trees, foliage, and unanchored mobile homes. No real damage occurs in building structures. Some damage is done to poorly constructed signs. |
| Storm Surge: 4-5 ft | Low-lying coastal roads are inundated, minor pier damage occurs, some small craft in exposed anchorages torn from moorings. |

Category 2 Hurricane—Moderate

| 96-110 mph | Moderate damage: Considerable damage is done to shrubbery and tree foliage; some trees are blown down. Major structural damage occurs to exposed mobile homes. Extensive damage occurs to poorly constructed signs. Some damage is done to roofing materials, |

windows, and doors; no major damage occurs to the building integrity of structures.

Storm Surge: 6-8 ft   Coastal roads and low-lying escape routes inland may be cut off by rising water 2-4 hours *before* the hurricane center arrives. Considerable pier damage occurs; marinas are flooded. Small craft in unprotected anchorages torn from moorings. Evacuation of some shoreline residences and low-lying island areas is required.

Category 3 Hurricane—Strong

111-130 mph   Extensive damage: Foliage torn from trees and shrubbery; large trees blown down. Practically all poorly constructed signs are blown down. Some damage to roofing materials of buildings occurs, with some window and door damage. Some structural damage occurs to small buildings, residences, and utility buildings. Mobile homes are destroyed. There is a minor amount of failure of curtain walls (in framed buildings).

Storm Surge: 9-12 ft   Serious flooding occurs at the coast with many smaller structures near the coast destroyed. Larger structures near the coast are damaged by battering waves and floating debris. Low-lying escape routes inland may be cut off by rising water 3-5 hours *before* the hurricane center arrives. Flat terrain 5 feet (1.5 m) or less above sea level flooded inland 8 miles or more. Evacuation of low-lying residences within several blocks of shoreline may be required.

Category 4 Hurricane—Very Strong

131-155 mph

Extreme damage: Shrubs and trees are blown down; all signs are down. Extensive roofing material and window and door damage occurs. Complete failure of roofs on many small residences occurs, and there is complete destruction of mobile homes. Some curtain walls experience failure.

Storm Surge: 13-18 ft

Flat terrain 10 feet (3 m) or less above sea level flooded inland as far as 6 miles (9.7 km). Major damage to lower floors of structures near the shore due to flooding and battering by waves and floating debris. Low-lying escape routes inland may be cut off by rising water 3-5 hours *before* the hurricane center arrives. Major erosion of beaches occurs. Massive evacuation of *all* residences within 500 yards (457 m) of the shoreline may be required, and of single-story residences on low ground within 2 miles (3.2 km) of the shoreline.

Category 5 Hurricane—Devastating

Greater than 155 mph

Catastrophic damage: Considerable damage to roofs of buildings. Very severe and extensive window and door damage occurs. Complete failure of roof structures occurs on many residences and industrial buildings, and extensive shattering of glass in windows and doors occurs. Some complete buildings fail. Small buildings are overturned or blown away. Complete destruction of mobile homes occurs. Shrubs and trees are blown down; all signs are down.

Storm Surge:
Greater than 18 ft

Major damage occurs to lower floors of all structures located less than 15 ft (4.6 m) above sea level and within 500 yards (457 m) of the shoreline. Low-lying escape routes inland are cut off by rising water 3-5 hours *before* the hurricane center arrives. Major erosion of beaches occurs. Massive evacuation of residential areas on low ground within 5 to 10 *miles* (8-16 km) of the shoreline may be required.

The Saffir-Simpson Scale first came into use by the National Hurricane Center in 1972.

Recommended Reading

Coulter, John, and E. E. Sprague. *The Complete Story of the Galveston Horror*. United Publishers of America, 1900.

Harrison, Dexter G. *Life's Ragin' Storms*. Baltimore: America House, 2001.

Larson, Erik. *Isaac's Storm: A Man, a Time, and the Deadliest Hurricane in History*. New York: Crown, 1999.

Menard, Donald. *Hurricanes of the Past: The Untold Story of Hurricane Audrey*. Acadiana, 1999.

Ross, Nola Mae Whittler, and Susan McFillen Goodson. *Hurricane Audrey*. Sulphur, La.: Wise, 1996.

Bibliography

Sources

Bartie, Maybell: interviews and correspondence, May 2005—February 2006.

Bredehoeft, Kathleen Phillips: interviews and correspondence, September 2004—January 2006.

Broussard, Clara E.: interviews and correspondence, December 2004—January 2005.

Broussard, Whitney, Jr.: correspondence, May 2005.

Clark, Sybil B.: interviews, December 2004—June 2006.

Fruge, Ethel Broussard: interviews, e-mail, and correspondence, December 2004—January 2005.

Griffith, Geneva E.: interviews and correspondence, September 2004—May 2006.

Griffith, Leslie: interviews and correspondence, September 2004—March 2006.

Heath, Theda Cagle: interviews and correspondence, September 2004—January 2006.

Richard, Elizabeth Phillips: interviews and correspondence, September 2004—January 2006.

Trahan, Elaine Broussard: interviews, e-mail, and correspondence, December 2004—January 2005.

Vineyard, Mary Ann Broussard: interviews, e-mail, and correspondence, December 2004—January 2005.

Newspapers

Much information, and factual verification of interviews, was derived from daily newspaper reports published in the months immediately following Hurricane Audrey (June 1957—November 1957), as well as the annual "anniversary" coverage of the storm. The following newspapers contributed greatly in my research:

Audrey Reporter (the American Red Cross publication during the aftermath)
Beaumont (Tex.) Enterprise
Cameron Parish (La.) Pilot
Lake Charles American Press (archives located in the Carnegie Library, Lake Charles, La.)
New Orleans Times-Picayune

Articles

Fogleman, Charles W., and Vernon J. Parenton. "Disaster and Aftermath: Selected Aspects of Individual and Group Behavior in Critical Situations." *Social Forces*, Vol. 38 No. 2, 1959.
Jones, Robert W. "The Tracking of Hurricane Audrey 1957 by Numerical Prediction." *Journal of the Atmospheric Sciences*, Vol. 18 No. 2, 1961.
Roth, David. "Louisiana Hurricane History: Late 20th Century." Lake Charles, La.: National Weather Service (also available on the NWS Web site).
Tisdale, John R. "Observational Reporting as Oral History: How Journalists Interpreted the Death and Destruction of Hurricane Audrey." *The Oral History Review*, Summer-Fall 2000.

Web Sites

http://en.wikipedia.org/wiki/Hurricane Audrey (encyclopedia)
http://lwf.ncdc.noaa.gov (National Climatic Data Center, NOAA Satellite and Information Service)

http://www.cameron.lib.la.us
http://www.explore-weather.com
http://www.home.att.net/~lv hayes/Genealog/Cems/Cam/sacrhear.txt
http://www.louisdl.louislibraries.org
http://www.rootsweb.com/~usgenweb/la/cameron/audrey.htm
http://www.srh.noaa.gov/srh/tropicalwx (Southern Region
    Headquarters, National Weather Service)
http://www.usatoday.com/weather
http://www.wunderground.com/hurricane/images
http://www2.worldbook.comwc/features/hurricanes/html/audrey

Libraries

The McNeese State University Library, Lake Charles, La. A treasure
trove of information lies within the archives, as well as the reference
section. Many of the sources are personal collections donated to the
university, including scrapbooks and historical photographs.

Index

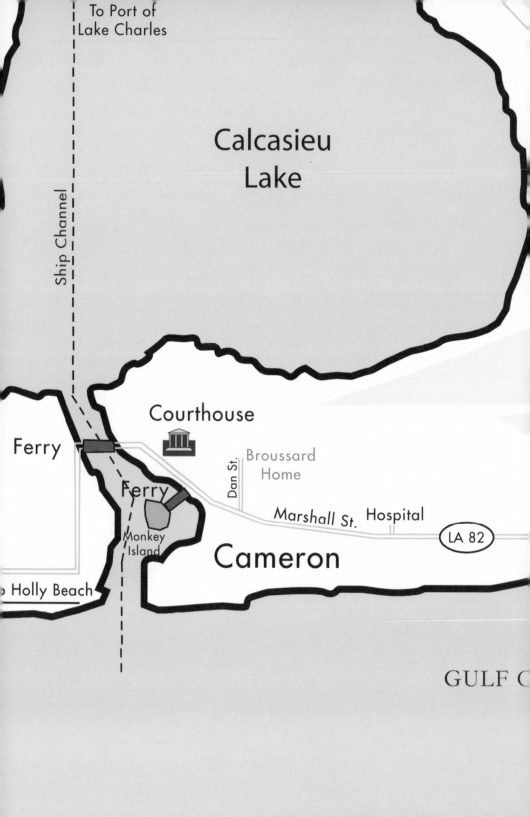

To Port of
Lake Charles

Calcasieu
Lake

Ship Channel

Ferry

Courthouse

Broussard
Home

Dan St.

Marshall St.   Hospital

LA 82

Ferry

Monkey
Island

Cameron

Holly Beach

GULF O

Map Not Drawn to Scale   COASTLINE OF CAM